THE HARDEST DAY

BATTLE OF BRITAIN

THE HARDEST DAY

18 August 1940

Alfred Price

ARMS AND ARMOUR PRESS

London   New York   Sydney

Dedicated to Guenther Unger and Harry Newton, whose terrible experiences on 18 August 1940 and subsequent friendship served as the inspiration for this book.

Published in Great Britain
in 1988 by Arms and Armour Press, Artillery House,
Artillery Row, London SW1P 1RT.

Distributed in the USA by Sterling Publishing Co. Inc.,
2 Park Avenue, New York, NY 10016.

Distributed in Australia by
Capricorn Link (Australia) Pty. Ltd., P.O. Box 665,
Lane Cove, New South Wales 2066, Australia.

First published 1979
by Macdonald and Jane's Publishers Ltd,
Paulton House, Shepherdess Walk,
London N1 7LW.

British Library Cataloguing in Publication Data
Price, Alfred 1936–
Battle of Britain: The Hardest Day, 18 August 1940—2nd Ed.
1. World War 2. Battle of Britain, 1940 (August 18)
I. Title
940.54'21
ISBN 0-85368-831-1

Designed by Judy Tuke; picture sections designed by
DAG Publications Ltd. Printed and bound
in Great Britain by Mackays of Chatham, Kent.

Contents

Maps and Diagrams

Photographs

Flight Lieutenant Dunlop Urie's
  Spitfire.
Barrage balloons going down in
  flames near Portsmouth.
Oberleutnant Johannes Wilhelm.
Unteroffizer Karl Maier.
Hauptmann Horst Tietzen.
Oberleutnant Gerhard Mueller-
  Duhe.
Yesterday's enemies meet in
  friendship.

Introduction

On Sunday 18 August 1940 the Luftwaffe launched three major air assaults against targets in southern England. In the course of these and numerous smaller actions 100 German and 136 British aircraft were destroyed or damaged in the air or on the ground. On no other day during the Battle of Britain would either side suffer a greater number of aircraft put out of action. This book describes the events of that 24-hour period – Battle of Britain: the hardest day.

Author's Note

In this account all times have been adjusted to British Summer Time, in use in Britain on 18 August 1940. British Summer Time ran one hour behind the German *Sommerzeit* in use in the Luftwaffe.

In the case of witnesses the ranks, ages, positions and surnames (in the case of ladies who later married) are those on 18 August 1940.

Where possible German words have been anglicised in the text; thus Schöpfel is written as Schoepfel, Günther is written as Guenther and Fözö is written as Foezoe. German unit designations have been translated to their closest English equivalent: Fighter Geschwader for Jagdgeschwader; Bomber Geschwader for Kampfgeschwader; Dive Bomber Geschwader for Sturzkampfgeschwader; Tactical Development Geschwader for Lehrgeschwader; and Reconnaissance Gruppe for Aufklaerungsgruppe. Luftflotte has been translated as Air Fleet. Because no exact English terms exist for them, unit descriptions such as Staffel, Gruppe and Geschwader (plurals: Staffeln, Gruppen and Geschwader) remain in the German. Also, German rank titles have been retained (a list of comparative ranks is given in Appendix A).

In several publications the abbreviations Bf 109 and Bf 110 are used, respectively, for the Messerschmitt 109 and 110 (Bf for Bayerische Flugzeugwerke). In official wartime Luftwaffe documents, however, the abbreviations 'Bf' and 'Me' both appear frequently; so both are correct. In this book the less cumbersome abbreviation 'Me' is used.

Prologue

On Saturday 17 August 1940 Oberst 'Beppo' Schmid's 5th Directorate of the Luftwaffe High Command, responsible for Intelligence matters, issued its appreciation of the strength of Royal Air Force Fighter Command on the previous morning. The document* made interesting reading. It stated that, as a result of losses suffered during the previous six weeks' fighting over southern England and the Channel, Fighter Command was now down to its last 430 Spitfires, Hurricanes and Defiants; and of these only about 300 were thought to be serviceable. The distribution of these remaining combat-ready fighters was thought to be 200 south of the line Bristol to the Wash, 70 in the Midlands and a mere 30 in northern England and Scotland. And, even as the report was being issued, it seemed that the optimistic picture it presented had been overtaken by events: during the course of 16 August Luftwaffe units had claimed a further 92 British fighters destroyed.

Schmid's appreciation came as a welcome confirmation of the impression of the enemy already gained by Luftwaffe staff officers: that the foe was shaken and weakened and now was the time for boldness and daring, a time to abandon caution and rain blows at his vitals until resistance finally collapsed. Then, with Fighter Command out of the way, many German leaders believed that Britain's continued survival in the war could be measured in weeks rather than months.

On orders from the High Command operations directorate, officers at the Brussels headquarters of Generalfeldmarschall Albert Kesselring's Air Fleet 2 laid plans for an ambitious programme for the following day, 18 August: powerful assaults were to be launched against Kenley, Biggin Hill, Hornchurch and North Weald, the four major airfields on which the fighter defences of south-eastern England hinged. The plan was not without its risks, for never before had the Air Fleet hazarded so many of its bombers by day against targets so deep inside England. Simultaneously, to maintain pressure against the defences in south and south-western England, officers at the Paris headquarters of Generalfeldmarschall Hugo Sperrle's Air Fleet 3 planned to hurl against targets in the Portsmouth area more Stuka dive bombers than had ever before been committed in a single attack.

If events unfolded according to the German design, Fighter Command's dwindling strength would be caught between the hammer and the anvil: either the defending fighters would be destroyed on the ground or, if they rose in strength to try to parry the blows, they would be cut to pieces by the escorting Messerschmitts.

The feelings of optimism for the immediate future were not confined to the higher echelons of the Luftwaffe. By the 17th the heady elation of impending victory had also pervaded the front-line airfields in France,

* Given in Appendix D.

Belgium and Holland. Thirty-year-old Leutnant Hans-Otto Lessing, who
flew Messerschmitt 109s with Fighter Geschwader 51 based at Wissant near
Calais, conveyed the mood of the time in a letter home:

17.8.40

My Dear Parents,

This morning it is foggy and there is little on before noon. So at last I
have the chance to write to you. I am sorry you have had to wait so long but,
as you will certainly have heard, we have been very busy. During the past
few days, each day has seen three or four large attacks mostly against
targets in the London area.

Yesterday I scored my fifth victory (that includes two barrage balloons,
which count as one victory). That is rather few considering the many
opportunities we have had, but they do not always go down when one
shoots at them. Also I have had some bad luck with my machine. Once I was
in a beautiful firing position and my guns would not work – I was in a terrible
mood for the rest of the day.

Yesterday I shot an enemy fighter off the tail of a Ju 88 bomber, but I
was too late to prevent hits being scored. Two of the bomber crew were
wounded and it made an emergency landing at Lille. That was the 100th
victory of our Gruppe. And of these Hauptmann Tietzen, my Staffel
commander, alone has 19! I witnessed most of his kills. It is fantastic, the
way he shoots. He is the boss, he moves us into position and selects the
victims, and we have to do little more than cover him. There is a wonderful
sense of teamwork in the Staffel. With his 20th victory, the Ritterkreuz will
be due. For me, the award of the Iron Cross, First Class, has been imminent
since my fourth kill.

Our own losses are only moderate. Seven in the entire Gruppe, and of
these three certainly survive in captivity. We are in the Geschwader of
Major Moelders, the most successful Geschwader. Ours is the most successful Gruppe and our 5th Staffel, with 37 victories, the most successful
Staffel.

During the last few days the British have been getting weaker, though
individuals continue to fight well. Often the Spitfires give beautiful displays
of aerobatics. Recently I had to watch in admiration as one of them played a
game with 30 Messerschmitts, without itself ever getting into danger; but
such individuals are few. The Hurricanes are tired old 'puffers'.

This is only a short letter. One would have to write a book to give even a
brief picture of events. I am having the time of my life. I would not swap
places with a king. Peacetime is going to be very boring after this!

Your

Hans-Otto

Thus the stage was set for the hardest-fought day of the Battle of Britain,
Sunday 18 August; and before its end Hans-Otto Lessing would go to his
death together with Hauptmann Horst Tietzen, the Staffel commander he
admired so greatly.

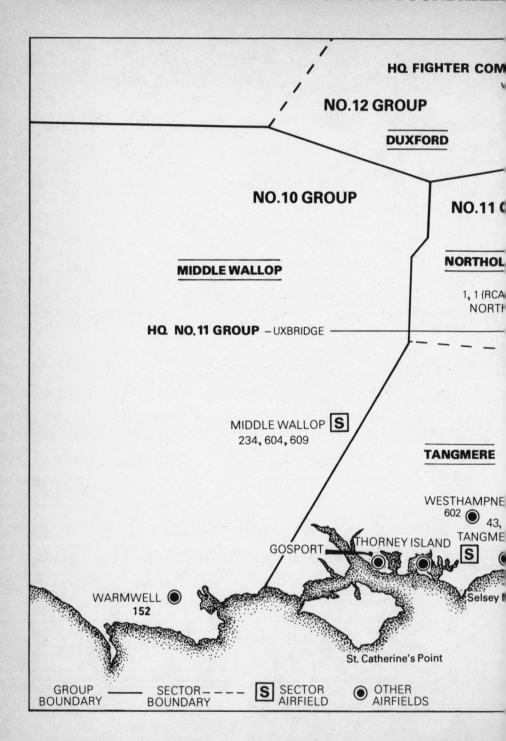

HQ FIGHTER COM

NO.12 GROUP

DUXFORD

NO.10 GROUP

NO.11 G

MIDDLE WALLOP

NORTHOL

1, 1 (RCA
NORTH

HQ. NO.11 GROUP – UXBRIDGE

MIDDLE WALLOP [S]
234, 604, 609

TANGMERE

WESTHAMPNE
602 ⊙ 43,

GOSPORT THORNEY ISLAND TANGME
[S]

Selsey

WARMWELL ⊙
152

St. Catherine's Point

GROUP BOUNDARY ———	SECTOR BOUNDARY – – –	[S] SECTOR AIRFIELD ⊙ OTHER AIRFIELDS

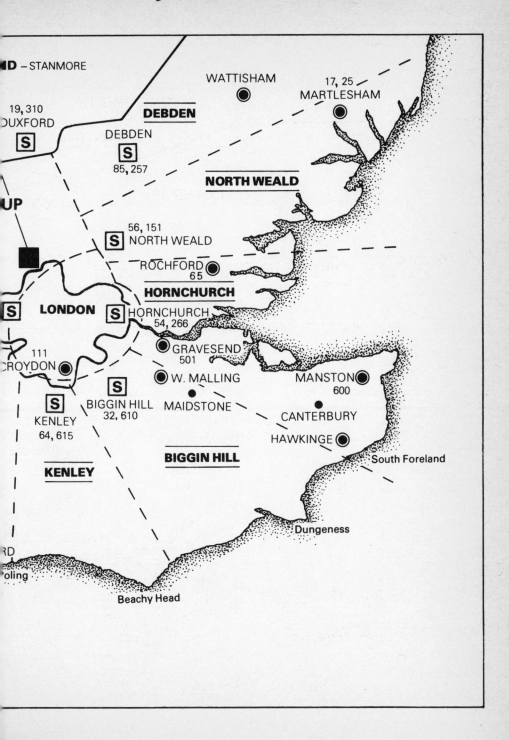

CHAPTER 1

Sunday 18 August 1940

Strategy is often likened to a game of chess, [but it is] quite different! In chess, you make your plans and opening moves, get your pieces in balance, and then say 'Check, and whatever you do I shall checkmate you in three moves; so you may as well throw your hand in now.' Whereupon your opponent concedes victory. Not so in warfare! When you say 'Check', your opponent may reply 'No, you are quite mistaken. This is where the fighting is going to begin!'
FIELD MARSHAL LORD MONTGOMERY

During the two months since the Dunkirk evacuation at the beginning of June 1940 German air activity over Britain had built up gradually, rising to a crescendo at the end of the second week in August. The Battle of Britain was now in full swing, with hard-fought actions over England on the 12th, 13th, 14th, 15th and 16th, during which 194 German aircraft and 85 British fighters had been destroyed. The Fighter Command airfields at Lympne, Hawkinge, Manston, Martlesham Heath, Croydon and Tangmere had all been hit hard; but of these only Tangmere was one of the all-important Sector control stations, and its ability to direct fighters was not impaired. The radar stations at Dover, Rye, Pevensey, Dunkirk and Ventnor had also come under attack, but only at Ventnor was serious damage caused and it was still inoperative.

On the 17th there had been an ominous quiet, as if the Luftwaffe had stopped to draw breath before its next great exertion. In the unofficial diary of No 32 Squadron at Biggin Hill, Squadron Leader Michael Crossley had scribbled: 'Not a single sausage, scare, flap or diversion of any description today. Amazing. Heavenly day too.'

On the evening of the 17th Alfred Duff-Cooper, the Minister of Information in Mr Churchill's government, delivered a radio broadcast to the nation calculated to raise spirits. He taunted Adolf Hitler to carry out his threat of invasion:

> We should not have liked him to come before we were ready to receive him, but we are quite ready to receive him now and we shall really be very disappointed if he does not turn up. We can assure him that he will meet with that welcome on our shores which no invader has ever missed. This was to have been a week of German victory; it has been a week of British victory instead.

Duff-Cooper went on to review the successes of the British defences during the past week and discussed the large number of German aircraft claimed shot down, 429 during the previous six days. He said that the figures had been 'very carefully checked' and 'we have only counted as dead birds those which have actually been seen to fall'. We shall see later just how carefully the figures had in fact been checked.

Some of those who heard Duff-Cooper's remarks would remember them with bitterness when the bombing resumed on the following day. They felt that his speech had goaded the Luftwaffe into action once again, but this was not the case: the German plans had been laid and, speech or no speech from the British Minister of Information, the attacks on the Sunday would go ahead if the weather allowed.

Other war news in the British press centred on the successes claimed for the Bomber Command attacks on targets in Germany on the night of the 16th/17th, notably the new synthetic oil refinery at Leuna, the Zeiss works at Jena and the Messerschmitt works at Augsburg. In Africa British and Commonwealth forces were being pulled out of Somaliland, under pressure from 'overwhelming Italian forces'. In north Africa the land front was generally quiet, though Royal Navy warships had bombarded Italian positions at Bardia and Capuzzo.

From the still-neutral United States the main news item was that Mr Wendell Willkie had accepted the nomination as Republican candidate for the Presidency. In his speech of acceptance Willkie discussed the Roosevelt administration's decisions to strengthen the US armed forces and to allow the delivery of war material to Britain: 'I wish to state that I am in agreement with these two principles as I understand them, and I don't understand them as implying military involvement in the present hostilities.'

In Britain, life went on with as much normality as the war allowed. 'Dear Octopus' was running at the Adelphi Theatre and 'Rebecca' was playing at the Queen's. There were daily matinees of 'A Midsummer Night's Dream' at the Open Air Theatre in Regent's Park. The Empire cinema Leicester Square was showing 'North-West Passage' starring Spencer Tracy; and at the Warner there was 'The Sea Hawk' with Errol Flynn, Flora Robson and Claude Rains.

Some of the newspaper advertisements now make quaint reading. Marshall and Snelgrove's August Coat Presentation included 'Really practical Winter Coats' from 6½ guineas. De Reszke minor cigarettes were selling at 6½d for ten, plain or cork tipped. And the luxury Green Park Hotel was offering rooms 'with full air raid shelter facilities' from 7s 6d per night (special terms for HM Forces).

A few of the statements in the newspapers could have fitted into today's issues without comment. For example, an editorial in the *Observer* of 18 August stated:

> Railway charges may have to be further increased but the public, like the Cornishmen, 'will know the reason why.' The necessity and equity of higher fares must be thoroughly established before assent is given to a demand which would make the whole apparatus of business and life more costly and give us a further impetus towards inflation.

In Germany most of the nation's leaders planned to spend a quiet Sunday 18 August. On the previous evening Adolf Hitler, now aged 52, had arrived at the 'Eagle's Nest', his mountain retreat high in the Bavarian Alps near Berchtesgaden. He intended to remain there a few days, unless the air battle taking place over Britain changed the political situation sufficiently to warrant his return to Berlin. One of the Fuehrer's few appointments that day was with Vidkun Quisling, the leader of the puppet government in Norway.

Reichsmarschall Hermann Goering, 47, was spending the day at his country estate, Karinhall, near Berlin. He had summoned from battle his two most famous and successful fighter pilots, Majors Werner Moelders and Adolf Galland, to award them with pilot's badges in gold and promote them to take command of their respective fighter Geschwader. All three men were, therefore, far away from the action about to take place.

Joseph Goebbels, 42, planned his usual daily conference at the Propaganda Ministry in Berlin, to review the general line the German newspaper reports and radio broadcasts were to take. He was particularly keen that editors should not issue premature reports that London was on the point of collapse. Since the previous day, Saturday, had been quiet, newspapers were to 'review the most reliable reports over the last few days, in order not to allow the tension to relax'.

Whichever course of action the German armed forces adopted for the rapid subjugation of Britain, Fighter Command of the Royal Air Force had first to be smashed as an effective fighting force. How could this be done?

Essentially there were four methods open to the Luftwaffe: air attack on militarily or economically important targets, to force the British fighters into the air where they could be destroyed by the German escorts and the bombers' defensive fire; air attack on the British fighter airfields, to put them out of action and destroy fighters on the ground; air attack on the British fighter control system and the radar stations, to put it out of action; and air attack on the factories which produced the fighters. Attacks aimed at all four of these targets were planned for 18 August. Yet clever targeting would avail the Luftwaffe little, if it lacked the forces necessary to attack the targets effectively; what forces were available at this stage of the battle?

On 17 August the three Air Fleets involved in the battle possessed the serviceable aircraft listed overleaf.

Also available for the battle was a special reconnaissance Gruppe* operating under the direct control of the Luftwaffe High Command. On 17 August it possessed 28 serviceable aircraft of assorted types, in some cases still in the experimental stage.

Generalfeldmarschall Albert Kesselring, the 45-year-old commander of Air Fleet 2, had come to the Luftwaffe from the army in 1933. An able adminis-

---

*The Gruppe was the basic flying unit in the Luftwaffe; at this stage of the war it had a nominal strength of three Staffeln each of nine aircraft plus a staff unit of three, making a total of thirty. Three Gruppen, plus a staff of four aircraft, made a Geschwader with a nominal strength of 94 aircraft.

Air Fleet	2	3	5	Total
Single-engined Fighters (Messerschmitt 109)	480	265	35	780
Twin-engined Fighters (Messerschmitt 110)	126	68	20	214
Single-engined Bombers (Junkers 87)	42	234	–	276
Twin-engined Bombers (Junkers 88, Heinkel 111, Dornier 17)	469	299	100	868
Four-engined Bombers (Focke-Wulf 200)	–	7	–	7
Long-Range Night Fighters (Junkers 88)	14	–	–	14
Reconnaissance Aircraft (Junkers 88, Heinkel 111, Dornier 17, Messerschmitt 110)	26	26	15	67
Total	1157	899	170	2226

For a more-detailed break-down of the German forces, by units, see Appendix B. Air Fleet 5 was based in Norway and would play virtually no part in the action on 18 August; it is included here only for completeness.

trator, in 1936 he was appointed to Chief of the General Staff of the Luftwaffe. Now, in the summer of 1940, his Air Fleet had its headquarters in Brussels and embraced all the combat units based in Holland, Belgium and France as far west as the Seine.

Kesselring was a German officer of the old school, firm but humane and courteous with his subordinates and greatly respected by them. Lacking any deep technical understanding of aircraft, Kesselring behaved like a father trying to keep up with a son whose knowledge has outstripped his own: before conducting an inspection of a flying unit he would read up on some small part, for example the fuel injection system of the Jumo engine. Then he would ask probing questions on this one part. Word soon got around about this practice, however, and there was some amusement during inspections as his subordinates waited to discover which piece the Generalfeldmarschall had read about. Behind this harmless piece of fun, however, was an enhanced respect for a commander seen to go to such trouble to impress those under him.

The rest of the German combat units in France, those to the west of the Seine, came under Air Fleet 3 commanded by 55-year-old Generalfeld-marschall Hugo Sperrle who had his headquarters outside Paris. Sperrle, remembered for his great bulk and the monocle he habitually wore in his right eye, was once referred to by Hitler as one of his 'most brutal-looking generals'. He had served in the Imperial Flying Service during the First World War and moved to the army in 1919 when German military flying ostensibly ceased. In 1935 he transferred to the new Luftwaffe and advanced rapidly: in the following year he went to Spain, to command the Luftwaffe flying units supporting General Franco during the civil war. In contrast to Kesselring, Sperrle was rather like the British archetype of a German general, an aloof figure who rarely spoke to his subordinates and who was a stickler for protocol. Rarely, if ever, was he seen to smile; some said that if he did, his face would crack!

In the summer of 1940 the aircraft types equipping the German combat units were in each case effective modern machines as good as or better than their equivalents in other air forces.

The Messerschmitt 109E, which equipped all of the single-engined fighter units during the battle, had a maximum speed of 357 mph and was armed with two 20-mm cannon and two rifle-calibre machine guns. A formidable aircraft in the right hands, it had been designed for the short-range interceptor role. As a bomber escort its great shortcoming was that, with tankage for only 88 gallons of fuel, its radius of action with an allowance for combat was about 125 miles; in other words it was effective only as far as London, from the German fighter bases in the vicinity of the Pas-de-Calais. This limitation would be one of the decisive factors in German fighter escort operations during the Battle of Britain.

Of the Messerschmitt 109 Oberleutnant Gerhard Schoepfel, who flew this type with Fighter Geschwader 26 from Caffiers, commented 'It was superior to the Hurricane and, above about 6,000 metres (about 20,000 feet), faster than the Spitfire also. I believe that our armament was the better, it was located more centrally which made for more accurate shooting,' he recalled. 'On the other hand, the British fighters could turn tighter than we could. Also, I felt that the Messerschmitt was not so strong as the British fighters and could not take so much punishment.'

The German twin-engined fighter, or 'Destroyer', units were equipped with the Messerschmitt 110, a two-seater with a maximum speed of 336 mph armed with two 20-mm cannon and four rifle-calibre machine guns firing forwards; for self-defence there was a single machine gun firing rearwards. This long-range fighter carried three times as much fuel as the Messerschmitt 109 and its effective radius of action of 350 miles took in almost the whole of England and Wales from bases in northern France. At this stage in the war the Messerschmitt 110 was the best *twin-engined* fighter in service in any air force. Certainly it was greatly superior to the Blenheim which was its equivalent in the Royal Air Force squadrons. If the Spitfires, Hurricanes and Messerschmitt 109s could be likened to sports cars, however, the Messerschmitt 110 was like a family car and far less nimble than the others. 'Because the 110 was so heavy it was difficult to manoeuvre it into a firing position on the enemy fighters,' recalled Leutnant Joachim Koepsell who flew this type with Destroyer Geschwader 26. 'So, although we had the heaviest armament of any fighter in the battle, it was very difficult to bring that armament to bear.'

Of the German bomber types the smallest, the slowest and the shortest-ranging was the Junkers 87, the single-engined two-seater with the fixed undercarriage and the distinctive cranked wing, which everyone called the 'Stuka'.* Flat-out without its bombs, its maximum speed was only 232 mph; laden with bombs and flying in formation, it cruised at 160 mph. It carried three machine guns, two firing forwards and one rearwards. With a bomb load of about 1,000 pounds, its radius of action was roughly the same as that of the short-legged Messerschmitt 109s which had the difficult task of escorting it. For all of its disadvantages, however, the Junkers 87 did have one outstanding advantage: the pin-point accuracy of its steep-diving attack,

---

* In fact Stuka was short for *Sturzkampfflugzeug* (dive bomber) and was a generic term used in the Luftwaffe to cover all aircraft employing this mode of attack.

made at angles of between 70 and 80 degrees. With its air-brakes extended under the wings, the bomber dived almost vertically under full control, enabling the pilot to line up accurately on his target and hold it in his sight until he reached his bomb-release altitude at about 2,300 feet (700 metres). During the 18 August action the extreme accuracy of the dive-bombers' attacks would enable them to cause damage to their targets out of all proportion to the number of aircraft involved or the tonnage of bombs dropped.

Contrary to what some accounts have suggested, the dive bombers were not vulnerable to fighter attack during their dives; indeed, the only time the Junkers 87 was *not* vulnerable to fighter attack was during its dive. 'In the dive they were very difficult to hit, because in a fighter one's speed built up so rapidly that one went screaming past him', remembered Flight Lieutenant Frank Carey who flew Hurricanes with No 43 Squadron from Tangmere. 'But he couldn't dive for ever . . .' At the bottom of the dive after it had pulled out, climbing slowly away, the dive-bomber was extremely vulnerable. 'Stukas were my favourite opposition', recalls Carey.

Another favourite misconception concerns the wind-driven sirens fitted to the wings of the Junkers 87, intended to demoralise those on the receiving end of the attack; if some accounts and television films are to be believed, the dive-bombers never went anywhere without them. In fact, by the Battle of Britain, most of the Stuka units had removed the sirens from their aircraft. 'They were slow enough without that extra drag', commented Major Helmut Bode of Dive Bomber Geschwader 77.

Next in importance in the German bomber force was the twin-engined Dornier 17, which carried a crew of four and a normal defensive armament of four hand-held machine guns. This aircraft had a maximum speed of 255 mph; over Britain, however, it usually flew at its formation cruising speed of 180 mph. Against targets anywhere in the southern half of England, the Dornier carried a bomb load of 2,200 pounds. Unique amongst the aircraft to see combat in any number during the Battle of Britain, the Dornier 17 had air-cooled engines; and air-cooled engines, lacking the fragile system of radiators and coolant pipes necessary for liquid-cooled engines, were far less vulnerable to enemy fire. This was one of the factors which would enable the Dorniers to regain friendly territory despite quite remarkable battle damage. By the summer of 1940, however, the Dornier 17 was being phased out of service in favour of the higher performance Junkers 88.

The twin-engined Junkers 88 also carried a crew of four and a defensive armament of four hand-held machine guns. Over short ranges it could carry double the bomb load of the Dornier, or the same 2,200 pounds over a far greater distance. It had a maximum speed of 286 mph, or it would cruise in formation at about 190 mph. Remarkably strong and manoeuvrable, the Junkers 88 was the best and most versatile twin-engined bomber in service anywhere in the summer of 1940. It was stressed and equipped to carry out precision dive-bombing attacks, or it could make horizontal attacks like any other medium bomber. 'The Dornier 17 was a much steadier aircraft than the Junkers 88', remembers Unteroffizier (Corporal) Guenther Unger, 22, who flew both types with Bomber Geschwader 76. 'To get the most out of the Junkers one had to be a good pilot, it was a more demanding aircraft. At the higher speeds the Junkers was very manoeuvrable and easier to handle than the Dornier; but at the lower speeds it was the other way round and for that reason some of the pilots converting from the Dornier to the Junkers 88 made heavy landings to start with.'

The Junkers 88 was also modified for use as a long-range fighter, and in this role it carried a forwards-firing armament of one 20-mm cannon and three machine guns and in addition it could carry a few small bombs. Night Fighter Geschwader 1 operated this type during its night intruder missions against Bomber Command airfields in Norfolk and Lincolnshire.

The most numerous of the German bomber types in service was the twin-engined Heinkel 111, which carried a crew of five and a defensive armament of five machine guns. Against targets in southern England it usually carried a bomb load of just under 3,000 pounds. The Heinkel had a maximum speed of 258 mph, but usually cruised in formation at 180 mph. One unique feature of this aircraft was that the pilot sat far back from the nose for most of the flight, submerged inside the structure of the aircraft. This gave aerodynamic cleanliness, but it left the pilot with a poor view above or to his right, and he could see practically nothing behind. Leutnant Walter Leber of Bomber Geschwader 53 recalled the Heinkel as being 'a nice machine to handle, very strong and fast for its time, though its defensive armament was rather weak'.

During the Battle of Britain the hand-held machine guns fitted to the German bombers did not prove very effective in deterring attacks by British fighters. Most of the German bombers were well provided with armour plate, however. The Heinkel 111, for example, carried some 600 pounds of steel plating to protect the pilot and crewmen. A further refinement fitted to the German bombers which enabled them to absorb punishment was the self-sealing fuel tank. As the Luftwaffe had learned during the Spanish Civil War, ordinary light alloy fuel tanks were extremely vulnerable to enemy fire. If they were punctured and the petrol escaped, the aircraft might run out of fuel before it could regain friendly territory. If the leaking petrol caught fire the danger was more immediate: it was usually only a matter of minutes before something important, like a wing, burned away or the fire reached the bomb load. An armoured jacket for each of the fuel tanks would have been one answer to the problem, but the weight penalty would have been far too great. So before the war German technicians developed a new and rather clever type of fuel tank. The tank itself was made of a thin fibrous plastic material, surrounded by layers of, in turn, thick leather, thick crude rubber, two layers of thin rubber and an outer layer of thick vulcanised rubber. If the tank was hit, the bullet or shell fragment would pass clean through the various layers and the wall of the tank, allowing the fuel to run out. Almost immediately the petrol came into contact with the crude rubber, however, the latter swelled up and sealed off the hole. When the aircraft returned to its base the tank had to be changed, a fairly lengthy task; but at least the aircraft and its crew had been able to get back.

For very long-range over-sea armed reconnaissance missions, the Luftwaffe had seven of the four-engined Focke-Wulf 200 Condors serviceable on 17 August. This aircraft, a converted air liner, had five fuel tanks installed in the fuselage to extend its operational range to over 2,000 miles, sufficient to take it far out over the Atlantic. During the summer of 1940 Bomber Geschwader 40 began sending its Condors on shuttle missions round the west of the British Isles, flying between its bases in western France and southern Norway. During these flights the aircraft carried a crew of five, an armament of one 20-mm cannon and three machine guns, and six 550-pound bombs. To survive, the Condor had to stay well clear of the areas patrolled by British fighters; lacking armour and self-sealing fuel tanks, this rather fragile aircraft could not absorb much punishment.

The majority of the German photographic reconnaissance aircraft were normal bombers or twin-engined fighters fitted with cameras. One exception to this, however, was the Junkers 86P high-altitude spy plane, the true predecessor of the infamous U-2 which was to hit the headlines some twenty years later. The Junkers 86P was powered by a pair of two-stroke double-supercharged Diesel engines, specially developed for high-altitude operations. The two-man crew was housed in a pressurised cabin; it was a necessary refinement, for the aircraft could ascend to altitudes around 38,000 feet, far higher than any other aircraft in service at the time. From this vantage point a pair of huge cameras, each larger than a domestic cooker and weighing about 150 pounds, surveyed the world passing below through 75-cm Zeiss telephoto lenses. A single frame on the large 30-cm-square negatives would take in an area the size of the city and dockyard of Portsmouth, with sufficient resolution to show the existence of anything the size of a family car or larger. The Junkers 86P carried no armament, armour or self-sealing tanks and its cruising speed was only about 160 mph; its sole protection lay in its superb high-altitude performance. On 17 August the Luftwaffe High Command's special reconnaissance Gruppe reported that it had two Junkers 86Ps on strength. Both were serviceable.

Flying high to keep out of the reach of British fighters, the German reconnaissance aircraft brought back copious film of the airfields in southern England and the Midlands. But, because they were taken from so high an altitude, the photographs lacked the resolution to enable photo interpreters to identify the types of aircraft seen on the airfields. The aircraft were counted, but could be described only as 'single-engined', 'twin-engined' or 'four-engined'. This lack of identification by type meant that the German photo interpreters could not tell which of the active airfields were used by fighters and which were used by other types of single-engined aircraft; it was a deficiency that would have an important effect on the action on 18 August.

During the Battle of Britain some of the German units were fortunate enough to operate from well-prepared permanent airfields but there were insufficient of these to mount a large-scale air offensive. The remaining units had to fly from airstrips hastily prepared on open land by men of the Todt Organisation. Typical of the latter was the airstrip at Cormeilles-en-Vexin about 20 miles north-west of Paris, the home of the IIIrd Gruppe of Bomber Geschwader 76 with thirty Dornier 17s. Before German troops had captured the area in June, the landing ground had been a cow pasture. Now it had been flattened to give the clear run of 800 yards necessary to get a full-laden Dornier airborne with a reasonable margin for safety. There were no concrete runways or taxi ways, or indeed any permanent facilities of any sort. The aircraft were dispersed and camouflaged along the edge of the wood which ran down the side of the landing ground. Some of the ground crewmen had built an improvised hangar out of wood from packing cases which would take one aircraft, but most of the engineering work had to take place in the open.

The men of the Gruppe were accommodated in abandoned houses in the villages round the airfield. Those of the 9th Staffel* were concentrated in Ableige in one-time holiday homes which had been systematically looted before the men arrived. The airmen, living out of their travel bags, slept on whatever bedding they could find. 'We did not mind the discomfort', recalled Guenther Unger. 'We thought we should be there for only a short time and then the war would be over.' The Staffel had its own 'Goulash Canon' (Luftwaffe slang for field kitchen) in the village and to supplement their diet the men would buy fresh food from the local inhabitants.

The 9th Staffel, on which Unger served, was one of the few units in the Luftwaffe which had specialised in very low-altitude attacks. During the campaign in France, just three months earlier, the unit had perfected its tactic of hedge-hopping all the way to and from the target to achieve maximum surprise. Attacks with 20-mm cannon (a special modification to the Dorniers of the Staffel) and small bombs had proved devastatingly effective against enemy airfields and supply lines. And losses had been low, only two crews during the campaign lasting six weeks.

The German bomber units were all based well back from the coast, both to render more difficult any attempt at a pre-emptive strike by the Royal Air Force and also to leave the Pas-de-Calais and Cherbourg areas free for the short-range fighter units.

During the battle the German fighter pilots enjoyed one important advantage over their counterparts in the Royal Air Force: their combat tactics were greatly superior. During the Spanish Civil War two young fighter pilots, Guenther Luetzow and Joachim Schlichting, in turn the commanders of the first unit to operate the Messerschmitt 109 in action, had developed a new family of air fighting tactics in which the keynote was flexibility. Their basic fighting unit was the Rotte, or widely-spaced pair of aircraft, flying about 200 yards apart almost in line abreast with the leader slightly ahead; each pilot concentrated his search inwards, so that he covered his partner's blind areas behind and below. In combat the leader did the fighting, while his

* Under the German system for designating units, the nine Staffeln within a Geschwader were numbered consecutively. Thus the 1st, 2nd and 3rd Staffeln belonged to the Ist Gruppe: the 4th, 5th and 6th Staffeln the IInd Gruppe: and the 7th, 8th and 9th Staffeln belonged to the IIIrd Gruppe.

The 'Cross-over' turn

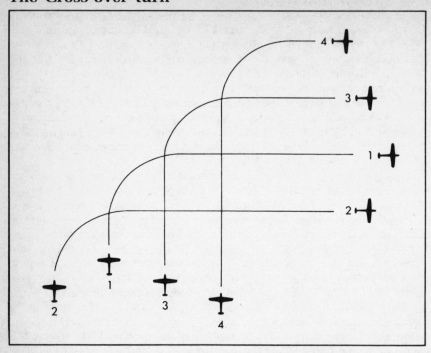

wing-man guarded his tail and kept watch to ensure that the pair were not taken by surprise. Two pairs of fighters made up a Schwarm of four aircraft, with the leading pair flying to one side and slightly ahead of the other. With its aircraft spaced 200 yards apart the Schwarm had a frontage of 600 yards, which meant it was impossible for the aircraft to hold their position in formation during a tight turn maintaining high speed. So the 'cross-over' turn was used: each pilot turned as tightly as he wanted to and simply rolled out on his new heading on the opposite side of the formation. A Staffel battle formation comprised three Schwarm formations, flying either in line astern or line abreast. If one aircraft in the Rotte or Schwarm was attacked from behind, a simple turn would result in the attacker being 'sandwiched'.

So far as the Luftwaffe was concerned, having good fighters, aggressive combat-experienced pilots and clever fighting tactics was one thing; bringing Fighter Command into action was quite another. Initially the Luftwaffe had tried to wear down Fighter Command by sending large 'free hunting' patrols with Messerschmitt 109s over southern England. At first Fighter Command did rise to this bait and in the ensuing combats suffered disconcerting losses.

'The means of gaining air superiority is the "free hunting" patrol, with the aim of bringing the enemy into action in the air and shooting down as many as possible,' wrote 48-year-old Oberst (Group Captain) Theo Oster-kamp who commanded the fighter units of Air Fleet 2 based in the Pas-de-Calais area. 'The enemy had to be sought over his own territory.' After some initial successes over England, however, these operations achieved little

'Sandwich' manoeuvre

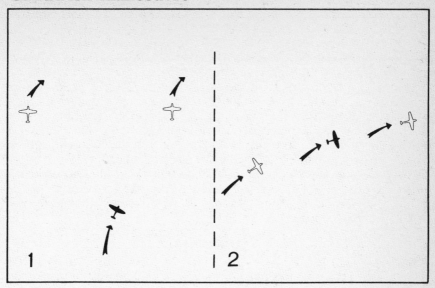

because the defending fighters became increasingly reluctant to come up and fight. 'The fighter incursions were tried at all times of the day and in changing strength: in Staffeln, Gruppen right up to several Geschwader at a time, at various altitudes. But successes became less and less and gradually these operations lost their meaning.'

The only way to force Fighter Command to come up and fight was to send in bombers to attack targets which the British had to defend. Then, when the defending fighters rose to engage, the German fighters could pounce on them. Yet this gave rise to its own problems. Above all, the German bomber force could not afford heavy losses during such actions: without its support an invasion would have been quite out of the question. So during these attacks a large proportion of the available German fighters had to remain close to the bombers to protect them. The German fighter pilots hated this restriction. 'The fighters flying with a bomber formation were always at a tactical disadvantage with respect to an attacking enemy, because they could neither determine the time of the attack nor exploit the advantages of height or the sun,' Osterkamp continued. The fighters providing close escort for a bomber formation had to throttle back to match their speed to that of their charges; so if the enemy attacked the German fighter pilots had first to accelerate to fighting speed and were vulnerable until they had done so.

Dominating all tactical considerations on the German side, during the Battle of Britain, was the short range and endurance of the Messerschmitt 109. Allowing for the climb to altitude, running at full throttle during combat and normal operational margins, this fighter could spend only about an hour in the air. To put it another way, operating from bases in the Pas-de-Calais area, it could spend only about twenty minutes over targets like Kenley which were some 95 miles away. And even that short time was possible only if the fighter pilots were permitted to make the most of their limited fuel; if they had to fly a zig-zag course to match their rate-of-advance to that of a formation of cruising bombers, the Messerschmitt's limited radius of action was further reduced.

By the middle of August the tactics used by the German escort fighters were a compromise between two conflicting requirements: on the one hand they had to protect the vulnerable bombers and provide moral support for their crews; on the other hand they had to be able to engage effectively those British fighters which the bombers drew up. Normally each bomber Geschwader of 40 to 60 aircraft had a close escort of one Gruppe of 20 to 30 fighters; these had to remain with the bombers and were allowed to engage only if the bombers they protected came under attack. A further Gruppe of fighters flew as extended escort, ahead of the formation and clearing the sky of enemy fighters in front.

In practice this meant that the indirect escort usually operated in the same general area as the bombers but independently of them. The bomber formation would usually join up with its close escort over or near the fighters' base airfield; from there the raiding force would usually head for its target by the most direct route, for any deviation would eat into the single-engined fighters' already-meagre fuel reserves.

For the Germans flying single-engined aircraft, especially those based in the west of France to whom an operational mission meant two long over-water flights and usually a fight in the middle, crossing the Channel was a harrowing experience. They coined their own word for the fear of it: *Kanalkrank* – Channel sickness. 'Either the water or the Spitfires, one was enough', commented 23-year-old Oberleutnant Julius Neumann of Fighter Geschwader 27, 'but both together was a bit too much.'

Even though it was summertime, the water temperature in the English Channel was rarely greater than 14 degrees centigrade. A man wearing a life jacket and normal flying clothing could survive in this numbing cold for only about four hours at most. If he was in a rubber dinghy a man could survive for days. But during this stage of the battle many of the German crews lacked this important aid to survival. Moreover to use their dinghy the Germans had to alight on the water in the aircraft, remove the pack and inflate the frail craft; if they baled out, they had to leave the dinghy behind.

If they were forced down in the sea, the worst off were the men on board the Junkers 87 dive-bomber with its fixed undercarriage. They faced a cruel dilemma: if the pilot tried to alight the aircraft on the water, the wheels were likely to 'dig in' and the Stuka would somersault on to its back giving the men inside little chance to get out; but if the crew baled out, they had to leave their precious dinghy behind. Some of the dive-bomber crewmen wore a camper's airbed underneath their parachute harness, tied round the waist with string. The idea was that if they parachuted into the sea they could blow up the air bed by mouth and lie on it out of the water. It was a perfunctory scheme, based more on what could be provided in a hurry using existing equipment than on what was really needed to sustain life until rescue came.

Several ex-members of the Luftwaffe believe that the fear of the sea was confined to their side alone. 'The British are a seagoing people and for them the sea is a friend. We are a land people and for us the sea is an enemy,' stated Major Eduard Neumann, a Messerschmitt 109 pilot with Fighter Geschwader 27. The fact was, however, that if they came down in the sea British and German aircrew were equally likely to die from exposure before they could be rescued, if they had no dinghy. At this stage of the war both sides' rescue services were woefully inadequate and were confined mainly to a few motor launches and spotter aircraft. The Luftwaffe operated some old Heinkel 59 biplane seaplanes as rescue aircraft, but these could not alight on open water if there was any sort of sea running.

In Britain Winston Churchill, 65, was spending 18 August at Chequers, the mansion in Buckinghamshire which is the Prime Minister's official country retreat. He does not appear to have had any notable appointments, though he was not idle. In two days he was to deliver a major speech before the House of Commons. The sentences he was to compose on this Sunday would long be remembered as a clarion call to action in the nation's hour of danger:

> The gratitude of every home in our island, in our Empire, and indeed throughout the world, except in the abodes of the guilty, goes out to the British airmen who, undaunted by odds, unwearied in their constant challenge and mortal danger, are turning the tide of the world war by their prowess and by their devotion. Never in the field of human conflict was so much owed by so many to so few.

At his headquarters at Stanmore Park the Commander-in-Chief of Fighter Command, 58-year-old Air Chief Marshal Sir Hugh Dowding, had worries that could not be soothed away with such rhetoric. The battle so far had imposed a terrible drain on his pilot strength, with 105 killed, wounded and missing during the previous nine days' fighting. His Command was now 209 pilots below its establishment, a deficiency of about 13 per cent. On the 17th Dowding had pleaded to the Air Staff for pilots to be transferred from other Commands and it had been agreed to move 32 to Fighter Command immediately; these men would require a rapid conversion training on to fighters, however, and it would be a few days before they were ready for action. The other reinforcement coming to Fighter Command was from the recently formed squadrons using trained pilots from abroad. One of these, No 310 (Czechoslovak) Squadron, had been declared operational on the 17th. A second, No 1 (Canadian) Squadron, was due to become operational on the 18th. Two further squadrons had been formed with Polish pilots, but neither was yet ready for operations.

Yet for all the British leaders' worries about the shortages of aircraft and pilots, Fighter Command was far from being the near-broken and exhausted force 'Beppo' Schmid's officers imagined it to be. On the evening of 17 August Fighter Command's squadrons possessed a total of 918 single-engined and twin-engined fighters, distributed as shown in table. This layout

Fighter Command Group areas

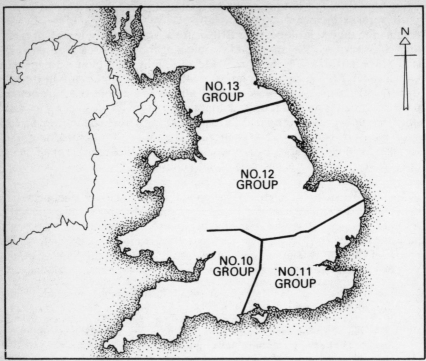

Serviceable Fighters

	No 10 Group	No 11 Group	No 12 Group	No 13 Group	Total
	10 Sqns	23 Sqns	16 Sqns	14 Sqns	62 Sqns
Spitfires	51	81	100	44	276
Hurricanes	69	245	85	150	549
Defiants	–	–	30	–	30
Blenheims	9	17	21	11	58
Gladiators	5	–	–	–	5
Total	134	343	236	205	918

For a more-detailed break-down of the strength of Fighter Command, by sectors, stations and squadrons, see Appendix C.

gave the defences considerable depth and provided Dowding with a large reserve of squadrons he could feed into the battle when he needed them. Throughout the Battle of Britain there was a continual movement of exhausted squadrons to the north and fresh or refreshed squadrons to the south.

Dowding himself was an exceptionally far-sighted innovator and a very capable administrator, who had personally overseen the build-up of his Command's now elaborate system of fighter control. Yet Dowding was an aloof complex figure, with none of the extrovert qualities one might expect from a fighter leader. He had gained the nickname 'Stuffy', and that summed up the opinion of him held by many of the more senior officers in Fighter Command. To the fighter pilots Dowding was like the character in a play who exerts a continual influence on events but who seldom appears on stage. 'He was so above us we never really thought of him', is a view often expressed.

Dowding would come down like a ton of bricks on anyone he felt had given less than his best; yet on occasions he demonstrated a remarkable compassion for those beneath him whom circumstances had pushed beyond their abilities. 'At the time we on the squadrons did not know anything about Dowding, either as a man or a leader. I met him for the first time when he visited Kenley', recalled 26-year-old Squadron Leader Don MacDonell who commanded No 64 Squadron there. 'During his visit a pilot brought in a Spitfire on a delivery flight; he landed it on the grass and stood it on its nose. Dowding slowly lifted his arm and pointed in the direction of the aircraft. "Arrest that man!" he boomed.' A posse of officers and the station warrant officer rushed over to the Spitfire and brought the pilot, a young sergeant, before The Presence. 'Dowding asked him how many hours he had flown in Spitfires. The sergeant, still a little shaken and practically in tears, replied with some very low figure like four or five. Dowding replied "We can ill afford to have Spitfires broken like that. You had better go and have a meal and go back to your base." ' The matter was closed.

While he concentrated his efforts on the weighty matters of administering to the needs of his force, and equipping it with the best that technology would allow, Dowding left most of the operational running of Fighter Command to his Group commanders. Each Group controlled the squadrons based within its geographical area. When the situation demanded it squadrons could be sent into action in the neighbouring Group's area, though usually they were directed by their parent Group.

Responsible for the vitally important south-eastern corner of England with the lion's share of the forces was No 11 Group commanded by Air Vice-Marshal Keith Park, a 48-year-old New Zealander who had flown fighters in France during the First World War. Over six feet tall, he was a gaunt, austere-looking man. Quietly devout, Park drew great strength and comfort from his prayers during the battle. He once confided to his personal assistant, 21-year-old Flying Officer Donald Wiseman, that had he not stayed in the Royal Air Force after the First World War he would probably have gone into the church. 'He drove himself harder than he drove anyone else. He could be very caustic towards anyone he felt was letting the side down. But I never saw him lose his temper with anyone or get het up,' recalled Wiseman. 'His heart was in the front line with his pilots.'

An effective and popular leader, Park had the great gift of making those serving under him feel that they mattered. He would often turn up at his airfields in his personal Hurricane, without ceremony or prior warning. Don MacDonell recalls his first meeting with Park: 'Once, during a period of bad weather, we had been released to 30 minutes and went to the Mess. We were there drinking coffee when a tall grey-haired man came in wearing a flying suit with no rank tabs. We did not pay him much attention, he was standing by the fire place.' The pilots thought he was probably a delivery pilot who had brought in a new aircraft. MacDonell walked up to him casually, introduced himself, and asked whether there was anything he could do for him. 'Yes,' the stranger replied, 'I'm your AOC!'* It was Park's way of finding out what went on in his Group without relying on the ponderous, and often fallible, official channels. Had the weather not been bad, as likely as not, Park would have asked to join in the Squadron's next practice scramble.

The individual Group commanders were responsible for the tactical handling of the fighter squadrons under their control; and during the Battle of Britain Park's tactics were conditioned by the geographical position of his area, at its nearest point only five minutes' flying time from the German airfields. If he ordered his Spitfire and Hurricane squadrons to scramble immediately the German formations began to move away from the Pas-de-Calais area there was time, just, to climb up and intercept a formation of high-flying bombers over the middle of Kent. Throughout most of the battle Park's squadrons had to go into action singly – there simply was insufficient time to assemble two or more into a larger fighting unit.

Commanding No 12 Group, bordering Park's and responsible for an area extending from Cambridgeshire to Yorkshire, was 48-year-old Air Vice-Marshal Trafford Leigh-Mallory. By all accounts Leigh-Mallory was an ambitious man. Ambition, in itself, is no vice but the No 12 Group commander allowed it to cloud his judgement on how the battle should be fought. As an Air Vice-Marshal Leigh-Mallory was senior to Park by about 1½ years and he felt that he, and not Park, should be running No 11 Group which was playing the major part in the battle; Dowding would have none of it. So, as the battle progressed, Leigh-Mallory became increasingly vocal in his condemnation of Park's single-squadron fighting tactics; the No 12 Group commander felt that many more enemy aircraft would be shot down if the squadrons went into action in twos or threes. Park reciprocated this hostility. The personal animosity between Leigh-Mallory and Park did not, however, have as great an influence on the Battle of Britain as some later accounts have suggested; by the time the rancour really developed, the battle would be in its closing stages. There is no indication that the men's feelings towards each other had any effect on the action on 18 August; during the day squadrons from No 12 Group would move south to protect No 11 Group airfields.

Commanding No 10 Group, defending the west country, was Air Vice-Marshal Sir Christopher Brand. Brand gave Park the fullest co-operation during the battle, and on 18 August would send squadrons to help defend airfields in the 11 Group area. Defending the outlying parts of the country, from Yorkshire to the Shetland Islands and including Northern Ireland, was No 13 Group under Air Vice-Marshal Richard Saul. This

* Air Officer Commanding

Group played a comparatively minor part in the battle, and none at all on 18 August.

Of the aircraft available to Fighter Command that with the highest performance was the Supermarine Spitfire and on the evening of 17 August Fighter Command had 276 of them ready for action. Powered by a 1,030 horse power Rolls-Royce Merlin engine, it had a maximum speed of 362 mph at 19,000 feet. It could climb to 20,000 feet in a little under eight minutes. At low or medium altitudes the Spitfire's beautifully harmonised controls made it a remarkably manoeuvrable aircraft. 'The Spitfire was a marvellous aircraft, streets ahead of the Hurricane,' felt 25-year-old Pilot Officer Colin Gray, who flew them with No 54 Squadron at Hornchurch. 'How the Spitfire compared with the Messerschmitt 109, we did not know at the time. Because they always seemed to be above us, they appeared to be faster than we were. They certainly did not appear to be more manoeuvrable.' The Spitfire was essentially a short-range aircraft, with a combat radius of action, with reserves, of about 130 miles and a combat endurance of about 50 minutes' flying time.

The Hawker Hurricane equipped the bulk of Dowding's squadrons, and on the evening of the 17th Fighter Command had 549 of them ready for action. The Hurricane was fitted with the same type of engine as the Spitfire but, because it was somewhat heavier, the Hurricane was about 35 mph slower in level flight and took nearly a minute longer to reach 20,000 feet. 'We envied the Spitfire people for their higher rate of climb and their better altitude performance,' recalled Pilot Officer Kenneth Lee, who flew Hurricanes with No 501 Squadron from Gravesend. 'On the other hand the Hurricane was easier to fly and a more rugged machine. So long as we had some Spitfires around to give us high cover, we were quite happy with the Hurricane to go in and attack the bombers.' In terms of radius of action and endurance, the Hurricane was as limited as the Spitfire.

Compared with the Messerschmitt 109 both of the main British fighter types were more manoeuvrable and, below 15,000 feet, the Spitfire was also faster. Above 20,000 feet, however, the Me 109 was faster than the Spitfire and it could out-run the Hurricane at all altitudes. The Messerschmitt 110 was inferior to both of the British types in speed, rate of climb and manoeuvrability, except above 20,000 feet where it had a slight edge over the Hurricane in speed and rate of climb. Both of the German fighters were fitted with direct fuel injection for their Daimler Benz engines, rather than the float carburettors fitted to the British fighters' Merlin engines. In combat this meant that the German pilots could push their fighters into negative-G manoeuvres, for example nosing over into the dive, and their engines kept running. If British pilots tried to follow, their carburettors ceased delivering fuel and the engines spluttered to a stop.

Both the Spitfire and the Hurricane were, for the most part, armed with eight Browning .303-in machine guns each with a rate of fire of 1,150 rounds per minute. Each gun's magazine housed 300 rounds, sufficient for about 14 seconds' firing. From the beginning of the war, however, more and more of the German aircraft were fitted with armour; to defeat this some Spitfires and Hurricanes had been fitted with the Hispano 20-mm cannon, a French-designed weapon with a formidable penetrative ability. Due to teething troubles, however, the early career of this cannon in the Royal Air Force was a sad tale of frequent stoppages and failures. On the evening of 17 August No 19 Squadron at Duxford had fifteen cannon-Spitfires ready for action. Also, at North Weald, No 151 Squadron operated a Hurricane fitted with a one-off installation with a single Hispano cannon under each wing. Flight Lieutenant Dick Smith, 25, used the cannon-Hurricane as his personal aircraft, a move which drew no objections from the other pilots. 'They regarded me as mad because with those two heavy guns, the normally highly manoeuvrable Hurricane became a heavy old cow', he recalled. With the extra drag of the cannon blisters, his Hurricane was hard pressed to exceed 300 mph and it was much slower than the others in rolls or turns.

The other two single-engined fighter types in Dowding's order of battle, the Boulton-Paul Defiant turret fighter and the Gloster Gladiator biplane, were considered unsuitable for combat against modern enemy single-seaters; the three squadrons equipped with them would see no action on 18 August.

The last of the types in the Fighter Command order of battle, the twin-engined two-seat Bristol Blenheim, had a maximum speed of only 285 mph and took about 13 minutes to reach 20,000 feet. When the Blenheim had first gone into service as a bomber three years earlier, in 1937, such a performance had been considered impressive enough for some of these machines to be modified and issued to fighter squadrons. In this role the Blenheim carried five Browning machine guns firing forwards and a single Vickers gun in the rear turret for self defence. By the summer of 1940 the Blenheim was clearly no match for any of the German fighters and in Fighter Command it was relegated to the night fighter squadrons where its long endurance was of value – it could fly patrols lasting more than four hours. In the summer of 1940 some of the Blenheims were fitted with the first primitive airborne interception radar sets. A few Blenheims were also operated by Coastal Command as long-range fighters and, from time to time during the Battle of Britain, these would become embroiled in combat with German aircraft.

The fighters were the 'teeth' of Fighter Command. But scarcely less import-ant were the 'eye' and 'brain' organisations, and the 'nervous system' which carried the information between them, to position the 'teeth' so that they could snap at the enemy with greatest effect.

By the summer of 1940 the chain of radar stations along the southern and eastern coasts of England and Scotland was able to detect and track incoming aircraft flying at any but the lowest altitudes; at the best altitude, around 20,000 feet, the detection range was about 100 miles. So that they could be identified on radar, British aircraft were now fitted with a device called IFF (Identification Friend or Foe) which produced a distinctive blip on the radar screens.

In considering the effectiveness of the British radar system, it should be realised that the device was still in its technical infancy. The plots obtained on the incoming raids, while accurate in range, were considerably less accurate in bearing. Thus a series of radar plots on a formation flying straight for a target, marked on a map, took the form of a zig-zag and often it took several minutes to deduce the line of advance of the raiders. Height-finding was crude and, on aircraft flying about 25,000 feet, unreliable. The least effective aspect of the early radars, however, was the measurement of the number of aircraft if a large formation was being plotted. By the look of the echo on the radar screen and the way it flickered, the man or woman operator was expected to make a 'guestimate' of the number of aircraft present. The accuracy of this depended on the skill (or luck) of individuals, and such reports could be gross under- or over-estimates ranging anywhere between one half and double the true enemy strength.

For the most part the radar stations were sited to look out to sea, and were not very effective in tracking aircraft once they had crossed the coast. The observation of the movements of aircraft flying overland was the responsibility of the Observer Corps, a volunteer organisation manning many hundreds of posts throughout the length and breadth of England. These posts were all linked in to the fighter control system by landline.

The sequence of events leading up to a fighter interception was as follows. First the radar stations, Fighter Command's long-range 'eyes', would detect the incoming aircraft. The radar plots were passed by landline direct to the filter room at the Fighter Command headquarters, at Stanmore Park to the north of London. At the filter room the radar plots were compared with the known positions of RAF aircraft; if none of the latter were in the area the plot was designated 'unidentified' or 'hostile'. The IFF device was a useful aid to identification but corroborative evidence was also required: electronic devices could go wrong, and there was always the chance that the enemy might succeed in imitating the distinctive IFF signals.

The radar plots designated 'unidentified' or 'hostile' were passed on by landline to fighter Group and Sector operations rooms, where they were plotted by means of counters on the situation maps there.

No 11 Group's headquarters, from which almost the whole of the British side of the action on 18 August would be directed, was situated at Uxbridge 15 miles to the west of London. The operations room was housed in a bunker nearly 100 feet below ground and resembled a small theatre. In the centre of the 'stage' was a large table bearing a gridded map of southern England and showing part of the north coast of France. About a dozen airmen and airwomen, under a sergeant, fussed round the table. The women plotters wielded rakes, similar to those used by croupiers, to push round small wooden blocks, carrying counters which showed the track number, the number of aircraft and their altitude; blocks representing friendly fighter squadrons carried a triangle with the squadron's number on it. The letter 'X' in front of the track number meant that it was not identified; 'H' meant it was hostile. At one end of the room was the 'tote' board, showing the current state of each of the Group's fighter squadrons: 'Released' (not available for action); 'Available' (airborne in 20 minutes); 'Readiness' (airborne in 5 minutes); 'Standby' (pilots in the cockpits, airborne in 2 minutes); airborne and moving to ordered position; in ordered position; enemy sighted; ordered to land; or landed and refuelling. Nearby was the weather board, showing the state of the weather at airfields in the area. It was the task of the plotters to up-date the situation map, the tote board and the weather board continually.

If it seemed there was a large raid in the offing, with several 'unidentified' or 'hostile' plots coming in from the filter room at Stanmore, the tension and excitement in the No 11 Group operations room grew and with them the level of noise. 'The whole thing could best be described as "organised chaos" ', recalled Aircraftwoman Vera Saies, 25, one of the plotters at Uxbridge. 'When things got going plots from the filter room were coming through at about five per minute on each track. Girls would be calling for new counters to up-date their blocks, runners would be dashing to get them from the table beside the plotting map. If one asked for one thing and one's neighbour asked for something else, it was a matter of who shouted loudest! It was all so unlike the quiet, relaxed atmosphere often depicted in films.' Looking down on the scene from the 'upper circle', behind a thick sound-proof glass partition which cut out the pandemonium from the plotting room, sat the duty fighter controller and his assistants. 'They seemed so calm, far removed from the hubbub below; if things there had been as chaotic as they were with us, I don't think we could have won the battle!'

The senior fighter controller at Uxbridge was 44-year-old Wing Com-mander Lord Willoughby de Broke. Between the wars his interest had turned to flying and after gaining his pilot's licence he had bought his own light aircraft. In 1935 he joined the Auxiliary Air Force, the week-end flyers, flying first Gladiators and later Hurricanes. Like many of the Auxili-ary pilots he was judged too old for combat flying when the war came, however, and early in 1940 he took up his new post at Uxbridge.

When the plots started to appear on the situation map it was up to the duty fighter controller, Park's personal representative, to 'set the stage' for the action by ordering up the squadrons and positioning them as he thought best. This process of positioning the fighter squadrons in readiness to meet the enemy raid could be likened to positioning rugby players in readiness to meet a kick-off from the opposing team: both had to be spread out roughly in position beforehand, because by the time the line of the opponent's thrust became clear there would be little time to rearrange the defence. Once the attackers started to move in, time was of the essence. 'Each minute of unnecessary delay waiting to make absolutely sure that the raid was coming in, meant about 2,000 feet of vital altitude our fighters would not have when they met the enemy,' recalled Willoughby de Broke. If, on the other hand, the controller ordered the fighters to scramble at the least sign of enemy activity, he stood the risk of his aircraft being short of fuel when the real attack came in. Once it was clear that a major attack was in the offing Park was informed and, whenever he could, he made his way to the operations

room. The Air Vice-Marshal would allow his controllers to continue directing the action, making suggestions where he thought necessary.

The controller at Uxbridge would order the fighter squadrons to
scramble and move to designated positions in readiness to meet the attacks.
Then, when the fighters were airborne, they were controlled from the
various Sector operations rooms. In other words the Group controller
decided which squadrons were to engage which enemy formations, and then
left it to his Sector controllers to bring this about.

The Sector operations rooms were smaller replicas of the one at
Uxbridge, little larger than a good-sized drawing room, with half a dozen
men and women plotters to keep the situation map up to date. There was no
glass partition separating the fighter controller and the plotters, so the latter
had to be far quieter than their counterparts at Group. From his position on
a raised dais overlooking the situation map, the fighter controller was in
radio contact with the leaders of the fighter units and directed them into
action. 'My job was not only to put the fighter squadrons in position to
intercept, but also put them into a position where they could intercept with
advantage,' Squadron Leader Anthony Norman, the senior controller at
Kenley, explained. 'So we would not aim them straight at the enemy formation; instead we would try to place them a little to the south, so that they
could attack from out of the sun and, if possible, with the advantage of
height.' The fighters had to be positioned within visual range, about eight
miles, of the enemy formation; once there, the fighter leader called 'Tally
Ho!' (to indicate he needed no further help from the ground), and led his
force in to attack. Eight miles might sound a long way, but for fighters
moving at four miles per minute seeking bombers moving at three miles per
minute there was little margin for error. A few patches of cloud in the wrong
place could mean that the opposing forces sailed past without seeing each
other.

Whatever the doubts nursed by the controller on the ground, it was
essential for the morale of the fighter pilots that he appear confident and in
complete control of the situation. The worst thing of all for those above was
an air of indecision from the controller. 'The important thing was to make a
right-enough decision, soon enough', commented Squadron Leader David
Lloyd, 30, the senior controller at Tangmere. 'If you then found that it
wasn't the right decision, it should be left as long as possible without doing
any damage before one gave the correct order. But one should never, never,
give contradictory orders one after the other.'

As the incoming raids crossed the coast of England and came within view
of the Observer Corps posts, the aircraft could be counted and the types
could usually be identified. This information was then passed to the various
Group and Sector operations rooms. If there was cloud or haze about,
however, the ground observers found it very difficult to keep track of the
movements of high-flying aircraft; this would pose a problem during the
action on 18 August.

As well as the fighters, the Sector operations rooms controlled the
anti-aircraft gun batteries in their areas. An army officer sat on the dais

beside each fighter controller and told his gunners when to come to readiness, when to open fire and, if friendly fighters entered the gun zones, when they had to cease fire.

By the summer of 1940 the system of fighter control masterminded by Dowding existed as a coherent organisation, covering the whole of southern and eastern England and Scotland. 'We had done literally thousands of practice interceptions during the phoney war,' recalled Anthony Norman. 'We were absolutely confident that nothing could come over the coast unseen by some element of the system.'

One unknown quantity prior to the Battle of Britain was the ability of the airwomen to stand up to the shock and carnage of battle. Many of them were employed at the front-line fighter and radar stations; would they be able to continue to perform their duties when these stations came under attack? In these enlightened times the answer is clear, but in 1940 a woman's place was very definitely in the home.

The entry of large numbers of women into the Royal Air Force brought other problems. David Lloyd remembers one airwoman at Tangmere who, in moments of excitement, took to using highly colourful language over the radio to fighter pilots. She was very good at her job as a radio monitor, but Lloyd's injunctions to her to moderate her speech were in vain. One day the station commander, Wing Commander Jack Boret, sent for Lloyd and said that there had been a complaint from the Air Ministry about his station's radio procedures and in particular the girl's language. Lloyd recalled 'I told Jack that I couldn't do anything with her, but that otherwise she was an excellent worker and a splendid girl. He said "Send her to me!" ' The following day, Lloyd was summoned to the station commander again. 'He said "That girl, she's absolutely infuriating!" ' Boret had given the girl a lengthy dressing down about her language and throughout it all she had stood demurely to attention in front of his desk. At the end of it, Boret told Lloyd, 'I said "Have you got anything to say for yourself?" And she said "Yes, Sir: balls!" ' On hearing this, Lloyd burst into a fit of uncontrollable laughter. 'The awful thing was,' Boret continued with an ill-concealed grin, 'that I couldn't help bursting out laughing myself!'

By the beginning of the Battle of Britain Fighter Command had good leaders, sufficient modern aircraft, and a system of fighter control which was workable and reasonably efficient. The force's greatest single weakness lay in the tactics its fighter pilots had been trained to use, before and after they made contact with the enemy.

Up to the late spring of 1940, Fighter Command had been preparing to meet a possible air attack on the British Isles coming only from due east, from Germany itself; prior to the German break-through in France in May, the possibility that France might fall and Britain would continue to fight on alone had not been a matter for serious consideration. An air attack mounted from Germany meant an air attack mounted beyond the radius of action of the German single-engined fighters; if twin-engined Messerschmitt

110s escorted the bombers they would be relatively few in number and they would have to fight almost at the limit of their radius of action.

In any case, before the war many had doubted whether high-speed dogfighting was even practicable between the latest types of fighter then entering service. The RAF Manual of Air Tactics, 1938 edition, had solemnly stated: 'Manoeuvre at high speeds in air fighting is not now practicable because the effect of gravity on the human body during rapid changes of direction at high speed causes a temporary loss of consciousness, deflection shooting becomes difficult and accuracy is hard to obtain'* So the main threat to Dowding's fighters engaging enemy bombers was thought to be not the enemy fighters, but the bombers' own return fire; before the war, the effectiveness of cross-fire from bombers flying in close formation had been greatly exaggerated.

With unescorted enemy bombers the prey, Dowding's planners had devised a system using tight formations to bring the fighter squadrons into contact with the enemy bombers, followed by set-piece tactics for the actual engagement. Moreover, because the bombers' return fire was considered dangerous, British fighter pilots were drilled to open fire at long range, 300 to 400 yards, then break away without closing to short range. These were the tactics Fighter Command's pilots had practised over and over again during the previous years. They were to prove utterly inappropriate to the battle in which the force now found itself.

In the Battle of Britain the biggest difference from the planned scenario was, of course, the presence of single-engined fighters escorting the German bomber formations. This meant that the British fighter squadrons, their pilots more concerned with maintaining position than keeping watch for the enemy, were highly vulnerable to surprise attack. And even if the squadron did reach the enemy bombers without interference from the escorts, it was rarely possible to employ the tactics for which the pilots had been trained. Sergeant John Etherington, flying Hurricanes with No 17 Squadron at Martlesham Heath, commented 'In peace time we had practised our set-piece attacks, but actual combat was nothing like that. Our CO would say "Attack! Attack!" and we would follow him. Whenever we mixed it with the Germans there was no time to organise attacks or anything like that. We just went in and had a go.'

The other big problem was that the fighter pilots had been trained to have a greater respect for the bombers' return fire than was necessary, with the result that attacks were broken off far too early. 'We had been taught, during the months before and during the early part of the war, to set our sights and open fire at over 300 yards then pull away', said Kenneth Lee. 'If we had been told to go in to 150 yards, we would have knocked down twice as many aircraft. We had been drilled in the old tactics so much that we did them automatically; we missed hundreds of opportunities.'

* It is interesting to note that almost exactly the same thing was said in the late 1940s, following the introduction of fighters capable of diving at supersonic speed, and again in the late 1950s with the advent of fighters capable of twice the speed of sound in level flight. The Korean and then the Vietnam air wars proved this to be false in each case.

Type of formation used by Fighter Command

When, following the campaign in France, the weakness of the British tactics did become clear, there was insufficient time for major changes. 'We knew that there was quite a lot wrong with our tactics during the Battle of Britain, but it was one Hell of a time to alter everything we had practised', explained Pilot Officer Bob Oxspring who flew Spitfires with No 66 Squadron at Coltishall. 'We had no time to experiment when we were in combat three or four times a day. Moreover we were getting fresh pilots straight out of the flying schools who were trained, barely, to use the old type of close formation; they simply could not have coped with anything radically different.'

Immediately before the battle the V formations used by the British fighters were widened out slightly, so that pilots could spend more time searching for the enemy rather than holding an exact distance from their neighbours; and one section of three, led by an experienced pilot, was stationed about 1,000 feet above the formation flying a weaving course and keeping watch for the enemy. These two steps greatly improved the search capability of the squadron, lessening the chances of being taken by surprise.

As we shall see, however, even the revised formation was inferior to those in use by the German fighter pilots.

As the Battle of Britain progressed and squadrons rotated between the No 11 Group area and quieter sectors to the north, the more enterprising commanders had the time to evolve more flexible tactics; and those pilots who survived found that going in to short range to finish off bombers was not so dangerous as they had been told. Bit by bit British fighter tactics evolved on a 'do it yourself' basis, at squadron level. Several commanders felt they could do no better than imitate the loose pairs and fours tactical formations used by the enemy.

At this stage of the battle one of Dowding's main concerns was the deficiency of 209 pilots in his operational squadrons; and things were getting worse, because the flying training organisation was not turning out new pilots as rapidly as their predecessors were being killed or wounded in action.

Moreover the pilots Fighter Command had lost were, in many cases, highly experienced men who had been trained in peacetime. Those who came to replace them were, for the most part, hastily trained and far from ready for action. One of these was 19-year-old Sergeant Harry Newton who arrived at No 111 Squadron at Croydon in June with only about 15 hours' flying time on Hurricanes; he was barely able to fly the aircraft, let alone handle it in combat. Newton's first interview with his new squadron commander was short: 'You will fly three hours in the morning and two each afternoon until you have 45 hours on type' he was told. By the latter part of June Newton had the requisite number of flying hours and was declared operational. He was luckier than many, for his squadron was not heavily committed during July and he had a little more time to adjust to the needs of battle. 'Gradually I gained experience of formation flying, operational scrambles, etc. My biggest worry was falling away from the fight and being called a coward.'

Much of the work of preparing the newcomers for operations fell on the already over-worked squadron commanders. Squadron Leader Don Mac-Donell, who commanded No 64 Squadron at Kenley, would try to fly with each of his new pilots before declaring them operational to give them some idea of what they would meet in combat. 'Young NCO and officer pilots would arrive on the squadron with only six or seven hours' flying time on the Spitfire. One or two practice sorties could make all the difference to their ability to survive in combat,' he recalled. 'If one could take them up one could point out their failings and tell them: "You won't survive ten minutes in battle if you fly like that!" The object was to tell them why and lead them round, not to frighten them.'

The half-trained newcomer's first meetings with the enemy were usually a fast-moving blur, with events moving too rapidly for him to grasp and which he would need luck even to survive. Kenneth Lee remembered one action during which No 501 Squadron was jumped by some Messerschmitt 109s: 'The word came over the R/T: "They're coming from the right. Break RIGHT!" There were two new fellows with us that day. One turned with us.

The other looked down in his cockpit to make sure his guns were switched on and when he looked up again we had all gone. For some reason the Germans did not hit him and he sailed on without seeing anything of the battle which must have been going on all around him.' The pilot landed half an hour after the rest of the squadron, oblivious of the mortal danger in which he had been.

Without the element of luck, a new pilot's first contact with the enemy could be fatal. Sometimes these men arrived on squadrons and died before anyone could get to know them. Lee remembered one new pilot 'who arrived in the morning in a Riley sports car and carried his stuff into the Mess. He took off in the afternoon with the Squadron and we never saw him again. The only reason I remember him at all was that we used his car for a couple of weeks before his family came to collect it.'

The main targets planned for attack on 18 August were the fighter airfields in south-eastern England. Of these the most important in No 11 Group were the Sector stations at Kenley, Biggin Hill, Hornchurch and North Weald, Northolt, Tangmere and Debden. The first five were situated along the periphery of the sprawling conurbation surrounding London. Tangmere was in the south of the Group's area, near Chichester; Debden was in the north, near Saffron Walden. Each of these airfields housed two or three fighter squadrons and had its own Sector operations room from which its fighters, and those from satellite airfields nearby, were directed into action. There were six satellite airfields, at Westhampnett, Croydon and Gravesend, Manston, Rochford and Martlesham Heath; Manston and Martlesham Heath each housed two squadrons, the remainder each housed one. Finally there was the forward operating airfield at Hawkinge, just inland from Folkestone.

Typical of the Sector airfields was that at Kenley in Surrey, 13 miles south of London. It dated from the end of the First World War and was built in what had been an area of relatively open countryside. Between the wars, however, the surrounding dormitory towns at Kenley, Caterham, Whyteleafe and Coulsdon, respectively to the north, south, east and west of the airfield, had all grown in size. By the end of the 1930s, in places low-density housing extended as far as the airfield boundary.

During the Battle of Britain Kenley was under the command of 38-year-old Wing Commander Thomas Prickman. The airfield was the home of two fighter squadrons: No 64 (with 17 Spitfires, of which 12 were serviceable on the evening of 17 August) and No 615 (with 22 Hurricanes, 16 serviceable on 17 August). An operational flying squadron can be likened to a spear: behind the short, sharp cutting edge there is a very long and heavy shaft. Kenley's 'cutting edge' comprised the Spitfires and Hurricanes, 23 of which would go into action on 18 August. Behind this 'spearhead', and necessary to give it accuracy and momentum and enable it to strike repeated blows, was the 'shaft' comprising some 30 officers, 600 airmen and 100 airwomen, plus about a hundred army anti-aircraft gunners and infantrymen to guard the airfield. Thus, for each fighter pilot who would take off from

Kenley on 18 August, there were 35 men and women on the ground directly or indirectly supporting his efforts.

Originally the landing ground at Kenley had been of grass, which meant that operations were not possible if the ground became sodden. Then, late in 1939, two 800-yard concrete runways had been laid at right angles to each other to allow all-weather operations. During the 18 August action, however, the fighters operated off either the runways or the grass, depending on which was the more convenient. Surrounding the landing ground was a concrete perimeter track nearly a mile and a half long; jutting from it, at irregular intervals, ran a dozen lead-offs to 8-foot-high earth-and-brick blast walls each looking, from above, like a letter 'E' and with accommodation for two fighters. Thus Kenley had protected dispersal points for 24 fighters; most of the remaining 15 were dispersed around the perimeter. Since they would obviously be a prime target for any German attack, the station's four hangars were used by aircraft only when strictly necessary for engineering work. One of the hangars, no longer required for its original purpose, housed the station's motor transport pool; and there was room to spare for part of it to be used for the private cars of station personnel 'strictly at the owner's risk'. The buildings and runways were camouflaged, as was the sick quarters which bore no conspicuous red cross.

The Sector operations building at Kenley stood on the eastern side of the airfield. Internally the building resembled its larger brother at Uxbridge, but externally it was quite different: the No 11 Group operations room was situated in a concrete bunker deep underground; that at Kenley was housed in a small bungalow-like building, its sole protection being a 6-foot-high blast wall round the outside and the camouflage netting festooned over it. Flying Officer Jack Hill, one of the officers working in the operations room, remembers seeing the building for the first time. Previously he had worked as an underwriter at Lloyd's, where there was a complete system of underground offices so that work could continue even if the main building was bombed; surely Fighter Command would have nothing less for its vitally important control centres? After he had been shown round Hill asked his guide 'Yes, but where's the proper underground one, the one we will use when things start happening?' He was told that there was none; he was looking at the place from which the fighters would be directed 'when things started happening'.

Dowding was fully aware of the vulnerability of his Sector operations buildings; and plans were in train for protected fighter control centres situated off the airfields. Following many years of financial stringency, however, his works services were now fully committed. Not until early in 1940, it will be remembered, had Kenley had even concrete runways or blast pens for its aircraft. In the meantime a site had been earmarked for use as an emergency Sector operations room in case the main one was hit: an empty butcher's shop in Caterham High Street nearly a mile away, so chosen because it was immediately over the main GPO telephone cable running through the area.

Kenley's primary defences were, of course, its fighters. Backing these, on the ground, were the station's anti-aircraft defences to combat attacks by enemy dive-bombers or low flyers. These two forms of attack were the most feared, for they were potentially the most accurate and therefore likely to be the most damaging.

Kenley's main gun defences comprised four 40-mm Bofors guns, powerful modern automatic weapons with a rate of fire of 120 rounds per minute. The 2-pounder high explosive shells from the Bofors were quite devastating against aircraft of 1940-vintage; if one of them exploded against a light-metal structure it would make a hole large enough for a man to climb through. The only thing to be said against the Bofors gun, in the summer of 1940, was that there were far too few to go round: more than twice as many would have been needed to protect Kenley properly. To make up the difference other less-effective weapons had had to be pressed into service. Kenley had two 3-in guns, obsolete weapons dating back to the First World War which fired 13-pound shells and, being hand served, had a maximum rate of fire of about 15 rounds per minute; used in the low-altitude defence role, the 3-in guns fired over open sights. There were about twenty old Lewis guns, infantry machine guns also dating back to the First World War; these were sited to counter both attack from the air and a possible attempt to seize the airfield in a land attack by paratroops. And there was at least one 20-mm Hispano cannon, an aircraft weapon fitted to a makeshift ground mounting. The Bofors guns belonged to the 31st Light Anti-Aircraft Battery, the 'Rough Riders'. The 3-in guns belonged to the 148th Light Anti-Aircraft Battery. Army gunners manned most of the Lewis guns; Royal Air Force gunners manned the rest and also the Hispano gun.

Finally, defending Kenley, there was the unconventional parachute-and-cable system in position along the northern side of the airfield just outside the perimeter track, with launchers at 60-foot intervals. Fired vertically upwards in salvoes of nine or more as enemy aircraft came in at low altitude, this device comprised a 480-foot length of steel cable carried 600 feet high by a rocket; at the top of the trajectory the cable was released, a parachute opened and suspended the cable hopefully in the path of the enemy aircraft. If the latter struck the cable a second parachute opened at the bottom of the line and the unfortunate aircraft was left towing away the contraption. If the cable was picked up on one or other wing, there was a good chance that the aircraft would go down out of control. This 'secret weapon' had not been used in action before 18 August.

Each of the airfields in the No 11 Group area possessed similar defences, which were reasonably effective against aircraft flying at altitudes up to about 7,000 feet. Above that altitude heavy anti-aircraft guns with predictor control were necessary, if there was to be any chance of inflicting damage on the raiders.

The part played by the heavy anti-aircraft gun batteries during the Battle of Britain has usually been neglected. The task of the heavy gun defences was four-fold: first, to shoot down or damage enemy aircraft; secondly, to split up the enemy formations so that the fighters could engage the bombers more

Parachute and Cable

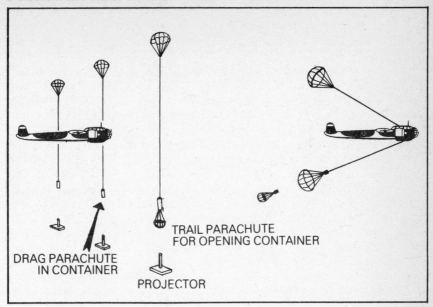

TRAIL PARACHUTE
FOR OPENING CONTAINER

DRAG PARACHUTE
IN CONTAINER

PROJECTOR

easily; thirdly, to indicate the position of enemy aircraft to the fighters; and fourthly, to prevent or hinder accurate bombing. And while they were only rarely successful in achieving the first three of these, the gunners were consistently able to achieve the fourth.

Three types of heavy anti-aircraft gun were in service: the 4.5-in, the 3.7-in and the 3-in. The first two of these, the 4.5-in and the 3.7-in, were modern guns effective over 26,000 feet. The last, the obsolete 3-in gun which dated back to the First World War, was effective only to about 14,000 feet. Usually heavy anti-aircraft guns were sited in fours, with a range-finder and predictor. The latter calculated the point in the sky where the aircraft *would be* when the shell reached it. Taking as an example an aircraft 6,000 yards from the gun, the shell would take about 10 seconds to reach its target; if the aircraft was moving at 180 mph, however, it would cover half a mile during the time-of-flight of the shell. So at the time of firing the gun barrel had to be aligned on a point half a mile in front of the aircraft. The predictor and range-finder operators calculated this lead distance and also the time-of-flight of the shell; the latter was set on the shell's clockwork fuse, to explode it in the right place. Of course, the pilot of the aircraft could avoid the shell by jinking his aircraft from side to side; but he could not do this and carry out an accurate bombing run, nor could he do so and hold his place in formation.

Whenever possible, bombers were routed to fly round the areas defended by heavy guns. Or, if they had to fly through these areas, they would usually do so at altitudes around 15,000 feet. As a rough guide, anti-aircraft fire became half as effective for each 5,000 foot increase in the

Operation of Barrage Balloon

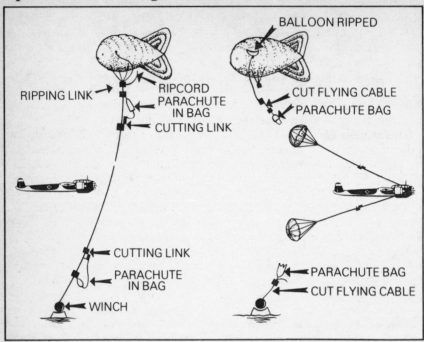

altitude of the target aircraft; that is to say, compared with the effectiveness at 5,000 feet, the guns were half as effective at 10,000 feet and only a quarter as effective at 15,000 feet. On the other hand, the greater the altitude from which the bombs were released, the lower was their accuracy. Again as a rough guide, and other things being equal, under operational conditions bombing errors from 15,000 feet were about twice as great as those when the bombs were dropped from 5,000 feet. To sum up: the lower the bomber flew the greater were the chances that its bombs would hit the target; but also greater were the chances that it would be hit by anti-aircraft fire. In the narrowest sense, every German bomber which attacked from 10,000 feet or higher represented a minor victory for the heavy anti-aircraft gunners.

In south-eastern England the heavy gun defences were concentrated round London itself, on either side of the Thames Estuary, covering the ports of Dover, Folkestone and Harwich, Ipswich, Portsmouth and Southampton, and at a few of the more vulnerable airfields.

During the battle, life for the gunners was often hard. Gunner Peter Erwood, 18, serving at a 3.7-in gun site near Dover with the 75th Heavy Anti-Aircraft Regiment, remembers the Battle of Britain as 'one almost continuous grind of carrying ammunition (two 56-pound cartridges in a 28-pound steel box, 140 pounds in all, one per man), changing gun barrels when they were worn down (1 ton between eight men, lifted nearly 5 feet) and long periods of duty. We worked bloody hard,' he recalled, 'with none of the glamour enjoyed by the fighter pilots.'

A further aspect of the defences was the network of searchlight sites dotted over southern and eastern England, with about two miles between each. Each site was served by ten men and equipped with a searchlight, a sound locator and a single Lewis gun manned at all times by an air sentry. These small camouflaged sites, difficult to pick out from the air until the Lewis gun opened fire, would serve as an additional hazard to German aircraft flying to and from their targets at low altitude.

Finally there were the barrage balloons, 1,523 of which were in position on the morning of 18 August. These ungainly hydrogen-filled gasbags, 62 feet long and 25 feet in diameter, had a maximum flying altitude of about 5,000 feet. Usually they were dotted in a random pattern over the target to be defended, as a deterrent to low-flying aircraft and dive-bombers. If an aircraft struck the cable, a pair of explosive cutters severed the wire strands at the top and the bottom and the aircraft was allowed to carry the cable away with it. Attached to each end of the cable, however, was an 8-foot diameter canvas parachute; when fully open, these exerted a combined drag of 7 tons at 200 mph, more than six times the engine thrust of the most powerful German bomber. It was sufficient to stop an aircraft in its tracks and send it spinning down out of control. The main balloon-defended areas in south-eastern England were London, Chatham and Dover, Harwich, Portsmouth, Gosport and Southampton.

Air operations are critically dependent on the weather. On the evening of 17 August the weather over southern England was dominated by an area of intensely high pressure to the west of Cornwall. For the past few days cooler air spilling out of the bottom of this almost-stationary anti-cyclone had been creeping underneath the warmer air lying over the land mass. The resultant condition, with a blanket of relatively warm air suspended above cooler air close to the ground, is known as a temperature inversion. It is a stable condition, which acts as a barrier to hold smoke and industrial haze in place and prevents them from dispersing upwards. This haze had gradually been thickening for the past few days and it would have its effect on the aerial fighting on the 18th. It was high summer, however, and the haze would be scarcely noticeable to those on the ground. The Saturday had seen English summer weather almost at its best with a warm sun, almost clear blue skies and a crimson and gold sunset. The forecast for the 18th was that the south of England would enjoy similar weather, at least during the morning and early afternoon.

A long-drawn-out confrontation between two major air forces is a continuous affair. Part of each force is always active as each side attempts to maintain its pressure on, or extend its knowledge of, the other. Thus, as midnight on 17 August passed and the new day began, the wombling desynchronous engine note of German bombers was audible over several parts of England and Wales. Fourteen Heinkel 111s of Bomber Geschwader

27 attacked airfields and harbour installations in the west. Their bombs damaged a warehouse, a dry-dock, a granary and a railway siding in Liverpool and one man was wounded. In Aberavon and Coventry there was further slight damage to property. The rest of the bombs fell on open ground.

At the same time fourteen Heinkels of Bomber Gruppe 100 attempted a night precision attack on the Nuffield factory at Castle Bromwich near Birmingham, which had just started to mass-produce Spitfires. To find their target the German crews used a complex beam system code-named X-Geraet (later, in November, the Gruppe would use this system when it marked Coventry for the devastating attack by the rest of the German bomber force). On this occasion, however, the Gruppe did not achieve spectacular results: the bombs fell in open fields, uncomfortably close to the Castle Bromwich factory but without causing any damage to it.

Over the eastern half of England the Luftwaffe sent single aircraft, to lay mines off the coast or to make harassing attacks on the airfields used by RAF Bomber Command. One of the intruders, a Junkers 88 of Night Fighter Geschwader 1, fell foul of a Blenheim of No 29 Squadron piloted by Pilot Officer Richard Rhodes. It was a fine night, with visibility about 10 miles in the bright moonlight. Rhodes sighted the enemy aircraft but, in spite of a 35-minute chase with the lumbering Blenheim's throttles wide open, he was unable to close within normal firing range. Other Blenheims were ordered to try to cut off the intruder's escape, but none succeeded in making contact. Finally, as the raider crossed the coast near Spurn Head soon after 3 am, Rhodes received orders from the ground to fire at the enemy and hope for a few lucky hits. Some 400 yards behind his quarry Rhodes lined up his sights then pressed the firing button for two long 8-second bursts, until the hiss of compressed air escaping from the breech blocks showed that he had fired all 2,397 rounds in the magazines of his five forwards-firing machine guns.

Some of the rounds must have struck the enemy aircraft, however, for now it slowed down and entered cloud still pursued by the Blenheim. 'We came out of cloud and there, about 150 yards behind us and to our left, was the enemy,' recalled Rhodes's gunner, Sergeant 'Sticks' Gregory. 'I don't know who was the more scared, me or the Germans.' Gregory swung round his turret and fired a short sighting burst with his Vickers gun at the aircraft, which he took to be a Heinkel 111, then emptied the rest of the 100-round drum in a single long burst. Flames licking its cockpit and starboard wing, the damaged aircraft spiralled down gently through the patchy cloud and crashed into the sea. There were no survivors from the Junkers 88's three-man crew; the war had claimed its first lives on 18 August.

Afterwards Rhodes and Gregory landed at Digby and excitedly described their long chase and ultimate success, in the squadron's crewroom. At this time a victory at night was a great rarity and there were congratulations from everyone except the squadron's armament officer, a Warrant Officer, who burst into the room carrying the Vickers gun Gregory had used. 'Who was the gunner on that aircraft?' he demanded. Gregory said that he had been. 'Well you're on a charge,' the Warrant Officer said, 'look at the barrel of this gun!' The Vickers had not been designed for such harsh usage and Gregory's long bursts had ruined it. Salvation was close at hand, however. The squadron commander, Wing Commander Stan Widdows, spun round and declared, 'I think we can ignore that, Chiefie; he's just shot down an aircraft with it.'

The only other German loss during the early morning darkness was a Heinkel 111 of Bomber Gruppe 100, returning from Castle Bromwich with a mechanical failure. It was wrecked when the crew made a crash-landing near Dinard, but nobody was hurt.

Also during the night of 17th/18th, Royal Air Force bombers were active. Bomber Command despatched 35 Blenheims to attack German airfields in France, Holland and Belgium; and 40 Wellingtons and 11 Hampdens were sent to bomb aircraft storage parks, railway yards and industrial targets in Germany and drop mines in the Elbe estuary. Coastal Command sent 11 Battle single-engined bombers to attack shipping in Boulogne harbour and 8 Blenheims to bomb barges in the port of Vlaardingen near Rotterdam. All of the bombers returned safely.

The British night bombers achieved no greater success than their German counterparts. Again there was sporadic bombing and damage to private property.

In the south of England first light came shortly after 5.10 am and by 5.50 am the sun's disc was clear of the eastern horizon. At the German bases in northern France, first light and sunrise came about five minutes later. By now almost all of the night raiders had landed; both sides began preparing for a day of hard fighting.

Shortly before first light Fighter Command's day fighting squadrons had begun to stir. Sleepy ground crewmen had been roused from their sparsely furnished huts beside the dispersal points, and started to get their dew-covered aircraft ready for immediate action. After their previous flights the fighters had had their fuel tanks, oxygen bottles and ammunition magazines replenished. The main thing to be done now was to run each fighter's engine to warm the lubricating oil, so that there would be no delay in getting airborne if the order came to 'scramble'. With two men lying across the tailplane to stop it from rising, each fighter's engine was run up to maximum revolutions and each of the two magnetoes was switched off in turn to check that the other was functioning. Then the engines were shut down and a refuelling tanker moved from aircraft to aircraft, topping up the depleted tanks.

At most of the squadrons each pilot now placed his parachute pack on the tailplane of his aircraft, the straps carefully folded, so that it could be put on in a hurry if needed. A few squadrons did things differently: at No 615 Squadron at Kenley, for example, the parachute pack was placed in the pilot's seat and the straps hung over the side of the cockpit, to save a few vital seconds in strapping in when the order came to 'scramble'.

Even before the sun had fully risen, a couple of squadrons roared into the air and moved to forward operating bases in the south-east of No 11 Group's area. No 65 Squadron sent twelve Spitfires to Manston, No 151 Squadron sent eight Hurricanes to Rochford, one of them Dick Smith's 'heavy old cow' fitted with cannon. When they arrived these aircraft were topped up with fuel. A few other fighters were sent off, in threes, to fly standing patrols over the convoys of shipping moving back and forth along the east coast of England.

Now each fighter on the ground stood ready for immediate action, chocks in front of the wheels and an electric starter trolley plugged into its side. The early morning ritual complete, silence returned to the fighter airfields punctuated only by the softer notes of nature's own dawn chorus.

For the British pilots now was the time of waiting and, for some, thinking about what the day might bring. Men sat around in their flying kit and lifejackets, some trying to snatch a little more sleep, some reading, some playing cards. For men tensed up for action, this waiting was the worst part of war. 'From time to time the telephone would ring and whenever it did there was a ghastly silence,' recalled Don MacDonell. 'The orderly would answer it and often one would hear something like: "Yes, Sir . . . yes, Sir . . . . Yes Sir . . . Sergeant Smith wanted on the phone." And everyone would breathe again.'

In the various Fighter Command operations rooms the members of the 'graveyard shift', on duty throughout the night, saw out its last few boring hours. Leading Aircraftman Fred Bailey, 26, a plotter in the operations room at Kenley, recalled that it had been a very quiet night in his Sector. Those on duty sat around drinking tea or reading books while some of the WAAFs knitted, filling in time until they were relieved at 8 pm.

Before any attack could be mounted, the German commanders needed confirmation that there had been no unexpected change in the weather pattern. Accordingly, immediately after sunrise, Weather Reconnaissance Staffel 51 sent a Heinkel 111 round the Scilly Isles and up to the Bristol Channel to report on the cloud moving in from the west.

The next German aircraft to take-off was a four-engined Focke-Wulf 200 Condor, which left Bordeaux at 6.06 am. It was to carry out an armed reconnaissance over the Atlantic, flying in a wide sweep to the west of the British Isles with the intention of landing in Norway about 11 hours later.

By 7 am the day was already well advanced for many, though for others it was just beginning. At Kenley Aircraftman Laurence Bell, 26, rose after spending an uncomfortable night bedded down on the floor of the station chapel, which had been pressed into use as overflow accommodation. He had just finished his 3-week recruit training and today he was to start work as an aircrafthand with No 64 Squadron with Spitfires.

In Clacton 23-year-old shop assistant Kathleen Venn was relaxing in bed for a few more minutes before getting up, her thoughts on how the day would go in spite of the war. Today was her wedding day and the ceremony was booked for the early afternoon in St James's Church. Since it might be in the thick of the fighting if the Germans invaded, Clacton now resembled a ghost town; its children had been evacuated to safer areas, many of its shops were closed down and several houses had been boarded up or taken over by the Army. It was going to be a quiet wedding, with no choir and few guests. Nor was Kathleen Venn even to be permitted the luxury of a honeymoon, for on the very next day her husband-to-be had to leave her to join the Royal Air Force.

At Ableige, just to the north of Paris, Unteroffizier Guenther Unger and Feldwebel Wilhelm Raab and their comrades of the 9th Staffel of Bomber Geschwader 76 had finished breakfast and were now moving to the disused school which was used as a briefing room. Rumour had it that there was something big on.

During the early part of the morning half a dozen German reconnaissance aircraft, Dornier 17s, Junkers 88s and Messerschmitt 110s, fanned out over southern England to take photographs and report on the weather. For the most part these came and went without interference, though at 7.20 am the crew of one Dornier did get a nasty fright when they stumbled upon a convoy off the Essex coast protected by three Hurricanes of No 257 Squadron and escaped only after a long diving chase. Apart from the occasional 'scramble' to chase away these reconnaissance aircraft, and a few standing patrols mounted over convoys, the morning was relatively quiet for Fighter Command.

For the millions of men, women and children living in the south-eastern corner of England, the Sunday morning brought with it yet another baking-hot summer's day. The sun beat down out of the deep blue sky, rapidly evaporating the morning dew. Only the more observant noticed that immediately above the horizon in every direction was a bank of haze, which bleached the sky to a dull off-white and shrouded high objects on the ground more than a mile or so away. For some of the people the Sunday was a day of relaxation just as in peace time, with church for the devout and cycle trips or countryside rambles for the more energetic. Yet many more found themselves engaged in work connected in some way or other with the conflict. Some toiled to raise crops in their gardens, for the growing of food had been elevated from productive pastime to patriotic duty. In threatened areas many worked on the erection or improvement of their Anderson shelters, simple structures of corrugated steel plates which could be assembled like some outsize Meccano set to provide protection for an entire family. For the members of the Home Guard and the many first-aid and civil defence units, war was a part-time activity; and Sunday morning was the time to learn the skills which the long-expected battle might demand from them.

The first deaths in Britain that day due to enemy action occurred during the morning at Hook in Hampshire. A disposal team from No 48 Section, Royal Engineers, was digging down to an unexploded bomb dropped a couple of days earlier, when it went off. Five sappers were killed and their section leader, Lance Sergeant William Button, was hurled a considerable distance and badly concussed. Nevertheless he helped the two other survivors to safety, before summoning help.

The Luftwaffe did not intend to allow the relative calm over southern

England to continue much longer, however. Soon after dawn the bomber airfields to the north of Paris and around Amiens had started to hum with activity, as bombs were moved into position beside the aircraft and then loaded on board. Air Fleet 2 was making last-minute preparations for large-scale attacks on two of No 11 Group's most important airfields.

CHAPTER 2

The Lunchtime Engagement

Confusion in battle is what pain is in childbirth –
the natural order of things.
GENERAL MAURICE TUGWELL

On the prediction of fine weather over southern England for much of 18 August, staff officers at Kesselring's headquarters at Brussels issued executive orders for the morning's operations. Units of Air Fleet 2 were to carry out the previously planned attacks on targets 1017 and 10118 in the Luftwaffe catalogue: the British fighter airfields at Biggin Hill and Kenley. The former was allocated to Bomber Geschwader 1, based at airfields around Amiens, which was to send in sixty Heinkel 111s; the latter was allocated to Bomber Geschwader 76, based at airfields immediately to the north of Paris, which was to attack with forty-eight Dornier 17s and Junkers 88s. Not only was the force attacking Kenley smaller than that attacking Biggin Hill, but each Dornier 17 and Junkers 88 carried only about two-thirds the bomb load of the larger Heinkel 111; it was confidently expected, however, that the more-precise attack methods planned for the Kenley attack would result in it receiving a similar level of destruction. Fighter Geschwader 3, 26, 51, 52, 54 and Destroyer Geschwader 26, all based in the Pas-de-Calais area, were to provide the necessary close escorts and free-hunting patrols to cover these attacks.

Both of the target airfields were also the sites of the all-important Sector operations rooms, from which the British fighters were directed into action. These airfields had been selected for attack only because they were known to be amongst the largest ones operating fighters, however; the German Intelligence service had no knowledge of the Sector operations rooms there. But if these poorly protected buildings could be hit, and those inside killed or wounded, it would be a body-blow to the fighter control system in these Sectors.

In the austerely furnished disused school room at Ableige, near the airfield at Cormeilles-en-Vexin, the assembled crewmen of the 9th Staffel of Bomber Geschwader 76 ceased their chatter as the unit's popular commander, 27-year-old Hauptmann Joachim Roth, entered the room. Without formality he began his briefing. The unit's objective today was the airfield at Kenley, one of the most important British fighter bases, situated on the southern edge of London. He pointed it out on the wall map. For the first time, he continued, the Staffel was to attack a target in England at low altitude; it was to use the same hedgehopping tactics which had proved so devastatingly effective during attacks in France. As usual, Roth himself was to fly as navigator in the lead aircraft. The nine Dornier 17s were to cross the

English Channel at low altitude and make their landfall just to the west of Beachy Head; from there they were to skirt round the south of Lewes, pick up the London to Brighton railway, and follow its general line to the target.

The crews were to concentrate their attack on the hangars and buildings at the southern end of the airfield. Glossy prints of aerial photographs were then passed round for the crews to look at and the individual buildings were pointed out to them. Feldwebel Wilhelm Raab recalled that it was the only occasion on which he had seen such prints passed round during a briefing; obviously the target was considered to be of especial importance. For this attack each of the bombers was to carry twenty 110-pound bombs, each fitted with a new type of fuse which would function effectively if they were released from 50 feet or higher; the type of bomb previously used by the Staffel had had to be released from twice this height, making the unit's Dorniers correspondingly more vulnerable to ground fire.

The daring attack by the 9th Staffel was to be part of a complex pincer attack on Kenley involving the entire Geschwader. First, a dozen Junkers 88s of the IInd Gruppe were to approach from high altitude and carry out a precision dive-bombing attack on the hangars and airfield buildings. Next, five minutes later, twenty-seven Dornier 17s of the Ist and IIIrd Gruppen were to attack from high altitude and crater the landing ground and knock out the ground defences. Finally, five minutes later still, the 9th Staffel was to go in and finish off any buildings still standing. It was a bold and imaginative plan and one which, if it succeeded, would wreck Kenley from end to end. The high-flying bombers were to have a full fighter escort; the low-flyers would have to rely on stealth to avoid trouble, on their routes to and from the target.

Compared with the complicated effort planned by Bomber Geschwader 76, the attack by Bomber Geschwader 1 on Biggin Hill scheduled to take place five minutes later was an unsophisticated affair. Sixty Heinkel 111s were to go in at high altitude in three closely spaced waves, with fighter escort, and knock out the airfield.

Today the 4th War Reporter Detachment of the Luftwaffe chanced to be visiting the two bomber Geschwader, and no fewer than eight reporters and cameramen were to fly with the raiders. Two of these, reporter Georg Hinze and photographer Rolf von Pebal, were to go with the 9th Staffel. Two other 'passengers' were to go with the low flyers: Hauptmann Gustav Peters, to gain experience of low-altitude bombing operations; and the highest-ranking officer on the mission, Oberst (Group Captain) Otto Sommer, a staff officer, there to gain operational experience.

Shortly before 9 am the first of the German bombers, Heinkel 111s of Bomber Geschwader 1, began to get airborne from their bases at Rosiéres-en-Santerre and Montdidier near Amiens. 'The metal birds were soon roaring into the sky. Others moved in to make up a Geschwader formation, as it had so often been practised in exercises,' wrote war reporter Bankhardt flying with the Ist Gruppe. 'Suddenly the radio operator interrupted my thoughts: "Herr Leutnant, I have just received a radio message. The Geschwader is to split up and return to base by Staffeln." "Damn shit!"

murmured the pilot, as he turned away as ordered. Shortly afterwards he landed the kite smoothly, in spite of the heavy bomb load on board.'

On landing the crews were informed that the whole operation had been postponed by two and a half hours, due to unfavourable weather conditions over southern England. The problem was that the layer of haze, sealed in by the temperature inversion, had concentrated to produce a zone of reduced visibility up to about 4,000 feet. This would certainly affect the dive-bombing and low-altitude attacks planned by Bomber Geschwader 76. The situation was likely to improve with time, however: as the sun rose higher and warmed the ground, the temperature inversion should lift and visibility close to the ground would improve.

The postponing order had reached the Bomber Geschwader 76 airfields to the north of Paris in time to prevent the take-off: the Ist Gruppe at Beauvais, the IInd Gruppe at Creil and the IIIrd Gruppe (which included the 9th Staffel) at Cormeilles-en-Vexin. 'We spent the whole of the morning kicking our heels by our aircraft' Guenther Unger afterwards wrote. 'We had stripped off in the marvellous weather and were sunning ourselves, for the take-off had been delayed. Gradually we became impatient. Were we going to be sent home to our billets today without flying a mission, as had happened so often in the past?'

During the mid-morning the British fighters were still being scrambled from time to time, to intercept or at least drive away the bothersome German reconnaissance aircraft which ventured over southern England. The intruders proved fleeting targets, however, and for the most part their crews were able to shake off the pursuing fighters. The sole exception was a Messerschmitt 110 of the 7th (Reconnaissance) Staffel of Tactical Development Geschwader 2. Possibly the crew felt themselves safe at 31,000 feet, for their flight path took them in over Kent and Sussex, then boldly across the Thames estuary to Essex. Elements of five fighter squadrons were ordered to intercept and the Messerschmitt was finally sighted at 11.30 am off the Essex coast by five Spitfires of No 54 Squadron led by Flight Lieutenant George Gribble. The fighters climbed to engage and the first to get within range and open fire was Pilot Officer Colin Gray. He fired off a long burst, causing both of the enemy aircraft's engines to smoke. The Messerschmitt dived away with the Spitfires in pursuit and the remaining four Spitfires fired bursts at it in turn. The German aircraft was last seen at low altitude going down thoroughly ablaze and with pieces falling off it, as it disappeared into the haze near the French coast. Soon afterwards it crashed into the sea, killing both men on board.

The period of relative inactivity at the German airfields lasted until 11 am, by which time the reconnaissance aircraft over southern England were reporting that the haze was thinning out. The planned attacks could start again. As before, the first to take-off were the Heinkels of Bomber Geschwader 1. 'One circuit of our base, then we set course for England. On the way to the coast the other Staffeln joined up. It made an impressive picture: the whole Geschwader with about sixty aircraft, just like on an exercise flight,' wrote Gefreiter (Leading Aircraftman) Willi Wanderer, a gunner with the IInd Gruppe. 'Soon it was going to be in earnest and the pilot gave the order "Prepare the guns!" I checked each of my two guns twice, to be on the safe side. At the French coast we joined up with our fighter escort. To the left and the right of us the sky was full of small black specks.'

Bomber Geschwader 1 formed up and picked up its escorts relatively easily. It was not so simple for Bomber Geschwader 76. In the area round Calais, where the Dorniers and Junkers 88s were to link up with their escorting fighters, there was 8/10ths cloud cover with a base of 6,500 feet and tops around 10,000 feet. As the bombers climbed through this layer their formations lost cohesion and valuable time had to be lost in orbiting while they reformed. Finally, at 12.45 pm, about six minutes late, Major Theodor Schweitzer led the Dorniers of the Ist and IIIrd Gruppen on to a westerly heading towards their target; already they had overtaken the Junkers 88s of the IInd Gruppe, which should have been five minutes ahead of them. These delays were to have ominous consequences for the low-flying 9th Staffel.

Soon after 12.50 pm 27-year-old Oberleutnant Gerhard Schoepfel, temporarily in command of the IIIrd Gruppe of Fighter Geschwader 26 while his friend Adolf Galland was in Berlin, crossed the coast near Dover with the leading fighters. His Messerschmitt 109s and those from Fighter Geschwader 3, about forty in all, were to roam ahead of the raiding force to disrupt the British fighter attacks before they could develop. About 25 miles behind Schoepfel came the high-altitude raiding force bound for Kenley: twenty-seven Dorniers of Ist and IIIrd Gruppen of Bomber Geschwader 76, with their close escort of some twenty Messerschmitt 110s of Destroyer Geschwader 26; and close by the Dorniers, though they should have been about 15 miles in front, were the Junkers 88s of the IInd Gruppe escorted by Messerschmitt 109s of Fighter Geschwader 51. About 15 miles behind these bombers came the sixty Heinkel 111s of Bomber Geschwader 1 bound for Biggin Hill, escorted by some forty Messerschmit 109s of Fighter Geschwader 54. The huge phalanx of aircraft droned its way westwards at three miles per minute, arrayed for battle above 12,000 feet. Meanwhile, some 50 miles away to the south-west, the nine Dorniers of the 9th Staffel were half-way between Dieppe and Beachy Head, skimming low over the waves and bent on sneaking under the British radar beams unobserved. Altogether, the raiding force comprised 108 bombers and about 150 fighters.

Meanwhile, in England, attentive eyes had been following the progress of the German formations, apart from the one at low altitude. Soon after noon the radar station at Dover had begun reporting activity over the Pas-de-Calais area. During the next forty minutes this activity had steadily increased until by 12.45 pm the filter room at Fighter Command headquarters was issuing plots on six separate concentrations of enemy aircraft. On the situation maps at the various operations rooms a rash of markers began to appear over the Straits of Dover and extending south-eastwards over France. The radar operators estimated the total strength of the raiding forces at 350, nearly one-third more than were actually approaching.

In the underground operations room at Uxbridge Park's controllers disposed No 11 Group's fighters for the riposte.* One Squadron, No 501 with twelve Hurricanes, was already airborne and on its way back to Gravesend after spending much of the morning at the forward operating base at Hawkinge near Folkestone. Pilot Officer Kenneth Lee and his comrades were winging their way homewards, happy in the knowledge that the Squadron was due for a rare afternoon off. It was not to be, however. The pilots' reveries were interrupted by orders from their ground controller to climb to 20,000 feet and patrol over Canterbury. Within minutes eight further squadrons were scrambling into the air to join them: two from Kenley, two from Biggin Hill and one each from North Weald, Martlesham Heath, Manston and Rochford. Squadron Leader Don MacDonell describes what it was like to lead the Spitfires of No 64 Squadron off from Kenley in a scramble take-off:

> When the order came, the orderly answering the telephone would shout 'SCRAMBLE!' at the top of his voice and each pilot would dash for his aircraft. By the time one got there a mechanic would already have started the engine; the other would be holding the parachute up and help me strap it on. Once that was done I would clamber into the cockpit. He would pass my seat straps over my shoulders and help me fasten them. When I gave the thumbs-up he would slam shut the side door and I would pull tight the various straps. Next I would pull on my helmet, plug in the R/T lead, and check that the engine was running properly. If all was well I would wave to the groundcrew to pull away the chocks, open the throttle, and move forward out of my blast pen and across the grass to the take-off position. Once there I would line up, open the throttle wide and begin my take-off run with the rest of my pilots following as fast as they could. The whole thing, from the scramble order to the last aircraft leaving the ground, took about a minute and a half.

When he was airborne MacDonell informed the Kenley controller, Anthony Norman, who told him to climb to 20,000 feet over base. While the rest of his Spitfires formed up behind him MacDonell climbed in a wide spiral, throttled back slightly to allow everyone to get into position. Once the formation was complete he opened his throttle again, to gain altitude as rapidly as possible.

At the same time as the fighters were roaring off the ground, Air Raid Warning Red came into force in eastern Kent. Along a wide swathe, from Margate in the north to Hastings in the south and extending inland past Ashford, the sirens moaned their note of warning. Men, women and children, many of whom had been about to start their Sunday lunch, grabbed treasured possessions and made their way to the shelters.

* Official records do not state who was directing No 11 Group's fighters at particular times on 18 August, and over the years memories have blurred. Almost certainly, however, Lord Willoughby de Broke was in overall control, with Park in the operations room overseeing him once the raids began to leave France.

By 1 pm the fighters initially assigned to meet the raids were all airborne and clawing for altitude as they moved into position. Five squadrons, Nos 17, 54, 56, 65 and 501, with seventeen Spitfires and thirty-six Hurricanes, were moving out to patrol the line Canterbury–Margate, to block any attack aimed at the port installations along the Thames estuary or the fighter airfields to the north of it. Four squadrons, Nos 32, 64, 610 and 615 with twenty-three Spitfires and twenty-seven Hurricanes, spiralled up into position over their bases at Kenley and Biggin Hill. Altogether there were 97 Spitfires and Hurricanes airborne to meet the attack. This meant two British fighters to every three German fighters, or two British fighters to every five German fighters and bombers. To Winston Churchill the pilots of Fighter Command might have been 'The Few', but to the Germans there would soon seem to be a disconcertingly large number of them around.

Nor was the whole of No 11 Group yet committed: three squadrons of Spitfires and Hurricanes in the Tangmere Sector, based near Chichester, were held ready to meet attacks coming from the south; and six more were in reserve to meet a possible follow-up attack from the south-east.

It was Oberleutnant Gerhard Schoepfel's lucky day. Soon after he had passed the coast, with the other Messerschmitts of his Gruppe spread out in a wide hunting formation behind him, he caught sight of the enemy. 'Suddenly I noticed a Staffel of Hurricanes underneath me. They were using the English tactics of the period, flying in close formation of threes, climbing in a wide spiral,' he afterwards wrote. It was No 501 Squadron, moving towards Canterbury and gaining altitude. Schoepfel beckoned to his pilots to remain above and give him cover while he went down, taking care to keep himself between his quarry and the sun. Under such circumstances a single aircraft might achieve surprise while several were almost certain to be seen. Like a cat stalking a bird Schoepfel waited until the Hurricane formation was moving away from him, then he pounced. With a couple of accurate bursts Schoepfel dispatched both of the Hurricanes weaving above the formation. Then he darted in to attack the formation itself. He fired one short burst into the Hurricane at the rear and it too went down in flames. 'The Englishmen continued on, having noticed nothing. So I pulled in behind the fourth machine and took care of him also, but this time I went in too close,' Schoepfel continued. Pieces of wreckage smashed into the Messerschmitt's propeller and oil spattered over his windscreen and down the sides of the cabin, leaving him unable to see a thing. Well satisfied with his work, Schoepfel swung round his Messerschmitt and dived away from the action.

Schoepfel's fourth victim had been Kenneth Lee, who knew nothing of the German's presence until he felt the thump of explosions behind him and metal smashing against his back armour. At the same time a splinter rammed into the calf of his right leg; he felt as if somebody had kicked him from behind, knocking his foot off the rudder pedal and up against the toe strap. The Hurricane shuddered and flames flickered back from the engine. Lee could see that the aircraft was doomed so he rolled it over on to its back, slid back the hood, released his seat straps and fell clear.

At this time there were persistent rumours that some Germans had taken to shooting up enemy pilots descending by parachute and Lee had no intention of suffering that fate. Mentally, he had prepared himself for this situation weeks before. He knew that he had baled out at about 17,000 feet so, with icy calmness, he pressed the button of his stop-watch and observed the seconds ticking by. Lee knew that a human body falls about a thousand feet in six seconds and he wished to get down to 6,000 feet before he pulled his ripcord. Accordingly, he did a free-fall descent lasting *sixty-six seconds*. 'I had never been told how to put out my arms to stabilise myself in the fall; as a result I tumbled head-over-heels the whole way down and became completely disorientated. When I finally did pull the ripcord I was on my back. The parachute streamed back between my legs and I was very lucky not to get tangled up in the lines,' he later recounted.

Profiting from the failings of the tight-combat formation still in use in many Fighter Command squadrons, Schoepfel had been able to knock down four Hurricanes in two minutes, killing one pilot and wounding three others. As he departed, other members of his Gruppe dived on the survivors of No 501 Squadron and an inconclusive dogfight followed.

Bomber Geschwader 76 made a fine sight as it advanced towards its target, with the close escort of Messerschmitt 110s in position above and behind. 'The English coast comes into sight. "Prepare for action" orders the Staffel commander. We cross the coast of England in tight formation,' wrote war correspondent Raimund Schulz, flying with the Ist Gruppe. 'To the left of us everything is quiet but to the right, from Dover, the first black and white flak-bursts appear. I concentrate on searching for enemy fighters. The sky is filled with our machines.'

From the cockpit of his Messerschmitt 109 Hauptmann Hannes Trautloft, 28, leading the IIIrd Gruppe of Fighter Geschwader 51 flying close escort for the Junkers 88s bound for Kenley, also noticed the flak bursts. 'Flak comes up from Dover, but the shells burst too low. Probably they are marking our position for the British fighters. Now we are over England, laid out beneath us in the sunshine. Below us, nothing stirs. The inhabitants have taken cover, but the hum of the motors of so many German aircraft must be audible in the deepest shelter', he afterwards noted in his diary.

By luck rather than calculated design the German bombers' course took them some 15 miles to the south, and out of sight of, the main British fighter concentration in the Canterbury–Margate area. Now the bombers had in front of them a clear run of 40 miles, before they would have to face the four squadrons of fighters climbing into position over Kenley and Biggin Hill.

At 1.03 pm the bombers passed over Ashford, following the Folkestone –Reigate railway line which conveniently led most of the way to their target. From the front room of her home in Godinton Road, 16-year-old Peggy Marsh watched the Dornier formation droning majestically overhead as though performing some courtly minuet. She thought it strange that the enemy aircraft could have got so far without the sirens sounding; only later did she discover that the local siren had not sounded when all the others had.

The opposing forces at 1.04 p.m.

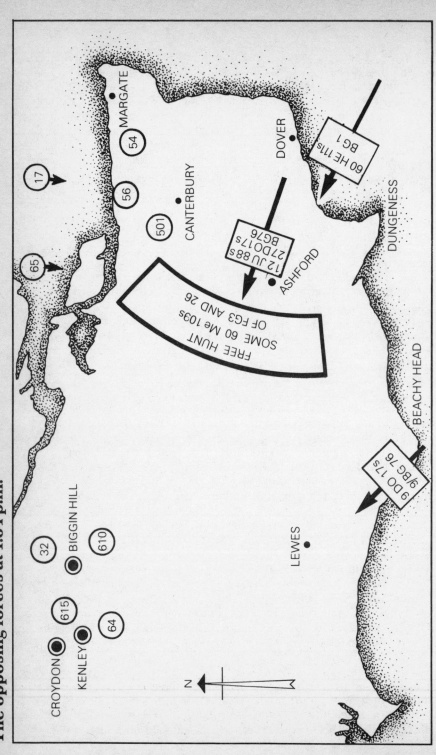

CROYDON

KENLEY

BIGGIN HILL

615

32

610

64

17

65

56

54

MARGATE

501

CANTERBURY

DOVER

ASHFORD

12 JU 88s
27 DO 17s
BG76

60 HE 111s
BG1

DUNGENESS

FREE HUNT
SOME 60 Me 109s
OF FG3 AND 26

LEWES

9 DO 17s
9/BG 76

BEACHY HEAD

N

'Wasn't I glad we hadn't heard it at twenty-to-one. Mum would never have sat down comfortably to dinner if she'd known', she afterwards confided in her diary.

Wilhelm Raab was worried. At the same time as the high-altitude raiding force was passing Ashford, the nine Dorniers of the low-flying 9th Staffel were nearing the south coast of England unseen on the British radar screens. Raab had been on several low-flying attacks before, but never on one which had involved a sea crossing. Now, with Beachy Head looming menacingly on his right, he felt the spidery tingle of fear running down the back of his neck. What if there were flak positions on the cliffs, able to fire down on the bombers? He felt naked and helpless: there was not a single tree or fold in the ground he could use for cover. If the shooting did start Raab would have known what to do to avoid it; but waiting to be shot at, that he found the most terrible thing of all. Many of the German crewmen now donned the special steel helmets they wore during low-altitude attacks.

The first shots fired at the Dorniers did not come from the land, however. As Roth led his Staffel in, flying so low that the propeller slipstreams left wakes across the surface of the sea, the bombers passed a couple of Royal Navy patrol boats. The German crews observed the flashing light demanding a reply of recognition and, when this did not come, the sailors opened up an ineffective machine gun fire. If the shots did nothing else, they relieved some of the tension on board the Dorniers roaring low over the coast.

Less obviously to the German crews, but far more ominously, Observer Corps post K3 situated on top of Beachy Head had seen their approach and reported it: nine Dorniers at zero altitude heading north-west. The warning was immediately telephoned to the Observer Group Headquarters at Horsham, thence to the fighter Sector stations in the area including that at Kenley.

Thirty-six-year-old Margaret Birch and her husband, Jim, were working in the garden of their home at Houndean Rise, Lewes, when they caught sight of the Dorniers to the south of them, flying close to the ground over the

Approximate positions of the opposing forces, 1.04 pm. The leading raiding force, comprising 27 Dornier 17s and 12 Junkers 88s of Bomber Geschwader 76, bound for Kenley, is just passing Ashford. Escorting the Dorniers are some 25 Messerschmitt 110s of Destroyer Geschwader 26; escorting the Junkers 88s are some 20 Messerschmitt 109s of Fighter Geschwader 51. The nine low-flying Dorniers of the 9th Staffel, also bound for Kenley, have just crossed the coast near Beachy Head. About to cross the coast, between Dover and Dungeness, are 60 Heinkel 111s of Bomber Geschwader 1 escorted by some 40 Messerschmitt 109s of Fighter Geschwader 54. Flying ahead of the bombers and their immediate escorts are some 60 Messerschmitt 109s of Fighter Geschwader 3 and 26 on a free-hunting patrol. Of the British squadrons the only one to have made contact with the enemy so far was No 501, which had lost four Hurricanes in quick succession to Gerhard Schoepfel. The other units ordered to the Canterbury–Margate area, Nos 17, 54, 56 and 65 Squadrons, with a total of 17 Spitfires and 36 Hurricanes, failed to make contact with the German formations during the initial stage of their penetration. Climbing into position above their airfields at Kenley and Biggin Hill are Nos 32, 64, 610 and 615 Squadrons, with a total of 23 Spitfires and 27 Hurricanes.

valley of the River Ouse, below the high ground on which they stood. 'We just stood and looked down at the pencil-like planes, creeping along with the South Downs as a backdrop,' she recalled. The aircraft remained in sight for nearly a minute; no markings were visible, but she remembers feeling that there was something sinister about both their appearance and their behaviour.

Wing Commander Thomas Prickman, the station commander, was in the Kenley operations room when the counters marking the low-flying Dorniers appeared on the situation map there. His fighter control officer, Squadron Leader Anthony Norman, had been busily passing instructions to the station's two fighter squadrons, Nos 64 and 615, to guide them into position to meet the high-altitude raiding force. At first the low-flyers seemed to be heading away to the west of them. Where on earth were they going?

Roth continued his north-westerly heading past Lewes until he picked up the London–Brighton railway line at Burgess Hill, then wheeled his formation round on to a northerly heading. The German commander's task, map-reading along the route at low altitude, was a difficult one: he had little time to identify landmarks as they raced beneath him and his visibility forwards was no better than the view from a 50-foot-high hill. Under such conditions one small town could look very much like another. He had chosen Burgess Hill as his turning point for two reasons: first, because it was at the junction of the railway lines from Lewes and Brighton to London; and secondly because on the eastern edge of the small town was the Keymer Brick and Tile Company whose kilns, topped by three high chimneys and four smaller ones, provided an unmistakable landmark. Several of the German crewmen recall passing low over the town. The people in the streets stood as if glued to the spot, gazing up at the unaccustomed sight of aircraft flying over so low. 'At first they did not take us for the enemy, not expecting German aircraft to be flying so low. Then the large crosses on our wings taught them otherwise and in the next instant they were scurrying for cover,' wrote Guenther Unger. Rolf von Pebal photographed the scurrying people in the streets, for posterity.

For those below, the scene was not so amusing. 'Just before lunch there was suddenly a huge noise in the sky and there were three German planes, only just skimming the tops of some oak trees near us, the crosses under their wings showing up very large and black,' recalled 44-year-old Muriel Bayfoot, on a visit to relatives in Burgess Hill with her husband. 'Off they went, machine-gunning the main street. As my father was walking down there I felt a bit worried, but he took cover in a nearby ditch.' As the formation passed over the centre of the town one of the German crewmen opened up with his machine gun at the 50-foot-high tower of the fire station. Bullets ricocheted off the houses and streets around, smashing windows and speeding the inhabitants in their dash for cover. There were no casualties.

The Dorniers hurtled northwards, passing Cuckfield and Balcombe. 'We zoomed over the English countryside, a few metres high. Every fold in the ground served as cover for us, each wood was exploited as a hiding place,' wrote Rolf von Pebal. 'We bounded over trees, undulating the whole time. A train rushed by underneath us. A couple of cyclists dashed for cover in the

Above Hermann Goering inspecting men of the 1st Gruppe of Bomber Geschwader 76, at Beauvais, during the Battle of Britain. To his right is Major Theodor Schweitzer, who led the high-level attack on Kenley on 18 August. (KG 76 Archiv) **Below** Generalfeldmarschall Albert Kesselring, commander of Air Fleet 2. **Right** : Generalfeldmarschall Hugo Sperrle, commander of Air Fleet 3. (via Dierich)

Scenes at the German fighter airfield at Caffiers near Calais home of the Messerschmitt 109s of the IIIrd Gruppe of Fighter Geschwader 26, from the album of Gerhard Schoepfel. **Above** Groundcrewmen constructing a sandbag blast pen to take one fighter. **Below** Engine change on a Messerschmitt 109 in the open.

Typical Gruppe formations employed by German bombers during the Battle of Britain. **Above** Dornier 17s (Schoepfel) **Below** Heinkel 111s (via Dierich)

Above The author outside the entrance to the underground bunker which housed the No 11 Group operations room at Uxbridge, photographed in 1978. **Below left:** Inside the operations room, nearly a hundred feet underground, from which the greater part of the British side of the air action on 18 August was directed. The senior fighter controller sat on the left, viewing the situation map through the sound-proof curved window on the right. **Below centre** View of the situation map and the WAAF plotters, from the fighter controllers' gallery. **Below right** View of the fighter controllers' gallery, from the plotting table. The WAAFs sitting at the dais were responsible for passing plots off the situation map back to the Fighter Command Filter Room at Stanmore, thus providing a running check on the correct positioning of markers.

Above The author beside the Sector operations building at Kenley, photographed in 1978. **Right** Squadron Leader Anthony Norman, the senior fighter controller at Kenley. (Norman)

Part of a remarkable series of photographs taken by a war photographer Rolf von Pebal, who accompanied the 9th Staffel during its low-altitude attack on Kenley on 18 August: **Top left** The Dorniers approaching Beachy Head at 1pm. **Middle left** Passing Beachy Head, two minutes later. **Bottom left** Unteroffizier Guenther Unger's Dornier soon after crossing the coast, with Seaford in the background. **Above** The railway halt at Southease, just to the south of Lewes. **Below** The scene at Cyprus Road, Burgess Hill, at 1.09pm with people dashing for cover as the Dorniers roared low overhead. The building with sandbags round it in the foreground was used as an air raid wardens' post.

Kenley seen from one of the Dorniers of the high-altitude raiding force, showing fires burning after the attack by the 9th Staffel. The German annotations show: 1 wrecked aircraft: 2 hangar on fire; 2a fire on the north side of the airfield; 3 crater on the runway.

ditch by the side of the road.' Many of the Germans commented on the wood and steel obstacles scattered over the fields, convincing proof of the British fears of attack by airborne troops. To keep out of each others' slipstreams the Dorniers flew almost in line abreast, bobbing up and down close to the ground like grass-track motorcyclists racing neck and neck.

Sixteen-year-old George Adams was with his father in the garden of their home in Mill Lane, Balcombe, when the Dorniers swept low over the roof of their house. When his father saw the black crosses under the wings of the bombers he made a dash for the open kitchen door, only to be bowled over as his wife and most of their six other children tried to run outside to see what the noise was about. By the time the two parents and their children had picked themselves up, the aircraft were out of sound and sight.

The Observer Corps posts passed back a steady stream of reports on the enemy raids advancing towards Kenley from both the south and east. From the situation in front of them, it was clear to Prickman and Norman that the Germans were attempting some sort of co-ordinated attack on their airfield or one of those nearby. The two squadrons already allocated to them were almost in position to meet the high altitude attack; they could not be diverted. No fighters had yet been allocated to deal with the low altitude attack. The sole squadron still on the ground in the Sector was No 111, with twelve Hurricanes at Croydon. Normally neither Prickman nor Norman had authority to order fighter squadrons into the air; that was the prerogative of Park himself and his controllers at Group headquarters. Sector controllers were permitted to take matters into their own hands if there was a danger of fighters being caught on the ground by an enemy attack, however. With two separate enemy forces moving in threateningly towards his airfields, Prickman now ordered all flyable fighters still on the ground at Kenley, and No 111 Squadron at Croydon, into the air in a 'survival scramble'; aircraft able to fly but not fight were to head northwestwards to safety. After take-off the twelve Hurricanes of No 111 Squadron were to assemble overhead Kenley at 3,000 feet; with a bit of luck they might be there in time to meet the low-flying attackers. Norman had one of his assistants telephone Group headquarters and inform them of the decision. Five miles away to the north east, in the operations room at Biggin Hill, Group Captain Richard Grice likewise ordered the rest of the fighters in his Sector to get airborne.

At 1.10 pm the German raiding forces came within 40 miles of the BBC high powered transmitter at Brookmans Park near Hatfield. In accordance with official policy, to prevent German aircraft using it as a beacon for direction-finding, it ceased transmitting. For millions of people, listening to the 1 o'clock news on the BBC Home Service, there was a sudden ominous silence.

At 1.19 pm the navigators in the low-flying Dorniers caught sight of the Reigate–Tonbridge railway line with its distinctive cutting and tunnel at Cuckseys, one of the navigational features which Roth had pointed out during the briefing. Half a minute later the aircraft passed low over Bletchingley, just six miles to the south of Kenley. There 27-year-old Lance Bombardier Wally Hatcher of 327 Searchlight Company, Royal Artillery,

Route of the 9th Staffel of Bomber Geschwader 76 from Beachy Head to Kenley

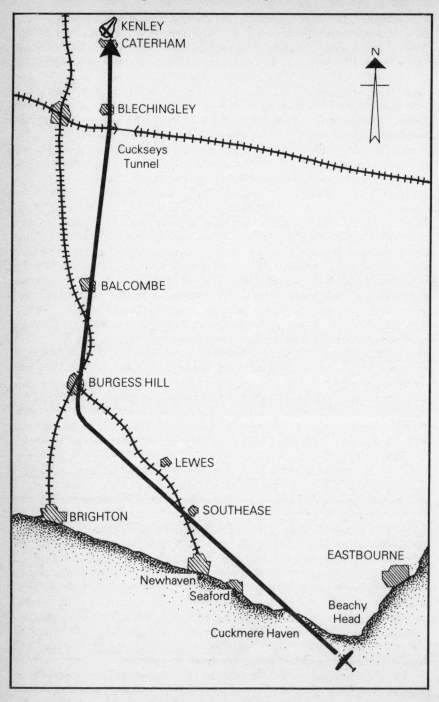

KENLEY

CATERHAM

BLECHINGLEY

Cuckseys
Tunnel

N

BALCOMBE

BURGESS HILL

LEWES

SOUTHEASE

BRIGHTON

EASTBOURNE

Newhaven

Seaford

Beachy
Head

Cuckmere Haven

commanding a ten-man detachment at the searchlight site, was supervising work on some equipment. Suddenly a Dornier passed low immediately to the west of the site followed by a second; then a third roared directly over the startled men. Hatcher leapt into the gun pit to steady the tripod mounting of the unit's single Lewis gun, and yelled at the air sentry to open fire. The gunner loosed off an entire drum of ammunition but to no avail; there was only the swish-swish-swish of bullets striking the ground, as one of the Germans replied. The men watched helplessly as the Dorniers continued relentlessly northwards.

Joachim Roth had achieved a clever piece of low-altitude navigation: after a sea crossing and a flight of 40 miles over unfamiliar enemy territory he had led his force to within two minutes' flying time of the target, right on time and exactly on the planned route. But where were the pillars of smoke rising up from the target in front of him, after the dive-bombing and high altitude attacks which should have prepared the way for his Staffel?

In the operations room at Kenley Anthony Norman watched the markers representing the two enemy raiding forces converging unswervingly on the airfield. He had disposed his squadrons as best he could. Now he broadcast to the station on the loudspeakers: 'Air attack imminent: all personnel not on defence duties to the shelters.' In the operations room the men and women had to remain at their posts, so he ordered them to put on their steel helmets. The task of plotting continued. Fully alerted, Kenley's gun crews were closed up, their barrels pointed expectantly to the south.

Leading Aircraftman Fred Bailey had been in the Airmen's Mess eating his Sunday lunch when the order came over the loudspeakers to take shelter. He had been working in the operations room all night and was now off duty for the rest of the day. On previous days there had been several such alarms and he was not particularly worried by this one. He and his friends picked up their plates and sauntered to the nearest shelter. There the men sat on the grass eating their meal, and watching the British fighters wheeling high overhead.

Aircraftman Laurence Bell and another new arrival on the station, Ken Winstone, were walking round to No 64 Squadron on the north side of the airfield when the call came to take shelter. Nothing much seemed to be happening so they continued their walk, enjoying the sun.

At 1.21 pm, with one minute to go to their target, the Dorniers of the 9th Staffel leapt the final hundred feet to clear the North Downs and the formation began to widen out as each crew prepared to go into the attack. The first sight the men had of Kenley was the roofs of the hangars, poking up out of the trees at the south side of the airfield. By now it was clear to Roth that the carefully-laid attack plan had somehow miscarried: there was no sign of any previous attack on the airfield. His Staffel was going in first. There was no time to consider the point, however, for already a Section of Hurricanes from No 111 Squadron was curving in behind the Dorniers and the German rear gunners were firing back at them.

Twenty-three-year-old Sergeant Harry Deacon of No 111 Squadron, going flat out in his Hurricane to catch up with the leading Sections, suddenly heard an excited shout in his earphones: 'Good God! Look at Kenley!' He glanced towards the airfield and caught a glimpse of several green-camouflaged aircraft streaking low over the dark rooftops of Caterham.

John Grohman, 15, was standing beside the air raid shelter with his father, mother and sister, in the garden of his home at Buxton Lane, Caterham, about 500 yards to the south of Kenley airfield. He heard a sudden noise 'like a lot of old motorbikes' and then the Dorniers roared overhead, so close that he was able to see the face of the navigator in the nose of one of them. The Grohmann family scuttled into their shelter.

Aircraftman Clifford Kenyon, 25, a trainee controller in the Sector operations room at Kenley, watched with a sense of detachment as the block representing the low-flying raiders was moved forwards on the map in front of him; now it was right on top of Kenley airfield.

At that moment the ground gunners at Kenley struck up their deadly martial overture. There was the distinctive boom-boom-boom-boom of the Bofors guns, firing off bursts of six or eight rounds in rapid succession; the much slower, more-measured, louder bark of the 3-in guns; and the almost apologetic stutter of first one, then two, then several Lewis guns chattering out rounds towards the attackers. The German gunners replied with their own cannon and machine guns. With shattering suddenness the sky over the airfield was criss-crossed with the flash of tracer rounds, from above seeming to form the spokes of a wheel with the Dorniers at the centre. 'The hail of light flak and machine gun fire showered around us, the red points of the tracer rounds came flying by', wrote Guenther Unger. 'I pushed the aircraft yet lower and went in exactly over the left-hand hangars.'

One of the first aircraft to be hit was that flown by Flight Lieutenant Stanley Connors, leading No 111 Squadron. His Hurricane may have been hit by the return fire from the German bombers, or by the gunners at Kenley, or both. The fighter broke away from the fight and turned northwards for Croydon, but crashed into the ground shortly afterwards killing Connors.

The remaining Hurricanes in Connors's section now pulled violently upwards and away, out of the inferno of fire over Kenley. Once they were safely clear they sped round to the north side of the airfield, ready to catch the raiders as they emerged. To the Germans it seemed that the fighters must have come from Kenley itself, especially as two Hurricanes were seen taking off as the Dorniers were running in to bomb. In fact these were two late-starters from No 615 Squadron, scrambling off the ground for safety.

Leading Aircraftman Fred Bailey, sitting on the grass beside his shelter with his friends, found that he had a more pressing engagement than Sunday lunch as the bombers suddenly appeared over the spinney on the south side of the airfield and the firing began. The men's plates went flying as they all dived into the slit-trench, ending up in a heap on the floor. 'Someone landed on top of me! One of the bombs thudded into the house nearby, in which we were billeted, and the next thing we knew one end of the slit-trench was filled with rubble. We had got into our shelter in the nick of time!'

Aircraftmen Laurence Bell and Ken Winstone were strolling along one

The 9th Staffel of Bomber Geschwader 76

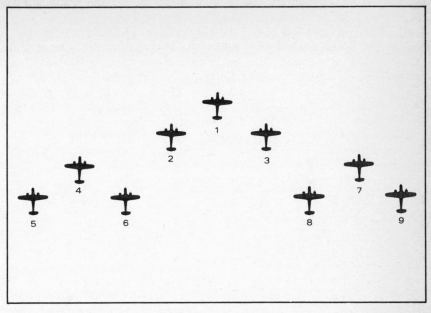

The 9th Staffel of Bomber Geschwader 76. Aircraft 1: navigator Hauptmann Roth (the Staffel commander), pilot Oberleutnant Lamberty; 2: pilot Unteroffizier Maassen; 3: pilot Feldwebel Raab, navigator Leutnant Wittmann; 4: pilot Feldwebel Petersen, navigator Oberleutnant Ahrends, passenger Oberst Sommer; 5: pilot Unteroffizier Unger; 6: pilot Feldwebel Reichel, passenger Rolf von Pebal, war photographer; 7: pilot Oberleutnant Magin, navigator Oberfeldwebel Illg, passenger Georg Hinze, war reporter; 8: pilot Unteroffizier Schumacher; 9: pilot Feldwebel Stephani.

of the roads round the airfield, on their first day with No 64 Squadron, when they noticed several twin-engined aircraft coming in from the south looking as if they were about to land. 'I didn't know they had Blenheims here,' commented Winstone, 'I thought they had only Hurricanes and Spitfires.' Then the pair saw the guns opening fire and the bombs begin to fall, and they quickly appreciated the value of some knowledge of aircraft recognition. 'I ran towards the nearest shelter,' Bell recalled, 'and was about to dive down it when Ken dragged me away shouting "Don't go down there you fool – it's No 13!" So we dashed to the next one, No 15.'

The Dornier leading the left-hand section in the German formation, piloted by Feldwebel Johannes Petersen, may have been hit during the attack by Connors's Hurricanes. For some reason, Germans in other aircraft recall, this aircraft ran in across the airfield much higher than the others. Several of the ground gunners singled it out and flayed it with their fire. The Dornier burst into flames but continued on.

Guenther Unger, piloting the aircraft to the left of Petersen, had lined up on one of the hangars when a burst of Lewis gun fire knocked out his right

Positions of witnesses on Kenley airfield

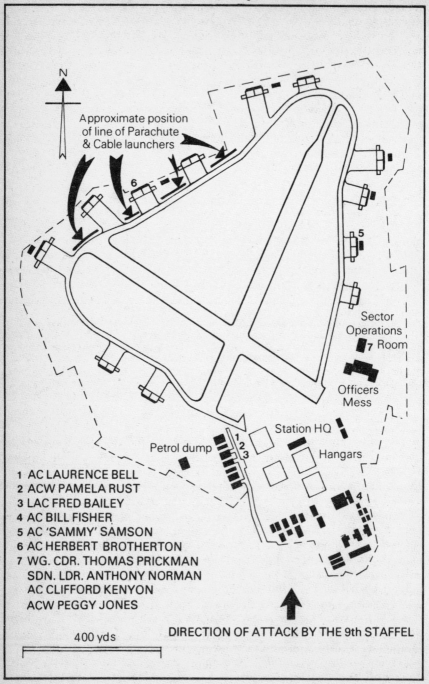

N

Approximate position
of line of Parachute
& Cable launchers

6

5

Sector
Operations
7 Room

Officers
Mess

Station HQ

Petrol dump

1
2
3

Hangars

4

1 AC LAURENCE BELL
2 ACW PAMELA RUST
3 LAC FRED BAILEY
4 AC BILL FISHER
5 AC 'SAMMY' SAMSON
6 AC HERBERT BROTHERTON
7 WG. CDR. THOMAS PRICKMAN
   SDN. LDR. ANTHONY NORMAN
   AC CLIFFORD KENYON
   ACW PEGGY JONES

400 yds

DIRECTION OF ATTACK BY THE 9th STAFFEL

engine. He feathered the propeller and struggled to hold the Dornier straight, as the navigator released the twenty 110-lb bombs in a long stick.

Unteroffizier Schumacher, on the right of the formation, watched fascinated as the bombs from the leading aircraft rammed into the hangars. 'Other bombs were bouncing down the runway like rubber balls. Hell was let loose. Then the bombs began their work of destruction. Three hangars collapsed like matchwood. Explosion followed explosion, flames leapt into the sky,' he later wrote. 'It seemed as if my aircraft was grabbed by some giant. Bits of metal and stones clattered against the fuselage; something thudded into my back armour and splinters of glass flew. There was a smell of phosphorus and smouldering cables.' Schumacher's airspeed indicator, turn-and-bank indicator, artificial horizon and fuel pressure indicator all gave crazy indications. It also seemed that his left motor had been hit: it belched brown smoke and the revolutions started to fall.

In the operations room Anthony Norman broadcast a final call 'Bandits overhead!' then braced himself, half expecting the walls to cave in at any moment. There was an indescribable din as the Dorniers passed low overhead, accompanied by the staccato banging of the guns and the louder crashes of the exploding bombs. The building shook and Aircraftwoman Peggy Jones, 18, plotting the movements of the British fighters, just had time to shout 'Look out!' as a notice board fell off the wall and narrowly missed Warrant Officer Richard Case.

Oberleutnant Hermann Magin, piloting the Dornier leading the right-hand section, was just lining up his target when a Lewis gun round hit him squarely in the chest. 'Suddenly the pilot slumped forwards and cried "*Nach Hause!*" (take me home!). Then his left hand fell from the control column, dripping blood', wrote war reporter Georg Hinze. The bomber would have smashed right into the ground had not the navigator, 28-year-old Oberfeldwebel Wilhelm-Friedrich Illg, leaned over the unconscious pilot and grabbed the control column. Illg pulled the aircraft straight, then eased it up to gain height and shouted the preparatory order 'Prepare to jump!' 'The aircraft in front of me went into a tight turn to the right, the formation split up and it was every man for himself' noted Feldwebel Stephani, who had been flying the aircraft to the right of and behind Magin.

One of the buildings hit during the attack was that used as a headquarters by the detachment of Scots Guardsmen responsible for the ground defence of the airfield. Second Lieutenant J. Hague was buried underneath the debris but, despite considerable pain from a crushed shoulder, he extricated himself and then, with bullets flying all around, directed his men to safety. Also under fire Lance Corporal Gale, with two ribs broken by the blast from an exploding bomb, rescued from the building a man more severely injured than himself and carried him outside.

In her shelter Aircraftwoman Pamela Rust, 18, sat huddled with her friends singing 'Ten Green Bottles' at the tops of their voices, trying unsuccessfully to drown out the 'great blasting crashes that shook the trench and hurt your ear drums' and convince themselves that they were not afraid.

As the Dorniers skimmed low across the airfield after releasing their bombs, Aircraftman D. Roberts waited for them by the northern boundary with his parachute-and-cable launchers primed for action. Three of the bombers were heading straight towards him, slowly gaining height. When the leader came within range he pushed his firing button and with a whoosh the line of nine rockets soared upwards.

Wilhelm Raab had tried to shoot up a refuelling tanker on the airfield with his 20-mm cannon, but the weapon had jammed at the critical moment. He had just passed over the vehicle when a terrifying scene unfolded before him. 'Suddenly red-glowing balls rose up from the ground in front of me. Each one trailed a line of smoke about 1 metre thick behind it, with intervals of 10 to 15 metres between each. I had experienced machine-gun and flak fire often enough, but this was something entirely new.' Raab had no idea how high the fire-balls were going to go nor what lay concealed in the smoke trails, but obviously the spectacle had not been laid on for his health. He eased the aircraft up a little, then yanked the right wing down and pushed on the left rudder to put the Dornier into a bank, to try and pass between two of the smoke trails. 'Everything seemed to be going well – then I felt a hefty tug on my machine. "Now they've got us," I thought, "we are going to smash into the ground." ' Raab's radio operator, Unteroffizier Erich Malter facing rearwards, suddenly noticed a line of small white parachutes hanging in the sky above him. 'Then there was a blow and a fantastic confusion in our aircraft. I was tossed about like a flowerpot. Then I heard the pilot cursing and swearing.'

The Dornier was still flying, however. Raab's quick thinking had saved it from disaster by an incredibly narrow margin. Because the aircraft was banking at the time it struck the cable, the latter had slid off the wing before the lower parachute had time to open and take effect. Raab waggled the controls and, to his immense relief, they functioned normally. Elated by his narrow escape, he pulled the wings horizontal and eased the aircraft down, to take advantage of cover from the ground sloping away to the north of the airfield.

Feldwebel Petersen's already-blazing Dornier was not so lucky. It ran into one of the hanging cables, the parachutes functioned as intended, and the unfortunate machine was literally plucked out of the sky. It smashed into 'Sunnycroft', a bungalow adjoining the airfield, killing all five men on board including Oberst Sommer who had flown with the crew to gain first-hand experience of combat.

Oberleutnant Rudolf Lamberty held the Dornier down low after his Staffel commander Joachim Roth, sitting next to him, had released the bombs across the hangars. As they roared across the airfield they, too, were horrified at the sight of the row of rockets snaking upwards in front of them. Lamberty immediately pulled his aircraft up to give him a bit of room to manoeuvre to avoid the smoke trails and whatever they contained. In this he succeeded but at that moment a Bofors shell smashed into his left wing beside the engine, blowing out a gaping hole. The wing fuel tank was torn open and the petrol gushing out exploded into fire. Lamberty feathered the propeller of the dying engine as he fought to hold the Dornier in the air.

The parachutes-and-cables were to cause alarm to both sides, that Sunday lunchtime. Frank Clark, 42, an auditor with London Transport, emerged from the shelter in his garden at Beverley Road, Whyteleafe, on the north-eastern edge of the airfield, as the bombs ceased exploding. Suddenly he was shaken to see a cluster of white parachutes descending in front of him. He exclaimed to his wife Lilian 'Good Gracious! Parachutists!' It seemed as if the expected German invasion was beginning right in front of them. Others thought so too. William 'Jigger' Lee, 37, the Duty Sergeant at the Police station at Kenley village, received an excited telephone call from one of his constables that 'about 500' parachutists were dropping on the airfield. Lee rushed to the window and was just in time to see a few of the parachutes sinking out of sight behind the trees. He immediately relayed the message to the nearby Army barracks at Caterham.

In the Kenley operations room, Peggy Jones recalled, there was a sudden, almost unearthly silence. As the bangs and explosions ceased the tele-phones, on which the controllers and plotters depended to receive and pass information, went dead. The girls looked up questioningly at the officers on the dais and Flying Officer David Owen-Edmunds bellowed at them 'Don't just stand there, take cover! There's nothing you can do now!'

Pamela Rust and her friends were chattering away in their shelter on the south side of the airfield, relieved still to be alive when the bombs ceased exploding, when a man's head poked round the door and shrieked that there was an unexploded bomb lying against the earth bank which covered them. The WAAF Corporal calmly led the girls outside and Pamela Rust walked across the road when: 'I became aware of a crackling sound and turned round. Beyond our trench – perhaps 50 yards away – the hangars were ablaze; everything seemed to be burning fiercely in a pall of black smoke blowing across to the right. It was an immense sight and I was staggered – surely we weren't meant to be wandering around as we were, swinging our mugs and knitting bags.' The WAAF Corporal received little credit for her cool deed. Suddenly an officer wearing a steel helmet came bounding towards them: 'Get to shelter you silly women,' he shouted. 'The bombing has not finished yet!' The airwomen scurried down another shelter.

When Pilot Officer 'Dutch' Hugo of No 615 Squadron first glimpsed the Messerschmitt 109, it was already too late to do much about it. With 'A' Flight he had been orbiting at 25,000 feet, nearly five miles, above Kenley waiting for the enemy to come to him. The Germans did, with breathtaking suddenness, from out of the sun. Seemingly appearing from nowhere the Messerschmitt curved in behind Sergeant Walley on the starboard side of the formation, there was a flash of tracer and his Hurricane went down in flames. Hugo swung his aircraft round to engage the attacker but another Messerschmitt hit him first: 'There was a blinding flash and a deafening explosion in the left side of the cockpit somewhere behind the instrument panel, my left leg received a numbing, sickening, blow and a sheet of high octane petrol shot back into the cockpit from the main tank. My stricken Hurricane flicked over into a spin and must have been hit half a dozen times while doing so, as the sledgehammer cracks of cannon and machine-gun strikes went on for what seemed ages.'

Without conscious effort Hugo turned off the fuel and opened his throttle, to empty the carburettor and so decrease the risk of fire. The cockpit was awash with petrol and his clothes were saturated with it: the slightest spark would have turned him into a human torch. Finally the engine coughed and spluttered to a stop, the propeller slowed until it was just flicking over in the slipstream, he switched off the ignition and the immedate danger of fire was over. Hugo pushed the stick forwards and eased on rudder to pull out of the spin. He was just straightening out when there was a colossal bang behind him and the now-familiar sound of cannon strikes. 'I had the biggest fright of my life – I knew I was completely incapable of movement as a particularly vicious-looking Me 109 with a yellow nose snarled about twenty feet past my starboard wing, the venomous crackle of his Daimler Benz engine clearly audible. Round he came for another attack, and although I did everything I could think of, gliding without power has its limitations and the next moment earth and sky seemed to explode into crimson flame as I received a most almighty blow on the side of the head.'

Hugo came to, feeling sick and shaken, to find his aircraft spinning down again. Through a red haze he saw that he was now at 10,000 feet, so he had time to take stock of the situation. His head was aching savagely and the right side of his face felt numb. When he touched it, he found a jagged gash from the corner of his right jaw to his chin. His microphone and oxygen mask had been torn off his helmet and were now draped over his right forearm; the microphone had a bullet hole through it. The cockpit seemed to be filled with a fine red spray; it took Hugo some time to realise that the cause was blood running down his chest being whipped up by the wind whistling through the holes in the sides of his cabin. He slid back the canopy and gasped his lungs full of clean air.

The next thing Hugo knew was that the Messerschmitt was curving round for yet another attack. Enough was enough, he decided to bale out. Hugo rolled the Hurricane on to its back and pulled out the harness locking pin but, instead of falling clear, to his consternation he fell only about twelve inches – sufficient to project his head, arms and shoulders into the blast of the slipstream, which promptly slammed him back against the rear of the cockpit. Before the astonished pilot could decide what to do next the Hurricane solved the problem for him by pulling through a half loop. With a thump Hugo fell back into the cockpit, puzzled but at least able to reach the controls again.

Then he discovered why he had developed such a firm attachment to his aircraft: during the rush to strap in for the scramble take-off, sitting on his parachute in the seat, he had inadvertently taken one of his leg straps round the lever which raised and lowered his seat. Now his own fate was tightly bound up with that of his Hurricane. The next minutes saw Hugo, as he later described, 'as busy as a one armed one-man bandsman with a flea in his pants', trying to avoid the attentions of his persistent foe, finding and doing up his seat straps in readiness for the inevitable crash landing, and seeking out a suitable field. Finally he put down his battered Hurricane in a meadow near Orpington, and was picked up and rushed to hospital.

Fifteen-year-old Ned Walsh and his mother, father and five brothers and sisters were huddled in the shelter beside their home at Green Lane, Morden, when they heard the loudening roar of an aircraft coming towards them at full throttle. It passed low overhead, then there was a muffled 'boomph' and silence. Sergeant Walley's Hurricane had plunged straight into the ground about 350 yards from them into Morden Park Golf course, the unfortunate pilot still at the controls.

A third Hurricane of No 615 Squadron, that flown by Flight Lieutenant 'Elmer' Gaunce leading 'A' Flight, was set on fire; Gaunce baled out and landed with slight eye injuries. Pilot Officer D. Looker's Hurricane was also hit and damaged during the surprise German attack. He spun away from the formation, straightened out and took the damaged fighter in to Croydon airfield for an emergency landing. As he lined up for his approach, however, the station ground defences opened up a spectacular, though fortunately inaccurate, fire at him. Looker set the Hurricane down firmly and it skidded to a halt with its nose dug into the ground.

The successful German pilots were 26-year-old Oberleutnant Lother Keller and Leutnants Helmut Meckel and Landry of Fighter Geschwader 3, flying extended cover for the bomber formations now nearing their targets.

No 615 Squadron had suffered grievously in the process, but by keeping the German top cover busy it allowed other British fighters to approach the bombers unmolested. Down at 15,000 feet Squadron Leader Mike Crossley was leading the twelve Hurricanes of No 32 Squadron in a climbing turn above base, when he caught sight of a swarm of midge-like black dots emerging from the horizon to the south-east, too many and too far away for him to count: it was the delayed high-level attacking force bound for Kenley, comprising twenty-seven Dornier 17s of the Ist and IIIrd Gruppen of Bomber Geschwader 76 with their close escort of some twenty Messerschmitt 110s of Destroyer Geschwader 26.

Crossley called 'Tally Ho!' to inform his ground controller, Squadron Leader John Worral at Biggin Hill, that he had the enemy in sight and was going in to engage. Then he swung his squadron round and headed towards the raiders. As the Squadron Leader viewed the steadily sharpening cluster of dots through his windscreen they appeared to be almost stationary in space. That meant one thing: the two formations were heading nearly straight towards each other. They were closing at 400 mph, nearly seven miles per minute.

Several times Crossley had discussed with his pilots the advantages of the head-on attack as a method of breaking up an enemy bomber formation. He was sure that for the German crews, sitting unprotected in their glass-fronted bombers, this type of attack would be the most fearful of all; only those bomber pilots with nerves of steel would fail to be daunted by such a prospect, and those who broke formation would probably be picked off later. Now, for the first time, Crossley and his squadron had the opportunity to put the theory to the test. 'We sighted them as we were coming from Biggin, and swung round in front of them. We didn't have to work very hard to do it. The visibility was very good. I remember some cloud about but there was bright sunshine. We had plenty of time to line up,' remembered 22-year-old Pilot Officer Alan Eckford, flying close behind Crossley.

Keeping a wary eye for the German fighters he knew must be somewhere around, Crossley held his course. If possible he wanted to get in his attack and perhaps break up the bomber formation, before the escorts could intervene. In each Hurricane the pilot made his final checks for battle: that his gun safety switch and sight were 'on', and that his seat was lowered so that he had maximum protection from the engine in front of him and the armour plate behind.

For Flight Lieutenant Peter Brothers, 22, leading 'B' Flight behind and to the right of Crossley, knocking down these particular bombers was a personal matter: far below, living in Westerham village close to Biggin Hill, was his pregnant wife Annette. He felt sure that these raiders were making for Biggin Hill; and each one that got through represented a threat to his unborn child. Seconds later, however, Brothers was jolted out of his grim concentration on the bombers by the sight of other black specks moving down from above and rapidly across to his right: the German escorts swinging round to take the Hurricanes from behind. Brothers cursed them and peeled away, leading his Flight upwards and to the right to engage the escorts head-on. In no time at all the specks had grown in size and sprouted wings, then the wings bulged into engines: they were Messerschmitt 110s, their noses flickering as they opened fire with cannon and machine guns. Brothers zoomed towards them and fired back, the five other Hurricanes of his Flight close behind.

Intent on following one of the Messerschmitts, Brothers eased his stick further and further back, firing off short bursts each time he had the enemy in his sight. Then came an abrupt, terrifying silence: in concentrating on his shooting he had inadvertently pulled the nose of his Hurricane past the vertical; the reversed effect of gravity had closed the needle valve in the float carburettor, shutting off the fuel to his Merlin engine and bringing it to a spluttering stop. The fighter rapidly lost its momentum, shuddered, stalled, the left wing dropped violently and Brothers went spinning helplessly away from the fight.

While the rest of 'B' Flight wheeled round to hold off the escorts, Crossley with 'A' Flight continued in his headlong charge into the bomber formation. Crossley fired at one of the Dorniers and saw it pull upwards abruptly. 'The bombers were stepped up, in close formation. I remember thinking, as I was approaching the formation, that if I opened fire at the first one and then gradually lifted my nose and kept the button pressed, several would have to pass through my fire,' Eckford recalled. He picked out the leading bomber and opened up at it at a range of over half a mile. His plan to engage several bombers did not work, however, because he had not allowed for the tremendous closing speed. He found there was time to fire at only one of the bombers, before he had to push hard on his stick to avoid colliding with his victim.

The swiftness of 'A' Flight's attack is borne out by German accounts. 'Here comes the first fighter, from the left and ahead. Very suddenly he is before our eyes, like a wasp, dashing through the formation. I see the reddish tracer rounds flying back and forth. Everything is happening tremendously quickly,' wrote war reporter Raimund Schultz. 'Suddenly the fighters split up, then attack from ahead and from the side. Look out! The fighters come in so close that one could speak to them. Pull up! Good – he misses us,' wrote Hauptmann Rolf Schroeter leading the 8th Staffel.

As Eckford came out of the other side of the German formation he turned his head and saw the Dornier he had fired at pull up into a drunken half-roll, then spin away. At the controls of his victim was Oberleutnant Werner Stoldt, leading the 1st Staffel. The fighter's rounds had slashed through the windscreen, reducing the cockpit of the bomber to a bloody shambles in a fraction of a second. But Feldwebel Johann Beck, the navigator, in the most vulnerable position of all crouching over his bomb-sight in the perspex nose of the bomber, suffered only splinter wounds.

During all of this the Dornier's flight engineer, 27-year-old Oberfeld-webel Wilhelm Lautersack, had been lying on his stomach on the floor of the cabin, manning the rearwards-facing machine gun. The first thing he knew of Eckford's attack was the crash of machine-gun rounds striking the bomber and smoke starting to spurt out of the starboard engine. Then the bomber reared up and went into a spin and he was pinned to the floor by the vicious centrifugal forces. He glanced forwards to see his pilot slumped lifeless against his harness. With a strength born of fear Lautersack inched his way to the escape hatch in the floor of the cabin, released it, then tumbled out. After a long delay he pulled his ripcord and saw the canopy open above his head. 'I had always wanted to make a parachute jump,' he later recounted, 'but not like this!' The German flight engineer was not yet out of danger, however. First the escape hatch came past him uncomfortably close, flutter-ing like a falling leaf. Then came the Dornier, going down under power in a series of shallow turns. At one stage it seemed that it might run into Lautersack or his parachute, but finally it passed safely clear of him on its downward spiral. Soon afterwards he saw a rolled-up body fall clear of the aircraft and another parachute open. It was the navigator, Johann Beck.

Crossley's head-on charge into Bomber Geschwader 76 had knocked down one Dornier and caused damage to others. More importantly, how-ever, it forced several of the German crews to jink out of the way of the fighters during the critical phase of their bombing runs. These crews found themselves unable to re-align themselves on Kenley to begin new bombing runs on the airfield before the formation had flown past it, and instead their navigators picked out alternative targets on the ground. The result was that some of the crews attacked Kenley, some aimed their bombs at the railway lines to the north and east of the airfield, some continued on and aimed their bombs at Croydon airfield 3 miles to the north-west of Kenley, while others turned round for home without releasing their bombs.

Railway lines, however, though considered fair game by German crews with bombs to spare, were almost impossible to hit from 15,000 feet without resorting to 'stick' bombing: bombs released at intervals to produce a row of explosions on the ground. By aiming such a 'stick' of bombs across a railway line, hopefully one or two bombs would hit it. The trouble was, however, that the rest of the bombs fell on whatever happened to be alongside the lines. Thus, as well as bomb concentrations on and near Kenley and Croydon airfields, a scattering of bombs fell across private property alongside the railway lines running through Whyteleafe, Caterham, Coulsdon, Purley and Croydon.

In her home at Warren Lane, Hurst Green near Oxted, 31-year-old Mrs Doris Addison was in the kitchen preparing Sunday lunch. Her two children, 9-year-old Walter and 5-year-old Delma, 9-year-old evacuee Jimmie Murrell and his 12-year-old sister who was visiting for the day, had just come running into the house and were chattering excitedly about the formation of German bombers which had just passed overhead. There was a sudden terrifyingly loud bang, the house shuddered, then out of the kitchen window Doris Addison saw the remains of an aircraft skidding away from her across her husband's smallholding, shedding pieces as it went. It was Werner Stoldt's Dornier, shot down a couple of minutes earlier by Alan Eckford. The bomber's starboard wing had struck the house on the way past, wrenching it off and spewing out petrol which immediately caught fire. As flames began to engulf the side of the house, Doris Addison ushered the frightened children into the downstairs bathroom on the opposite side and lifted them one by one out of the window and on to the ground. Then she dashed back towards the fire bent on rescuing Bob, the family's pet spaniel.

Wilhelm Lautersack, who had parachuted from the Dornier, had other problems. Rumours of enemy fighters shooting up men descending by parachute were prevalent at that time in the Luftwaffe, just as they were in the Royal Air Force. Now Lautersack remembered them, as he saw a British fighter curving round towards him. With a deliberate movement he reached down and unlocked the quick-release buckle of his parachute harness; if the fighter opened fire he resolved to shed the parachute and fall to his death, rather than provide a living target for somebody's firing practice. After a couple of orbits, however, it was clear that the fighter pilot had no such intent. Lautersack re-locked his quick-release buckle.

To the German crewman it seemed that his parachute descent was normal enough. But in fact Eckford's rounds had carved scores of splinters off the Dornier's structure and many of them had slashed their way into Lautersack's parachute pack before he had baled out. The silken canopy had been badly lacerated, with the result that he came down very fast indeed. He hit the ground so hard that he sprained badly both knees and ankles. Lautersack released his parachute and the wind whisked it away. Then, with the British fighter still orbiting above, he lay helplessly on the ground where he had landed.

Immediately the low-flying raiders had left Kenley Aircraftman Sammy Samson, 24, was ordered out of his shelter to help start up one of the Hurricanes still on the airfield. With a flight sergeant and another airman he had walked only some 50 yards when his ears caught the unmistakable whistling sound of falling bombs: the high-flying raiding force had reached its target. The three men hurled themselves to the ground, which shook under the force of the explosions. They could feel the warm concussion as the blast swept over them, then came the blows from the earth and pieces of debris raining down from above.

Three quarters of a mile to the north of Samson, in Valley Road, Kenley, 24-year-old nurse Kathleen Rhodes was in an Anderson shelter with her fiancé and the mother and daughter from the house next door. 'The bombs were getting nearer and nearer. We just held on to each other and waited,' she remembered. Suddenly there was a terrific bang and everything went black: a bomb had exploded immediately outside the entrance to their shelter. Kathleen Rhodes regained her senses able to see hardly anything, there was so much dust in the air. As this began to settle she saw that her fiancé was lying across her, unconscious, his head in her lap. She found that she was trapped and unable to move; her own left arm was hanging down her back, almost severed by a bomb splinter. Her shoes had been blown off and she wondered whether her feet had gone too, because she could not see them. The woman from the house next door had been badly injured about the face and was lying back groaning, partially conscious; her daughter, dazed but otherwise uninjured, staggered out of the wrecked shelter to get help.

Three miles to the north, in Bingham Road Park, Croydon, 8-year-old Brian Cane had been playing football with some young friends when the sight of the large formation caught their attention. The children gazed up in awe at the armada passing overhead. Then, too late, the sirens started to sound and the bombs began to fall. There was instant confusion: the horror-struck boys stood paralysed, not knowing what to do next. Then a lady shouted: 'Run home to your mummies, quick! They'll be worried!' And run the children did, homewards, as fast as their legs could carry them. 'The owner of the ball kept calling "You've left my bloody ball!" We hadn't. I was clutching it firmly to my stomach, probably wishing it was my mother.' Half crying to themselves the children ran on, people shouting at them from all directions: 'Get off the street!' 'Mind the shrapnel!' 'Get home quick!' All of this, intermingled with the crumps of exploding bombs and the menacing drone of the aircraft. Finally a concerned lady insisted that the boys take cover in her house. They were ushered into the cupboard under the stairs and plied with milk, biscuits and toffee. 'I sat with my knees under my chin, pressing the football into my chest and remembering every good thing my mother had ever done for me.'

Three miles to the south-west Kathleen Rose, 24, a post office tele-graphist, had just come off shift and arrived at her home at Edward Road, Coulsdon, beside the main London–Brighton railway line, when the sirens began sounding. Her 64-year-old widowed mother was getting Sunday lunch ready, but as the noise built up overhead Kathleen insisted that they both take cover under the stairs: 'Shortly afterwards there was a terrific bang and the house shattered. Doors and windows came out, and dust fell everywhere. Something hit me hard in the middle of my back as I bent over my mother to protect her – she was frail and suffered from heart trouble.' Before the dust had time to settle they heard the shouts of men from the local working men's club, fighting their way through the rubble with their bare hands to get the women out.

Nearly four miles above the exploding bombs Oberleutnant Ruediger Proske, piloting a Messerschmitt 110 of Destroyer Geschwader 26, dived down to head off a re-attack on the bombers by No 32 Squadron's Hurricanes.

Squadron Leader Don MacDonell, leading the eight Spitfires of No 64 Squadron, had heard his controller, Anthony Norman, call 'Bandits overhead!' (as the low-flying Dorniers of the 9th Staffel swept over Kenley). To MacDonell, orbiting at 20,000 feet, the call seemed a little strange: 'Instinctively I looked up, but there was only the clear blue sky above me. I thought "My God! Where are they?" ' Then he looked down and saw a commotion below, too far away from him to work out exactly what was happening. 'I gave a quick call: "Freema Squadron, Bandits below. Tally Ho!" ' Then down we went in a wide spiral at high speed, keeping a wary eye open for the inevitable German fighters.'

While MacDonell's Spitfires were speeding down, the Messerschmitt 110s of the close escort had succeeded in getting between No 32 Squadron and the Dorniers. So Flight Lieutenant 'Humph' Russell, 26, shifted his sight on to one of the twin-engined fighters wheeling in front of him. He loosed off a 6-second burst and watched his incendiary rounds 'walking' along the fuselage of the enemy aircraft. Several of the German rear gunners replied with accurate bursts, however, and the Hurricane was hit wounding Russell in the left arm and right leg. Smoke began to fill the cockpit so he opened the hood, released his straps and leapt out. Russell's parachute opened normally but when he looked down he noticed that his leg was bleeding profusely. In his right hand he still clenched the ripcord of the parachute and now he tried to use it as an improvised tourniquet. It was useless: each time he knotted it, the stainless-steel wire simply unravelled itself.

The Dorniers of the high-level raiding force were turning for home as MacDonell's Spitfires dived past the mêlée and then zoomed up from underneath. The Squadron Leader picked one of the enemy aircraft, which he took to be a Dornier, and overhauled it rapidly. At 250 yards, from behind and slightly below, he pressed his firing button and held it down until he was at 150 yards then broke away. The target's right engine belched out a large cloud of black smoke, then started to burn. The left engine was also hit and left a thinner trail of smoke. The aircraft reared up on its tail, stalled, then spun almost vertically away. MacDonell felt sure he must have hit the pilot or the elevator controls, or perhaps both.

In fact the 'Dornier' MacDonell had attacked was Ruediger Proske's

Messerschmitt 110. The speed and angle of approach of the Spitfire had taken the German crew completely by surprise and the first thing Proske knew was when the bullets started to tear into his aircraft. With his engines losing power and his rear gunner hit and wounded, Proske felt he was in no position to offer a fight. He decided to 'play dead' and pushed open the throttles, then let go of the controls and allowed the Messerschmitt to go its own way. MacDonell testifies that it was a convincing demonstration. Proske let his aircraft spin through 6,000 feet, then pulled out and looked behind him. The ruse had been successful: nobody had followed. Proske turned south-eastwards for home. Both of his engines were trailing a lot of smoke but at least they were still running. The nearest friendly territory lay 80 miles away, about 25 minutes of flying time.

The twelve Junkers 88s of IInd Gruppe of Bomber Geschwader 76, instead of being the first to attack Kenley, were the last to reach it. And by the time they got there the dense smoke rising from the blazing hangars rendered the planned precision dive-bombing attack impossible – and, it seemed, unnecessary. Accordingly the force turned round and made for its alternative target, the airfield at West Malling. In his nimble Messerschmitt 109 Hannes Trautloft found the task of escorting the bombers frustrating. 'My Gruppe flew 500 metres above the Junkers 88s. Always I had to remember my orders: be ready to ward off enemy fighters. A few enemy fighters were reported high above us and, had we been on a free hunting patrol, we could have gone after them. But today we had to obey our orders and stick close to the Junkers 88s, keeping an eye on the British fighters,' he later noted. As the formation flew past Biggin Hill on its way to West Malling, anti-aircraft shells suddenly began bursting round the bombers. 'A Junkers 88 was hit and began to trail smoke from its left motor and started to straggle as its speed fell away. This aircraft received our special attention, lest it became an easy victim for the British fighters,' Trautloft's account continued. Then, suddenly, Spitfires and Hurricanes pounced on the German formation. 'They dived on us from all directions, trying to get at the bombers. We moved in to head them off. When the Tommies saw us coming they peeled away. Beneath me I saw an aircraft going down in flames, though I could not see whether it was a friend or a foe.'

The aircraft Trautloft had seen going down was almost certainly one of the Junkers 88s, knocked out of the formation by Pilot Officer Boleslaw Wlasnowolski of No 32 Squadron. Once separated from its protectors the bomber came under attack from no fewer than five other British fighters. Taking this incident as an example we can see how, in the absence of any centralised agency to check the British pilots' victory claims, gross errors were inevitable even though individual pilot's reports were usually honestly made. The Junkers 88 crashed in woods beside the church at Ide Hill, a small village 8 miles south-east of Biggin Hill and 3 miles south-west of Sevenoaks. Wlasnowolski claimed 'a Do 215' which 'dived into the ground and burst into flames, near a church about 6 miles S of Biggin Hill.' Peter Brothers, who had in the meantime recovered from his spin and rejoined the fight, claimed 'a Do 215' which 'hit the ground at Ide Hill'. Flight Lieutenant

James Sanders of No 615 Squadron reported that he 'together with another Hurricane accounted for a Ju 88 which crashed south of Sevenoaks'. Flying Officer James O'Meara of No 64 Squadron claimed a Ju 88 which 'being attacked by 3 Hurricanes and 1 Spitfire crashed about 4 miles E of Biggin Hill'. Flight Sergeant E. Gilbert and Sergeant A. Laws, also of No 64 Squadron, jointly claimed an 'He 111' which 'crashed and burst into flames beside a church south of Biggin Hill'. Because all of the Dorniers, Heinkels and Junkers 88s lost can be accounted for during this engagement, and no other German aircraft came down within 5 miles of Ide Hill, there is no doubt that these claims all refer to the same aircraft (obviously their shooting was more accurate than their aircraft recognition!). Gilbert, Laws and O'Meara were each subsequently awarded a '½ kill'; Sanders, Brothers and Wlasnowolski were each awarded kills. Thus the Junkers was counted 4½ times in the overall British victory total for the day. There were no survivors from the unfortunate bomber.

Rudolf Lamberty's Dornier was not going to hold together for much longer. The left wing of his aircraft, which had led the 9th Staffel in to attack Kenley at low altitude, was now well ablaze and the flames were so hot that he could feel their heat on his side. To make matters worse, as he and his comrades tried to extricate themselves from the hornets' nest they had stirred up, the Hurricanes of No 111 Squadron were curving in for the kill.

In his home at Littleheath Road, Selsdon, 31-year-old bank clerk Leslie Stevens heard the roar of low-flying aircraft approaching. He ran outside to see what was happening, in time to hear a crackle of gun fire and the clatter of glass falling from smashed windows and see the dust kicked up by bullets ricocheting off the ground around him. 'It was all over in a couple of seconds,' he remembered, 'I just stood there amazed, there was no time to throw myself to the ground.'

Rudolf Lamberty also saw the dust being kicked up in front of him, as the bullets fired from behind thudded into the ground. Then his assailant, Sergeant W. Dymond, roared past him close over his head. Next to attack was Sergeant R. Brown, who came in from the beam. Above the roar of his engines Lamberty heard a sound 'like a handful of peas thrown against a window pane' – the rounds striking his aircraft. The Dornier was now a flying time-bomb: at any moment the main spar might burn through and then the wing would collapse. Lamberty picked out a large stubble field in front and prepared for a crash landing.

Unknown to the German pilot the three men in the rear of the cabin were already leaving; they could see that a crash was inevitable and could do nothing to help. Two of them, Hauptmann Gustav Peters and Oberfeldwebel Valentin Geier, struck the ground before their parachutes had time to open fully and both suffered multiple injuries. Radio operator Feldwebel Hugo Eberhart realised the danger and, clambering half out of the escape hatch, grasped the aircraft structure with one hand and pulled the ripcord with the other. With a thwack the slipstream slammed open the parachute canopy and he was torn away from the aircraft, then deposited neatly on the ground with only minor injuries to his hand.

At about this time the crippled Dornier flew past some twenty men of the Addington Home Guard, attending a Sunday training session with their newly-issued rifles. Their commander, Captain Clarke, who had served with the Australian forces in France during the First World War, afterwards said: 'I gave the order for rapid fire, and my second-in-command directed the height of the firing. We saw the machine stagger and lose height, and then smoke began to issue from it.' The ragged outburst of shots from the ground passed unnoticed amid the flames and confusion on board the blazing aircraft.

Lamberty put the Dornier down hard on the ground and there was a splintering, rending crash as it skidded across the stubble surface, throwing up a cloud of dust. When it came to rest Lamberty threw off his straps and struggled desperately to get out of the blazing wreck. At first it seemed he was trapped: behind him the cabin was a raging inferno while in front of him was an array of smashed windows too small to crawl through framed by metal too thick for him to bend. Joachim Roth, the 9th Staffel commander, had still been sitting next to him during the crash landing; he had gone, obviously through the rear. Lamberty followed. Using his hands to pull himself over the burning metal of what had been the radio operator's seat, the pilot clambered out the escape hatch above the rear of the cabin and slid down the side of the aircraft to the ground. As yet he could feel no pain from his hands, though reaction was beginning to set in as he staggered weakly away from the aircraft. As he did so a posse of Home Guardsmen came running up, excitedly pointing their rifles at the Germans. Lamberty and Roth, both fearfully burned, raised what was left of their hands in surrender.

Wilhelm Raab had escaped from the parachutes and cables and now he held the Dornier close to the ground, hauling it round, over and behind houses, trees and barns to prevent the pursuing Hurricanes getting in accurate bursts. 'To the rear I fired magazine after magazine at the fighters. My steel helmet fell off and I had no time to put it on again. We were all sweating like bulls' wrote Raab's radio operator, Unteroffizier Erich Malter. 'The machine rushed on just above the surface of the ground. The fighters did not let up. At first they came from behind, then, on my fire, they separated and positioned themselves to the left and the right behind our machine. First the left one attacked; I had a jam and had to watch as the fighter came in to 20–30 metres. Then I cleared the stoppage and fired like mad at him.' Malter saw his rounds striking the fighter, which broke off the attack and curved away to the right. The second fighter closed in to 100 yards, fired off two long bursts, then broke away.

Once the Hurricanes had delivered their attacks on the low-flying Dorniers they had no alternative but to break away over or to the side of their prey; and when they did they were exposed to return fire, often at short range. The engagement was not one-sided.

Possibly the Hurricane Malter had hit was that flown by Pilot Officer Peter Simpson, 18, who had closed in fast on one of the Dorniers and fired off several bursts at it. The pilot recalled: 'As I broke away I presented him with a plan view of my belly and I heard bang-bang-bang-bang as my aircraft was hit.' Simpson's aileron control runs were severed and he no longer had full control of the Hurricane. His first thought was to gain altitude to bale out, 'But then I thought better of it, as my foot was hurting like Hell. There was a splinter in it.' Simpson looked round for a piece of clear ground suitable for a forced landing and almost ahead he saw one: the golf course of the Royal Automobile Club, at Woodcote Park near Epsom. Gingerly he took the Hurricane down and made a wheels-up landing on the practice fairway.

Feldwebel Otto Stephani had been engaged in a 180-mile-an-hour slalom over the Surrey countryside, hotly pursued by three Hurricanes, when an accurate burst thudded home. 'All at once the navigator turned to me and said "The flight engineer is dead and the radio operator severely wounded!" There was blood on my right hand,' he later recounted. 'In the machine there was a crazy confusion and, at the same time, we were coming under attack constantly from the fighters. We stayed very low, for that was our only chance of survival.' Stephani kept going, there was nothing else he could do. Beside him, the left motor was smoking strongly.

Sergeant Harry Newton had become separated from the rest of the aircraft of No 111 Squadron, and was orbiting to the east of Kenley at 3,000 feet. Suddenly his attention was caught by the sight of a stick of bombs exploding across a row of houses. 'For the first time in my young life – I was 19 years old – I realised what war really meant. Then I caught sight of a Dornier, low down. I remember thinking: "Here's one that won't get back!"' In fact the Dornier was that flown by Guenther Unger, limping away from Kenley with one engine shot out. Unger had released his bombs on the airfield during the low-altitude attack; those Newton had seen exploding had come from the high-altitude raiding force. Newton slid back his cockpit hood, so that it could not jam shut and trap him inside if it was hit, then pushed down his nose and swooped down to attack.

Unger's rear gunner, Unteroffizier Franz Bergmann, had seen the Hurricane curving after him and swung his machine gun to engage. Newton saw the tracer rounds coming towards him but thought 'You've got one gun, I've got eight – you don't stand a chance!' He fired one burst at the Dornier but the tracer seemed to go over its starboard wing tip. Newton continued, 'I thought "Just a slight correction and I've got him!" But just at that moment he got me, because my cockpit seemed to burst into flames.' With his hood open, the slipstream drew the flames backwards and upwards, right over the unfortunate pilot. Then the oxygen in his mask caught fire, burning it on to his face. 'Strangely I do not remember feeling any heat though I suppose I must have since my face was pretty badly burnt. I closed my eyes tightly – I wasn't going blind for anyone. But I was so annoyed at the thought of that Dornier getting away that I put my hand back into the flames, groped for the stick, made my correction and then loosed off a long burst in the direction of where I thought the Dornier was.'

Then Newton pulled his Hurricane into a climb, to gain height so that he could bale out. On the way up he could feel the flames all around him. They burnt through the three pairs of gloves he was wearing, through his flying suit and his trousers. As he felt the Hurricane going up he undid his seat straps and stood on his seat, braced against the canopy rather like a jockey, still with his eyes tightly shut. The Hurricane got slower and slower then, suddenly, the engine cut. Newton kicked the stick forwards, at the same time throwing himself to the left and pulling the ripcord. 'At that moment I opened my eyes, in time to see the tail of my Hurricane flash past my right ear, about a foot away. The next thing I knew the parachute had opened and the ground was coming up to meet me.' Newton looked down, to see a reception committee waiting for him: about fifteen soldiers, their bayonets fixed and rifles pointing straight at him. He shouted at them 'Put those bloody things down! I'm on your side!' The soldiers did. During the descent one of his boots fell off, the laces burnt away. He made a perfect landing near Tatsfield Beacon in Surrey, knocked his release box and the parachute came away cleanly and sailed off into a nearby hedge. About 50 yards away lay a burning heap of wreckage which, less than a minute earlier, had been a perfectly serviceable Hurricane.

Guenther Unger had watched the blazing Hurricane pull up and Harry Newton's body fall away from it. Thirty-six years would pass before the two men next saw each other. The Dornier had suffered further damage as a result of Newton's final, despairing, burst of fire. The tattered bomber was, however, still flying and Unger pressed on towards home.

No 111 Squadron could not keep up the frenzied pursuit for long. One by one the surviving Hurricanes ran out of ammunition, broke off the chase and turned round for home. It had been an action with several victims, but no real victor.

Navigator Wilhelm-Friedrich Illg had originally taken the controls of the Dornier, after his pilot had been hit during the low-altitude attack on Kenley, to gain height so that the crew could bale out. At first, with the unconscious pilot's legs jammed against the rudder pedals, he had found it impossible to turn the aircraft: alone, it headed almost due northwards away from the target, over the southern outskirts of London. Then Illg, helped by the flight engineer and war reporter Georg Hinze, succeeded in lifting the pilot out of his seat and laying him on the floor of the cabin. Illg swung himself into the pilot's seat and took the unfamiliar controls. He found that the aircraft responded so he turned it round on to a southerly heading for home, jinking the whole time to avoid the uncomfortably heavy fire coming up from the anti-aircraft guns defending the capital. 'The Oberleutnant [Magin] slid to the floor. He lay against the pilot's seat, stretched out on the floor of the cabin,' Georg Hinze afterwards wrote. 'The flight engineer removed the tourniquet from the first-aid pack and tied it round the arm of the wounded man. But already he noticed that the bullet, which must have come from a gun on the ground, had not only smashed the bone of the left arm but had penetrated the left side of the chest. Already the Oberleutnant's flying suit was red with blood.'

In an air action events follow each other with great rapidity: almost everything described in this narrative, from the time the 9th Staffel had begun its attack on Kenley until now, had taken place within just five minutes: between 1.22 and 1.27 pm on that fateful Sunday afternoon. The only events to continue outside this time span were the longer parachute drops: a man on a parachute falls at about 1,000 feet per minute and Russell, Gaunce, Lautersack and Beck had all baled out from above 10,000 feet.

It was 1.27 pm and the sixty Heinkel 111s of Bomber Geschwader 1 were running in to bomb Biggin Hill. Escorted by some forty Messerschmitt 109s of Fighter Geschwader 54, the bombers flew in stepped-up waves between 12,000 and 15,000 feet.

The attack by Bomber Geschwader 76 had drawn upon itself four of the five British fighter squadrons airborne in the area. The fifth squadron, No 610 with 15 Spitfires from Biggin Hill, fought a running battle with the escorts but found great difficulty in getting through to the bomber formation.

The only heavy anti-aircraft gun unit in the area, part of the 58th Heavy Anti-Aircraft Regiment, was located just to the south of Biggin Hill, equipped with four obsolescent 3-in guns. Early on the gunners were ordered to hold their fire, however, because British fighters were operating overhead.

As a result of this tying-down of the defences, Bomber Geschwader 1 was allowed a clear run to and from its target. 'We had expected some flak, but none came and we continued on to our target. The order "Bombs Away!" was given and down they rained. With a hissing noise our bombs fell away. Now, with a turn to the left, the target could be seen. A giant cloud of black smoke announced that the bombs had struck,' noted war reporter Bankhardt, in one of the Heinkels. 'A single flak position revealed itself, but nothing came near us. Is this the best the English can do? Or is the *englische Luftwaffe* already nearing the end of its tether?' Others in the formation felt the same way. 'No English fighter, no flak came near us. Where are the English? That was the thought that went through our heads. Nothing seemed to move and, quite unscathed, we set course for home,' commented Gefreiter Willi Wanderer. 'I could not even bring my machine guns into action. Pity – I should have liked to have taken a few pot shots at an Englishman. It was just like an exercise, flying above the sleeping English. Nobody in the Staffel had ever experienced such a quiet operational mission. Can it be that the "Tommies" are finished already?' As is so often the case in battle, some of the participants saw hardly anything of the action while others, nearby, saw rather too much for comfort.

Most of the people at and around Biggin Hill had plenty of time to take cover before the high-flying Heinkels bombed. The weight of the attack fell on the landing ground and the wooded area to the east of it; few bombs fell on the station buildings. Corporal Lesley Webber, 26, had been working on a Blenheim fighter on the south side of the airfield when the raiders approached. Since there was no air raid shelter nearby he and the three men working with him ran into the nearby wood and lay on the ground between the trees. It was nearly a fatal error, because the wood collected several bombs. When the explosions ceased the men stood up, ears ringing, the air around them filled with the smoke and debris of smashed trees.

Amongst those caught out in the open when Biggin Hill was attacked were Joachim Roth and Rudolf Lamberty, standing beside their still-burning Dornier. Unfortunately for them, the field they had chosen for their crash landing was a few hundred yards to the north of the Heinkels' target. As bombs began exploding around them, captives and captors hurled themselves to the ground.*

One member of Bomber Geschwader 1 who could have told his comrades what the British fighters were up to on that Sunday afternoon was Leutnant Rudolf Ahrens of the Ist Gruppe. This was his first operational mission and from the start things had begun to go wrong. Even before he reached the Channel one of his engines had started to lose power and slowly his Heinkel had fallen further and further behind the main formation. 'But this was my first mission and I did not think of turning back,' he later explained. Near Cranbrook a Flight of five Spitfires of No 65 Squadron, led by Flying Officer Jeffrey Quill, stumbled upon the lone bomber. Lacking fighter protection, it made an easy target. 'We took our time and carried out a classic No 1 attack on it, going in to fire one after the other,' recalled Pilot Officer Dave Glaser. The Spitfires broke away leaving the Heinkel badly shot up and with its port engine trailing glycol smoke. Obviously it was not going to get very far. Ahrens stopped the damaged engine, feathered the propeller and turned for home, struggling to hold the battered Heinkel in the air.

At about the same time as Bomber Geschwader 1 was attacking Biggin Hill, the Junkers 88s of Bomber Geschwader 76 carried out a dive-bombing attack on their alternative target at West Malling airfield.

Now began the most difficult phase of the action for the Germans: the withdrawal. By 1.30 pm the raiding forces were streaming back southeastwards over Kent, pursued by the vengeful Spitfires and Hurricanes from Kenley and Biggin Hill. Damaged aircraft of all types straggled behind the German formations, easy prey for the defenders if they could be found. The German fighter escorts, now beginning to run short of fuel, provided what cover they could.

With two other Hurricanes, Pilot Officer 'Polly' Flinders of No 32 Squadron pursued an enemy aircraft 'thought to be a Do 215' eastwards from Kenley (in fact it was one of the Messerschmitt 110 escorts). 'He immediately dived towards the ground. At 3,000 feet he levelled out and I found that I was gradually closing in. We passed to the north of West Malling and over Detling, I was at about 600 yards. A running fight then ensued', Flinders afterwards reported, with the German pilot 'doing barrel rolls and half rolls in an attempt to get rid of me. We were now down to 200 feet and as

* Due to the proximity of the Dornier's crash landing to Biggin Hill airfield, several accounts have stated that the 9th Staffel low-altitude attack was on this airfield rather than Kenley. In fact, neither British nor German official records make any mention of a low-altitude attack on Biggin Hill on this day.

The opposing forces at 1.29 p.m.

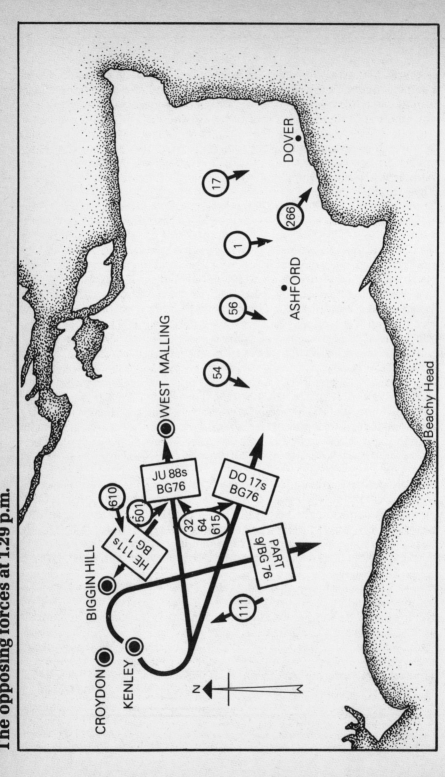

I knew that I had very little ammunition left I refrained from firing until I had a certain target.' The chase had been running for 40 miles when the Messerschmitt passed almost over the radar station at Dunkirk, 4 miles to the west of Canterbury. There, defending Bofors gunners of the 12th Light Anti-Aircraft Regiment were quick off the mark and they loosed off 47 rounds at the aircraft as it came past, hitting it on the wing and on the tail. Trailing smoke, the crippled Messerschmitt slowed up and Flinders was able to close in to 150 yards and fire off the rest of his ammunition into the enemy fighter. His victim burst into flames and dived into the ground at Harbledown, just to the north-west of Canterbury, killing both crewmen.

For Rudolf Ahrens and his crew on board their damaged Heinkel, the war would soon be over. Near Ashford, Squadron Leader Mike Crossley of No 32 Squadron came upon the limping bomber: 'I did a quarter attack on it and after about 5 seconds there appeared to be an internal explosion, and masses of bits flew off all round.' In fact the 'internal explosion' Crossley had seen was the bomber's oxygen bottles blowing up. Ahrens recalled that they 'exploded like grenades, wounding the flight engineer and blowing out the plexiglass in front of me.' The Heinkel's right engine was also hit in the attack, and the German pilot was forced to shut that one down too. Ahrens crash-landed his aircraft on Romney Marsh, near Snargate.

Ruediger Proske, nursing his crippled Messerschmitt 110 homewards on two damaged engines following MacDonell's devastating attack near Kenley, succeeded in avoiding the defending fighters. As he neared Dungeness, however, first one and then the other engine juddered to a halt. His radio operator, Unteroffizier Hans Moebius, was too badly wounded to bale out so Proske crash-landed the Messerschmitt on Derring Farm, Lydd, not far from Ahrens's Heinkel. The two men would get to know each other well during the long captivity which followed.

Oberleutnant Helmut Tiedmann, 22, flying a Messerschmitt 109 of Fighter Geschwader 3, had also had his engine damaged during a combat with British fighters. The glycol system had been hit, forcing him to shut down the engine and crash-land in open countryside at Leeds, 4 miles to the east of Maidstone. Tiedmann had time to get well clear of his aircraft, before Home Guardsmen arrived on the scene.

Approximate position of the opposing forces at 1.29 pm. The four German raiding forces over south-eastern England are all heading in different directions. The Heinkels of Bomber Geschwader 1 are bombing Biggin Hill; the Spitfires of No 610 Squadron try to engage them, but are held off by the Messerschmitt 109s of Fighter Geschwader 54. The Junkers 88s of Bomber Geschwader 76, having failed to attack Kenley, are moving in to attack West Malling; their escorts are battling with fighters of Nos 32, 64, 501 and 615 Squadrons. The Dornier 17s of the main force of Bomber Geschwader 76 are heading for home after bombing Kenley, under attack from elements of Nos 32, 64 and 615 Squadrons. The survivors of the 9th Staffel of Bomber Geschwader 76 are heading southwards for Beachy Head at low altitude, having attacked Kenley and shaken off the pursuing Hurricanes of No 111 Squadron. To the east Nos 1, 17, 54, 56 and 266 Squadrons, with 23 Spitfires and 36 Hurricanes, are moving into position to engage the German aircraft during their withdrawal.

Meanwhile, the surviving Dorniers of the bullet-torn 9th Staffel hugged the ground as they made their way towards the east coast. They had left behind the venomous Hurricanes of No 111 Squadron, but other pitfalls lay in wait for them. Guenther Unger came under uncomfortably accurate fire from a searchlight position in his path: 'One round from ahead smashed through the windscreen and glanced off my steel helmet, showering my face with glass splinters,' he later recalled.

Wilhelm Raab's Dornier had the bad luck to run over a military encampment. 'The English stormed out of their barracks, took aim and began shooting at us. Then Erwin Wittman cried out "Damn! I've been hit!" He pressed both hands to his right breast, blood trickling between his fingers,' Raab later wrote. The injured navigator, bleeding profusely, was helped to the floor of the cabin and an emergency dressing was pressed over the wound.

Nor was the action yet over for the 9th Staffel's adversaries, No 111 Squadron. Sergeant Harry Deacon was returning to Croydon after engaging the low-flying Dorniers, having been hit in the leg by return fire. As he neared Kenley at 250 feet, in some pain, trigger-happy ground gunners opened up at him. There was a resounding crash and the Hurricane's right outer wing section disappeared in a cloud of smoke. Deacon just had time to get out, before the fighter rolled on to its back and plunged into the woods below. His parachute opened in the nick of time, to deposit the badly shaken pilot on the ground. Then, to add insult to injury: 'The next thing I knew, a young fellow of about 18 stuck a shot-gun under my chin and asked "Do you speak English?" I left him in no doubt at all that I did!'

As the German raiding force began pulling back, Park's controllers slipped the leash on the fighter squadrons which had been waiting impatiently over the Margate–Canterbury area. Had the visibility been better, this would have been an excellent opportunity to hurl a concentrated force of 23 Spitfires and 36 Hurricanes (drawn from Nos 1, 17, 54, 56 and 266 Squadrons) at the raiders. But there were compelling arguments for splitting the force, for thickening haze made it impossible for the Observer Corps posts on the ground to track the movements of the German formations with sufficient precision for accurate ground control. A concentrated force of British fighters could inflict serious damage on the raiders only if they made contact with one of the main enemy formations; otherwise the blow would strike thin air and miss the enemy altogether. Instead of this all-or-nothing approach, Park's squadrons were ordered to fan out southwards over Kent and seek the enemy individually.

Thirty-nine-year-old Jim Hosmer, a railwayman and Home Guard corporal, was watching the German aircraft as they passed over Harrietsham, half way between Maidstone and Ashford. 'I remember my mother-in-law saying "Where are our fighters?" And right at that moment these Hurricanes were on to them and German aircraft seemed to be going down in all directions. It all happened so quickly, the Germans did not have any time to manoeuvre to avoid attack,' he remembered.

The victims were the Messerschmitt 110s of Destroyer Geschwader 26, their assailants the Hurricanes of No 56 Squadron. 'After being vectored about in various directions we suddenly found ourselves above and up-sun of a number of Messerschmitt 110s,' recalled Flying Officer Innes West-macott, 26. 'Delighted that we were for once not obviously outnumbered, we set about them and broke them up.' As he manoeuvred to attack, Westmacott witnessed an amazing sight: a Messerschmitt being attacked by a Hurricane, which was itself being chased by a Messerschmitt. A second Hurricane then joined in and attacked the second Messerschmitt, making four aircraft in line astern, twisting across the sky as though engaged in some crazy conga chain. The leading Messerschmitt was in 'dead trouble', West-macott observed, and beginning to trail smoke.

Westmacott picked out one of the Messerschmitts, closed in to 250 yards and gave it a 2-second burst. Then he moved in to 100 yards and fired two longer bursts and saw pieces break away from the enemy fighter. As he was closing in for the coup de grâce, however, another Hurricane attacked from his right and Westmacott was forced to break away. The pilot of the second Hurricane, Sergeant Clifford Whitehead, had been concentrating his atten-tion on the Messerschmitt and had not seen Westmacott. The Sergeant pilot opened fire at 200 yards and continued firing until he was at 100 yards. Larger pieces broke away from the Messerschmitt, which spun towards the ground.

Flying Officer 'Squeak' Weaver attacked another of the Messerschmitts and saw it dive into the ground at Bonnington, 8 miles south-west of Ashford.

Pilot Officer Maurice Mounsdon dived after yet another of the Messer-schmitts, which was itself diving away steeply to escape. The Hurricane gained rapidly, however, and Mounsdon had to throttle back to prevent himself overshooting. He put three long bursts into the violently evading German fighter and saw pieces fly off it. Then he broke off the attack as his victim went down in an almost vertical spiral dive.

From the ground, Jim Hosmer had also watched Maurice Mounsdon's Messerschmitt diving to its destruction. It disappeared behind some trees, then he heard the sharp 'boom' as it struck the ground about half a mile from where he stood.

'As so often happened, the sky seemed suddenly to be empty of aircraft,' recalled Innes Westmacott. Over the radio he could hear Flight Lieutenant Edward Gracie, his Flight Leader, calling his fighters together to reform. By now the patchy haze had thickened appreciably. 'Visibility was not good, but seeing a number of single-engined aircraft heading north-east I joined them, only to realise as I was coming up to the rear of their formation that they were Messerschmitt 109s!' Westmacott later wrote. His first inclination was to have a go at them. Then he remembered that he had used most of his ammunition. Deciding that discretion was the better part of valour he dropped back, thankful not to have been noticed, and headed for North Weald.

As the German aircraft reached the coast near Dover other British squadrons made contact. Here the haze patches were quite thick in places and fighters of both sides blundered about seeking out the enemy. Flight Lieutenant Harry Hillcoat of No 1 Squadron led two other Hurricanes in, to finish off a straggling Dornier of Bomber Geschwader 76; it plunged into the sea off Dungeness. Then one of Hillcoat's pilots, Pilot Officer George Goodman, spotted a Messerschmitt 110 flying low over the sea, streaming smoke from its left motor; probably it was a fugitive from No 56 Squadron's snap attack a couple of minutes earlier. Goodman went down after the German fighter, which jinked to avoid his fire but without success. After Goodman's first burst the left engine caught fire, after his second the right engine followed suit. Then his Hurricane was hit, as a Messerschmitt 109 came round to attack from behind and forced the British pilot to look to his own survival. Goodman hauled his fighter round in a steep turn to the right, and as he did so he caught a glance of the Messerschmitt 110 he had hit striking the sea. 'In the turn I made half a mile on the Me 109 and tried to climb in order to bale out, but saw the Me 109 gaining rapidly on me so I pulled the plug and made for home with the enemy aircraft gaining slightly,' he later reported. As Goodman pulled up over the coast at Rye the German pilot, probably running short of fuel, broke off the chase.

For 28-year-old Sergeant John Etherington, flying a Hurricane of No 17 Squadron, the business of blocking the German withdrawal seemed rather like standing in the path of a cattle stampede. Enemy aircraft of all types began streaming past, suddenly emerging out of the haze and then disappearing back into it. At first it was not too frightening. 'As we moved out over the Channel four Messerschmitt 109s passed a little way under us going south. We were there looking for bombers and left them alone; they took no notice of us,' Etherington recalled. Then Green Section, at the rear of the squadron formation, came under attack from enemy fighters, followed by Blue Section; Yellow Section broke away to give the others support. That left just Red Section continuing in search of enemy bombers: Squadron Leader Cedric Williams the squadron commander, Etherington, and Pilot Officer Neville Solomon weaving from side to side in the rear guarding their tails. 'Solomon suddenly disappeared. I never saw what happened to him, nor heard a peep from him. It was his first operational mission and we never saw him again,' Etherington remembered, 'so I began weaving from side to side to cover the CO's tail. There were just two of us, and what seemed like hundreds of enemy aircraft. I thought "How can we possibly get out of this?" And then, suddenly, the CO wasn't there either.'

Cedric Williams had stumbled upon three Dorniers emerging from the haze and went in to attack one of them, opening fire at 400 yards and closing in to 250 yards. The Dornier's left engine caught fire and he saw the bomber dive steeply away. Then, as he was breaking away, Williams saw that he was being attacked by a Messerschmitt 109. He pulled his Hurricane hard round to avoid the enemy fire, and three more Messerschmitts joined in. After a hectic series of diving turns, which took him almost to sea level, Williams succeeded in throwing off the pursuit. The Dornier he had attacked belonged to Bomber Geschwader 76 and one of those on board, war correspondent Hans Theyer, described how the aircraft had been attacked soon after leaving the coast of England: 'We fired every gun that could be brought to bear, loosing off magazine after magazine. Then the "gangster" came in behind our fin, carefully, so that we could not fire at him. He fired some bursts, then turned away.' With the Dornier's left motor badly damaged the German pilot, Unteroffizier Windschild, took the bomber down in a steep spiral turn and crash-landed near Calais.

After a frightening few minutes, both Williams and Etherington succeeded in joining up with some of the rest of the Squadron near Dover.

One fighter squadron was represented in the lunchtime battle without the knowledge of the 11 Group controller. Twenty-three-year-old Flight Lieutenant Bob Stanford-Tuck of No 92 Squadron, a 10 Group unit, had been visiting Northolt when the station's own squadrons had scrambled. Tuck decided to join in the fray alone; his radio was not tuned to the frequencies used by the 11 Group units. For an ordinary pilot to go into action in this way would have been an act of supreme folly. But Tuck was no ordinary pilot: with eleven previous victories to his credit, he was currently one of the top-scoring fighter pilots in the Royal Air Force. Tuck took off in his Spitfire and decided to orbit Beachy Head at 15,000 feet and await events. He had not been there long when a pair of German aircraft, which he took to be Junkers 88s, ran past him far below making for France at high speed. Tuck turned and, converting his altitude advantage into speed, rapidly overhauled the pair. Close to the water he pulled round and ran in to attack from head-on. Ignoring the tracer rounds streaking past his Spitfire, Tuck held his fire until he was satisfied he was well within range, then loosed off a short burst. It was sufficient. His opponent slid sideways into the sea, cartwheeled, and broke up in a flurry of white foam.

Still keeping up his speed, Tuck turned round after the second aircraft. Again he was able to overtake his enemy and again he turned in to attack from head-on. This time, however, the return fire was more accurate. 'Something very heavy' struck the Spitfire's engine, causing it to bump badly. Tuck opened fire and saw his rounds strike home, then pulled his fighter up into a zoom climb to gain some altitude in case his engine failed altogether. He glanced over his shoulder and saw his adversary making off at low altitude, seemingly in trouble. Since none was lost in the Beachy Head area at this time, the aircraft Tuck attacked cannot have been Junkers 88s. More likely they were Messerschmitt 110s of Destroyer Geschwader 26. The 'something very heavy' which struck Tuck's aircraft, probably a cannon shell, accords with this. Messerschmitt 110s carried cannon but Junkers 88s at this time did not.

As Tuck climbed away he had problems of his own. His propeller was damaged and knocked out of balance and the engine seemed as if it was trying to shake itself to pieces. Moreover the oil and coolant systems had been hit and were spilling their contents down the fuselage; the stench of glycol fumes wafted into the Spitfire's cockpit. Tuck succeeded in edging his fighter up to 4,000 feet by the time he reached the coast and for a time it seemed he might be able to reach one of the Fighter Command airfields inland. Near Tonbridge, however, his engine finally gave up and burst into flames. Tuck dived head-first over the wing and clear of his Spitfire, then pulled his ripcord. His parachute opened normally but he swung badly and struck the ground hard, wrenching his left knee and leg.

The Spitfires of No 266 Squadron were probably the last British fighters to engage during the lunchtime action, as they tried to do battle with a gaggle of Messerschmitt 109s making their way homewards at high speed. The German fighter pilots, probably almost out of fuel by this time, were in no mood to engage and dived away to the south-east.

Following his brush with Gerhard Schoepfel, and his lengthy, inexpert, tumbling, free-fall descent, Kenneth Lee parachuted to earth near Whitstable. The British pilot had not expected a hero's welcome, but he was rather taken aback by the reception he actually received. No sooner had he landed than an old man 'with an even more ancient firearm' advanced on him, slowly raising and lowering the barrel of the weapon in an unmistakable command to Lee to raise his hands. The pilot protested that he was British; but to no avail. Without uttering a word the man, obviously very frightened, repeated his demand. One did not argue with such people, and Lee complied. The pilot was then shepherded, limping, to a nearby road, the blood from his wounded right foot squelching in his boot. Shortly afterwards the pair came upon some soldiers and Lee was handed over to them; now he was able to establish his identity. Lee was helped over to a golf clubhouse nearby, where the soldiers' officer took him into the bar and bought him a drink. 'There I stood at the bar, wearing a Mae West, no jacket, and beginning to leak blood from my torn flying boot. None of the golfers took any notice of me – after all, I wasn't a member,' he remembered. 'Outside we could hear the battle still going on, with the roar of aircraft engines and the sounds of machine-gun fire. I remember one of the golfers coming into the clubhouse and indignantly exclaiming: "That burst of machine-gun fire when we were on the 5th made me miss my bloody putt, old chap!" They were far more concerned about their individual games of golf, than the battle going on overhead.'

Lying in a field near Oxted with his knees and ankles sprained, unable to move after his bone-jarring landing by parachute after being shot down by Alan Eckford, Wilhelm Lautersack was soon found by soldiers guided to the scene by the British fighter orbiting overhead. High above, the air battle was still in progress, with aircraft diving and machine guns rattling. Seeing that the German crewman was helpless the soldiers half carried, half dragged him to the side of the field, where the branches of a large tree gave their protection. Soon afterwards a vehicle arrived to take him to hospital.

After his fight with Guenther Unger's Dornier and the subsequent parachute descent, Harry Newton was picked up by soldiers and helped to a nearby pillbox to await an ambulance. He was a ghastly apparition, with one boot missing and the whole of his face, hands and clothing burnt or charred. As he shuffled along the road he passed a young couple who had been out for a Sunday ride on their tandem bicycle. On seeing Newton, the girl collapsed in a faint. Newton asked the soldier helping him what was wrong with the girl. The man replied, as gently as he could, that the reason for the young lady's distress was the pilot's terrible appearance.

Deep in shock, Newton's main worry was not for himself but for his parachute: he had signed for it and he had to have it back! Some soldiers retrieved it for him and, on examination, the canopy was found to have 36 bullet holes through it. Nobody had fired at him during his descent: one or two of Franz Bergmann's rounds had passed clean through the pack while Newton was still sitting on it in the Hurricane; they can have missed his body with less than half an inch to spare. Soon afterwards Newton was informed that a Dornier had crashed near Oxted, about three miles to the south of Tatsfield where he had come down. He never doubted that this was the bomber he had engaged. This was not Unger's aircraft, however: it was the aircraft of the high-altitude raiding force piloted by Oberleutnant Werner Stoldt, knocked down by Pilot Officer Alan Eckford during No 32 Squadron's head-on attack, from which Wilhelm Lautersack had jumped and which had crashed into Doris Addison's house. Harry Newton was whisked away to the hospital at Oxted, where he was put under anaesthetic and doctors worked to save the skin on his face and hands.

A small crowd of curious onlookers followed Joachim Roth and Rudolf Lamberty, as they were escorted away from their burning Dornier at Leaves Green and to the nearby road. Lamberty was still wearing his parachute but his hands were too badly burnt for him to undo his quick-release buckle. He tried to explain to one of the civilians how to release it, but by mistake the man pulled the ripcord and the silken canopy and rigging lines spilled out over the ground. Finally somebody undid the harness and the straps fell away. 'I asked them to get out of my pocket some cigarettes and matches and put the cigarette in my mouth and light it, as I couldn't. They did so. There was astonishment because they were English cigarettes – I had bought them in Guernsey a few days previously,' Lamberty recounted. Lamberty and Roth and the other three crewmembers of the Dornier, all with varying degrees of burns or wounds, were taken to the sick quarters at the nearby airfield at Biggin Hill.

After crash-landing on Woodcote Park golf course, following hits suffered while chasing the low-flying Dorniers of the 9th Staffel, Peter Simpson made a rapid exit from the cockpit of his Hurricane. Almost immediately he was confronted by a pair of fierce-looking golfers, one of whom brandished a club menacingly. They took him for a German – in the heat of the moment they failed to notice that his Hurricane bore Royal Air Force roundels. Simpson shouted to them that he was British and to prove it pulled out a packet of Player's cigarettes. This most fallible token of national identity was taken at its face value, and the hostility changed to concern. 'I jumped down off the wing, landed on the foot with the splinter in it and cried out with pain,' Simpson recalled. 'At that moment other people approached, one of whom said he was a doctor. He sat me down, took my shoe and sock off, and pulled out one of the splinters. My foot was all numb, with blood pouring out; I thought the whole foot was going to have to come off! But he said it was nothing serious.' Simpson's treatment was rather different from that meted out to Lee at Whitstable Golf Club. He was helped over to the Royal Automobile Club building and treated as an honoured guest, offered lunch and plied with brandy; though he did not normally drink spirits, Simpson decided that this was a special occasion. Finally, one of the club members drove him back to Croydon.

Following the crash-landing of his Heinkel on Romney Marsh near Snargate, Rudolf Ahrens and his crew clambered out of the aircraft carrying their wounded flight engineer. Ahrens then went back into the aircraft and set in operation the delay mechanism of the incendiary bomb, to destroy the aircraft and prevent it falling into enemy hands. He climbed out of the cockpit, in time to see Home Guardsmen advancing on the aircraft. Quietly the Germans surrendered, then Ahrens told the Home Guard commander to move everyone away from the aircraft: the pilot said that there were bombs still on board which might go off (in fact there were no high explosive bombs, Ahrens had jettisoned them, but he did not want anyone to interfere with the incendiary bomb about to ignite). The men moved a respectful couple of hundred yards away from the Heinkel, as other soldiers came running to the scene. The newcomers said that they had fired at the bomber immediately before it had crash-landed; would the German crew please confirm that they had been responsible for shooting it down? 'I could not grant them that success,' Ahrens commented. Then a vehicle arrived and the German crewmen were loaded on board. As he was being driven away, Ahrens heard the satisfying crackle of exploding machine-gun ammunition; the fire-bomb he had set had taken effect. The bomber's wounded flight engineer was rushed to Rye Memorial Hospital, but died there shortly afterwards.

After his unsuccessful attempt to improvise a tourniquet for his bleeding leg with his ripcord, while hanging from his parachute, 'Humph' Russell came to earth beside the railway track just outside Edenbridge. A railway-man working on the line was the first to reach him and, as luck would have it, the man had just completed a course in first aid. Delighted to have a chance to exercise his new-found skill, the man tore strips from the parachute and expertly bound up the wound, Russell was then rushed to the local hospital where he was treated by 'an excellent doctor who saved my leg, and kept me supplied with sherry all the time I was in hospital!'

On seeing the Messerschmitt 110 smash into the ground near Harriets-ham, Jim Hosmer slipped his arm into the Home Guard armband, grabbed his rifle, and hastened to the scene. 'As I was running to the wreck, carrying my rifle, somebody shouted "You won't need that! There won't be anybody there!" He was right. When we reached it one could hardly recognise that it had been an aircraft. It had gone through one hedge, across a road, and smashed into a bank on the other side,' he remembered. 'The whole thing was smouldering gently – there was very little left to burn. There were no survivors.'

Flight Lieutenant Bob Stanford-Tuck landed with his parachute beside Plovers, Lord Cornwallis's stately home near Tunbridge Wells. Tuck was taken to the house and, after a bath to clean off the oil that had spurted over him as he abandoned his Spitfire, he was invited to afternoon tea with the family.

As the last of the bombs ceased exploding at Kenley, Leading Aircraftman Herbert Brotherton, 24, cautiously opened the door of one of the shelters on the north side of the airfield and, blinking in the sunlight, peeped outside. He was greeted with a continuous strident blare sounding like an electric car horn. The noise came from the Spitfire lying on its belly in front of him, one of No 64 Squadron's aircraft which had been serviceable but for which there was no pilot to take it into action. One of the bombs from the high-altitude attack had gone clean through the concrete taxi-way beside the blast pen where the aircraft stood, and exploded in the soil underneath. The earthquake-like shudder from the explosion had been transmitted through the ground. It lifted the Spitfire bodily, released the undercarriage-down locks, and allowed the aircraft to slam down on its belly, forcing the wheels to retract into the wells in the wings. The horn Brotherton heard was fitted to warn the pilot if he throttled back with the undercarriage retracted, a safety measure to prevent accidental wheels-up landings. In this Spitfire the engine was not running and the undercarriage was up, so the electrical circuit was made and the horn sounded. Away to the south of the airfield, a thickening pillar of black smoke swirled upwards from the blazing hangars, a sombre backdrop to the bizarre scene.

On the other side of the shelter and much nearer to hand, the wreck of Petersen's Dornier was burning itself out in the grounds of a private house. Brotherton and some of his comrades rushed out to see if help was needed. As he crossed the lawn of the house he came upon the arm of one of the German crewmen, complete with sleeve, which had been torn off in the crash. 'I didn't feel squeamish. I remember looking at it and thinking that the hand was well manicured; on one of the fingers was a ring.' There was nothing anyone could do to save any other members of the German crew.

Around Kenley airfield there was ample evidence of the 9th Staffel low-altitude attack. Bombs had ricocheted across the ground, carving straight furrows through the soil. Several had failed to explode and now lay around the airfield and the camp buildings: because of their unexpectedly hot reception some of the German crews had released their bombs from too low an altitude for the fuses to function. One driver returned to the vehicle he had abandoned on the airfield to find that a bomb, going almost horizontally, had smashed clean through the cab without exploding. Nevertheless, sufficient of the bombs from the low-flying raiders had exploded to cause considerable damage; and by far the greater part of the damage was caused by the low-flyers.

About 600 yards away from Brotherton, on the southern end of the airfield, 28-year-old Flight Sergeant Reg Sheldrake emerged from his shelter to take stock of the situation. 'After the attack the station was a Hell of a mess. There was wreckage all over the place. We had no time to think about it, being more intent on rescuing the injured and putting out the fires.'

Sheldrake was responsible for the station's fire service, and directed the small Bantam fire engine into action. 'The hangar fires were very difficult to put out: the roofs were timber-framed and covered in asphalt, paint was stored there and some of the aircraft had petrol in their tanks. Once that lot got going, that was it.' The many unexploded bombs were a further hazard to the fire-fighters. 'I came across one in a hedgerow against the armoury, at the back of the motor transport section. I stumbled against it and it made me jump, I can tell you!' Sheldrake remembered.

There were other dangers: as the fires reached the oxygen cylinders stored in the hangars these exploded with considerable violence. Twenty-four-year-old Aircraftman Bill Fisher, a fitter with No 615 Squadron, recalled 'They went off with a fair old bang, hurling great chunks of iron in all directions.'

Sub-Officer Leo Dawe, 40, leading an Auxiliary Fire Service team based at Coulsdon about a mile from the airfield, was one of the first outsiders to arrive to assist with the fires at Kenley. Without waiting for orders he assembled his crew and they set out in their decrepit vehicle, a one-time London taxi, towing their Coventry Climax trailer pump. On reaching the camp the men found a standpipe, ran out their hoses and prepared to go into action for the first time. 'This was the moment we had been trained for. Hangars were ablaze from end to end, some with planes inside; outside were planes on fire. We decided to concentrate on the nearest hangar. Came the magic words "Water On!" then some delay before anything happened and then – not a blast of water, but a feeble trickle, which even in that urgent moment reminded me of the "Mannequin Pis",' Dawe later wrote. One of the bombs had fractured the station's water mains. Before Dawe could move his trailer pump over to one of the static water tanks, however, professional fire brigades from all over the area began arriving on the scene and started to bring the fires under control.

Bill Fisher joined in the rescue work round the gutted station sick quarters. The staff and patients had gone into the nearby shelter, which had been hit at each end by a bomb. The shock of the explosions had collapsed the ends of the shelter on the men and women inside. Amongst the dead was Flight Lieutenant Robert Cromie, a well-loved local doctor who had joined the Royal Air Force shortly before. Many of those in the mid-part of the shelter were dug out alive, though most had injuries. There were many more rescuers than either shovels or room to work with them. 'You took a shovel and dug and dug until you began to tire, then you handed it to somebody else,' Fisher recalled. One of the WAAFs dug out, Mary Coulthard, had sustained a nasty gash to her thigh from the sharp edge of her steel helmet; she sat down on the ground and bandaged the wound herself, without fuss.

The shelter which had been hit was No 13, the one Laurence Bell and his friend had almost entered, then rejected, during their mad scramble for cover when the Dorniers had begun their attack. He has been superstitious ever since.

Pamela Rust emerged from shelter a second time and surveyed the destruction. Inside one of the blazing hangars she could make out the

charred remains of aircraft. 'One hangar contained about fifty civilian cars –
one or two wheels and a few bits and pieces are about all that remain', she
noted in her diary. 'There was a dead bird in the gutter lying in a mass of
debris, bits and pieces of trees, wood, glass, telegraph wires, etc.' Two of her
Airwoman friends, Vera Nichols and Pam Kinahan, helped bandage one of
the wounded men who was bleeding profusely: 'He kept on calling for
something to put him to sleep but all the morphia had been destroyed when
the sick bay had been totally wrecked by a direct hit.'

With the station's doctor dead and the sick quarters wrecked, medical
teams had to be summoned from outside to help with the wounded. Ambulance attendant Maretta King and her driver were on duty at Sanderstead,
two miles to the north-east of Kenley, when the call came for assistance.
'Our first sight upon nearing the aerodrome was a terrific blaze. We were
then stopped by an Army officer who had a cut on his face and his arm in a
sling. With him were two of his men who, still amazed, told us they had not
expected to see him alive again as he had been in the sick bay which had
caught fire after a direct hit but miraculously he had got out alive,' she
recounted.

As the fires died down Bill Fisher and other airmen of No 615 Squadron
were ordered to the unit's wrecked hangar, to salvage everything possible.
'The heat from the fire had been so fierce that all the wood of my tool box
had disappeared; only the metal band was there; my saws and files were all
there, minus their wooden handles,' he recalled. 'The wooden roof of the
hangar was gone, and on the floor beneath were scattered the several
hundredweight of nails which had held it together.'

With several other airmen, Laurence Bell was ordered to the area of the
wrecked station headquarters to assist with the clearing up. Outside the
station chapel, where he had slept the previous night, stood a bomb stuck
nose-first in the ground. ' "Obviously a dud" said some of the 64 Squadron
old-hand airmen, who somehow got the tail-fins off and proudly collared
them as a trophy. They were very put out when a warrant officer came up and
told them off in very plain terms and made them build up a wall of sand bags
round it,' Bell recalled. 'This had been completed less than an hour when
the bomb went off with an enormous blast; but thanks to the warrant
officer's intervention there were no casualties as most of the blast went
upwards.'

Initially the fire and rescue services had been able to reach Kenley with
little difficulty, but later there were problems. The report of 'parachutists
descending on Kenley', passed back by Police Sergeant 'Jigger' Lee, had
triggered off an invasion scare. With other members of the Operations
Room staff, Clifford Kenyon suddenly received orders to take his rifle and
prepare to defend Kenley against an attack by enemy paratroops.
Apprehensively, he and his comrades took up positions round the perimeter
of the operations building. Meanwhile, off the airfield, police and Home
Guardsmen were erecting road blocks to seal off the airfield; patrols of
Army motor cycles, with sidecars fitted with machine guns, began roaring
round the streets seeking out the enemy. In his official report on the day's

events Mr N. Duncan, the senior regional Civil Defence officer, stated that
in some cases the arrival of services had been delayed:

> . . . due to the action of the police, who held up every vehicle they could and
> insisted on close examination of all credentials and did not appear to realise
> that speed was essential. In my own case I had a great deal of difficulty
> getting through, in some instances, and the police certainly appeared to be
> paying little attention to the Civil Defence armband. After a while I found
> the best method was to offer my blue Headquarters Pass and say 'Home
> Office' so that the police gave way. Home Guard were also active in this
> direction so far as I was concerned and much time was wasted arguing with
> isolated members of the force.

The scare reminded everyone of the dark rumours, current at the time but
never substantiated, that German paratroopers were sent into action wearing various disguises. As Maretta King left Kenley later in the afternoon, she
was warned to watch out for Germans 'in disguises such as nurses, vicars,
etc.'

At Kenley three out of the four hangars were gutted. The station headquarters was wrecked. So was the sick quarters, which bore no prominent
red cross and was camouflaged like the rest of the station buildings. The
officers' and sergeants' messes were both damaged, as were several other
buildings. Nine soldiers and airmen were killed in the attack and ten injured.
Four Hurricanes and a Blenheim were destroyed on the ground, two
Hurricanes and a Spitfire suffered damage. Four non-operational aircraft
were destroyed and one damaged. Numerous vehicles from the station
motor transport pool were wrecked when their hangar was hit. The billowing
pillar of smoke from the Kenley fires could be seen from Brighton, 34 miles
to the south.

The vitally important Sector Operations Room at Kenley had escaped
damage during the attack, but exploding bombs had severed some of the
underground cables to the building, including that to the main transmitter.
By judicious re-routing of calls through the surviving lines, however, signals
personnel enabled Norman and his staff to maintain contact with Group
headquarters and the other stations. After a hiatus of just over ten minutes,
Kenley's reserve radio transmitter was brought into use and Norman was
again able to contact his fighters which were airborne. The next priority after
that was to inspect the airfield and mark out a landing strip clear of craters
and unexploded bombs. Until this could be done, the fighters of Nos 64 and
615 Squadrons were instructed to land at the satellite airfield at Redhill. Six
did so. The other eleven missed the radio call and landed back at Kenley
without difficulty.

After the initial panic was over Aircraftman Sammy Samson climbed to
the top of one of the No 615 Squadron blast pens on the east side of the
airfield, and scanned the area around. From almost every direction he could
see the pillars of smoke marking the funeral pyres of wrecked aircraft: nearly
half a mile away to the north-west lay Feldwebel Petersen's Dornier; five
miles to the north-east lay Rudolf Lamberty's; four miles due east was Harry
Newton's Hurricane. To the south-east were three such pyres: five miles

away, Werner Stoldt's Dornier, three miles away was Harry Deacon's Hurricane and near it a Messerschmitt 110 knocked down in the mêlée over Kenley. And half a mile away to the south-west Kenley's own aircraft and hangars were burning themselves out.

In the populated area surrounding Kenley, civilians also began to take stock of the situation. Six miles to the south-east of the airfield, at Hurst Green, Doris Addison had gone back into her home to try to find Bob, the family's pet spaniel. One side of the house was burning, set alight by blazing fuel from Werner Stoldt's Dornier as it crashed alongside. She did not find the animal; in fact the singed and terrified dog had bolted from the scene and was whimpering in a field some distance away. Dick, her husband and part-time fireman, came dashing home and his comrades rapidly extinguished the flames. Lying on the ground around the house were nineteen of the 110-pound bombs carried by the Dornier; the twentieth had smashed through the kitchen wall and come to rest underneath the kitchen table. In fact the bomb had not been made live before the Dornier crashed, but Dick Addison had no way of knowing this. Bravely, he and a friend picked it up and gently carried it to a safe place at the end of the smallholding. Throughout it all the Addisons' chickens, all very frightened and some with feathers burnt away, were clucking noisily as they scampered aimlessly round and over pieces of wreckage of the bomber. Doris Addison was driven to Oxted Hospital to have treated the minor burns she had suffered during the hunt for Bob. As she arrived she saw a young fighter pilot being brought in with burns hideously worse than her own: it was Harry Newton.

In Valley Road, Kenley, half a mile to the north of the airfield, Kathleen Rhodes, her fiancé and the woman from next door were carefully extricated from the crumpled shelter which had saved their lives. As she was being carried to the ambulance she saw that the house she and her fiancé had been working on, which was to have been their home after their marriage planned in three weeks' time, was now a pile of rubble. To her trained nurse's eye it seemed that her shattered left arm would have to be amputated though, with some relief, she saw that although her shoes had been blown off her feet were still in place. Her fiancé, still unconscious, was bleeding profusely from a back injury. It seemed as if, in the split-second of the explosion, all of her life's dreams had been shattered*.

In the garden of his home at Buxton Lane, Caterham, about 500 yards to the south of Kenley airfield, 45-year-old Richard Grohmann poked his head out of the air raid shelter. Sadly he murmured to his wife, Winifred, 'I'm afraid the house has gone, dear.' His son John pushed his head round his father's arm to look outside, prepared for the worst. Outside, in whichever direction he looked, the sky seemed to be filled with a dull black fog, so thick that he could not even see the house ten yards away. Then, very slowly, the

---

* Kathleen Rhodes was to spend the following year in hospital. Her left arm was saved, though afterwards she would have only partial use of it. Her fiancé, Lionel Miller, made a complete recovery. When she came out of hospital their delayed wedding did take place and they are still together. The other injured occupant of the shelter, Mrs Bazin, also recovered.

'fog' dissipated until he was able to see first a little of the house, then more, then finally that it was intact. Later the family learned that a bomb had landed on a bunker full of coal four doors away; the explosion had pulverised the contents and blasted them high into the air, where the particles remained suspended for several minutes before descending to blanket the area around with fine black dust.

Two and a half miles to the north-west Kathleen Rose and her mother inspected their home, which really had been wrecked. 'After the dust had settled my mother remarked "Kath, our home is gone but I'm going to have my dinner." So she took it out of the oven – the gas main had been severed – and coolly sat where she could and ate her dinner.'

Two and a half miles to the east, 16-year-old apprentice motor mechanic Bryan Prosper and his parents climbed out of the Anderson shelter in the back garden of their home in Godstone Road, Whyteleafe, shaken after bombs had exploded nearby. Fortunately his mother had opened all the windows of their home because it was such a nice day: the glass panes had all survived, even though the blast had lifted more than a hundred tiles off their roof. Bryan Prosper inspected his home for internal damage and found that the main casualty was the sitting room. The blast of the bomb, passing over the roof, had neatly scoured the soot out of the chimney and deposited it in a thick black mess over everything, including the Sunday lunch his mother had served just before their dash for shelter. 'We spent the rest of the day cleaning and scrubbing the house, but thanking God that we were still alive,' he remembered.

The Prospers' next-door neighbours, the Freemans, who had had four bombs explode in their back garden, also emerged shaken from their shelter. Reg Freeman looked disbelievingly round him: where his kitchen garden and chicken run had once been, there was nothing but churned soil. Because the ground at the back of the house sloped back steeply, the blast had passed over his house also. Later he found his half-dozen Leghorn chickens, wrapped up in the wire of their run, still alive lying in the road in front of the house; shaken and subdued at first, they recovered from their experience in a couple of hours.

Across the Godstone Road from the Prospers and the Freemans, the Warners had their windows smashed and the ceilings knocked down by bombs in the same stick, aimed at the railway lines at the end of their garden. One piece of debris, a 25-pound cast-iron 'chair' used to fix a rail to its sleeper, had come crashing through the metal frame of one of the upstairs windows and ended up embedded in the mattress on one of the beds.

Approximately 150 bombs had fallen in the area surrounding Kenley airfield. Most people had taken cover in good time, however, and as a result casualties were relatively light. Six people had been killed and twenty-one seriously injured. Two of the deaths and most of the injuries were inflicted in Coulsdon, the town immediately to the north-west of the airfield, and most of the damage occurred there.

From the districts to the north and east of Kenley there came numerous reports of machine-gunning from the air, causing the death of one man,

Positions of witnesses around Kenley airfield

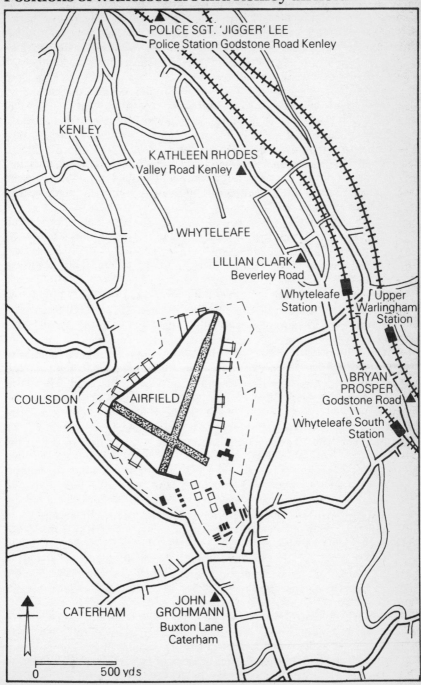

POLICE SGT. 'JIGGER' LEE
Police Station Godstone Road Kenley

KENLEY

KATHLEEN RHODES
Valley Road Kenley

WHYTELEAFE

LILLIAN CLARK
Beverley Road

Whyteleafe
Station

Upper
Warlingham
Station

BRYAN
PROSPER
Godstone Road

Whyteleafe South
Station

COULSDON   AIRFIELD

CATERHAM   JOHN
                GROHMANN
                Buxton Lane
                Caterham

0   500 yds

injury to others and some damage to property. This was not, however, the
wanton act of terror by the Germans that it appeared. As the crews of the 9th
Staffel had dodged in and out of any cover they could find, trying to shake off
the pursuing Hurricanes of No 111 Squadron, they were far too pre-
occupied to loose off at ground targets. But because the Dorniers flew so
low, the Hurricane pilots could fire at them only from above; and those
bullets which missed their target continued straight on into the ground. A
stray burst of just one second from a Hurricane, 160 rounds, could do a lot of
damage to a house. Almost certainly the rounds reported on this occasion
came from British, rather than German, machine guns. After his own
narrow escape air raid warden Leslie Stevens went into Selsdon Wood, a
local beauty spot behind his home, to look for possible casualties. He came
upon a courting couple looking very white and shaken, crouched beside a
tree several minutes after the aircraft had passed. A burst of machine-gun
fire had missed them only by inches.

At the remaining targets there was far less damage and far fewer casualties than at Kenley. Nineteen small bombs hit Croydon airfield, causing
damage to one hangar and the main terminal building. One soldier was
killed. A Hurricane of No 111 Squadron in the hangar was destroyed and
another suffered damage.

Surprisingly, in view of the scale of the attack by the sixty Heinkels and
the lack of interference from the defences, Biggin Hill suffered little damage. Thanks to the 'survival scramble' order, not a single aircraft was
damaged on the ground. One bomb landed on the shed housing the motor
pool, which was empty at the time; otherwise there was minimal damage to
the station buildings. Most of the 84 tons of bombs dropped by the Heinkels
fell on the landing ground itself or the woods to the east of it. There was
considerable cratering of the landing ground, but a clear area was soon
marked out and at no time was the airfield out of action. Two men were
killed on the station and there were some injured. After the attack WAAF
Sergeant Elizabeth Mortimer, an armourer, went out to help deal with the
many unexploded bombs. First these had to be marked with red flags, then
the disposal teams under Flight Sergeant Joe Hunt dug down to the bombs.
'During the defusing operation I acted as Hunt's assistant', remembered
Elizabeth Mortimer. 'We had a special tool which we used to short out the
electrical condenser fitted to the German bomb fuses, then the bombs could
be lifted clear.' Her plucky performance did much to stiffen the morale of
the men working beside her.

The dive-bombing attack on West Malling, which served as an advanced
landing ground for fighters from the Kenley and Biggin Hill sectors, caused
some damage to hangars and the destruction of three Lysander army co-
operation aircraft. There were no casualties.

During their return flights some of the raiders of Bomber Geschwader 76
with bombs remaining had dropped them on alternative targets along their
route. Thirteen 110-pounders fell on Paddock Wood railway junction near
Tonbridge, setting fire to twelve railway wagons and causing damage to
three cottages; there were no casualties. And at Rye, on the south coast,

twenty-eight 110-pounders fell across buildings near the railway line and caused the destruction of eleven houses and serious damage to eleven more; three people were killed and three more injured.

Although the raiding force had now left the coast and was clear of British fighters, home was still a long way away for some of the German crews. This was particularly so for the low-flyers of the 9th Staffel who, in order to reduce to a minimum their time over England, now had to make the longest over-water flights back to France. Of the seven surviving Dorniers one was being flown by its navigator, Wilhelm Illg, with the gravely wounded pilot lying on the cabin floor beside him. Feldwebel Raab had a seriously wounded navigator. Feldwebel Stephani had a badly damaged aircraft, a dead flight engineer and a seriously wounded radio operator. Unteroffizier Unger's Dornier had suffered damage to both engines, as had that of Unteroffizier Schumacher. Feldwebel Reichel was returning on one engine. Indeed only one of the Dorniers, that piloted by Unteroffizier Maassen, lacked serious damage or a dead or wounded crewman.

Maassen, Raab and Schumacher left the south coast of England together, the bullet-torn remnant of the proud formation that had gone in some forty minutes earlier. About half way back across the Channel, Schumacher began to run into trouble. 'We left the English coast and joyful expressions appeared on all faces, but the battle was not yet over. The left motor began to give up, visibly losing revolutions. A long line of black smoke trailed behind us. The speed fell and unfortunately I had no way of knowing what it was because the airspeed indicator was shot to pieces,' he later wrote. The only indication he had that he was slowing up was that his comrades were drawing further and further away in front. He pushed forwards his right throttle to get full revolutions from the engine and lowered the flaps a little, in an attempt to gain more altitude. Slowly the aircraft edged up to about 350 feet, then: 'Suddenly a shudder went through the aircraft and it appeared that it was about to break up. I switched off the ignition to the defective motor and the machine began to sink slowly. I tried to open the throttle to the right motor even further, but the lever was already hard against the stop.' Schumacher told his crew to prepare to ditch, and the men braced themselves in their seats. The pilot set down the Dornier as gently as he could, but with a Force 4 sea running the arrival was anything but smooth. As the bomber hit the sea the water smashed in the perspex nose and the crew were engulfed by the sudden inrush of cold water. Gasping for breath, the men scrambled out of the escape hatch at the rear of the cabin and into the water, taking their dinghy with them. As they pushed themselves clear of the sinking Dornier, the flight engineer failed to inflate his life jacket for some reason and was drowned. With some difficulty the three survivors inflated their dinghy, and boarded it.

When Schumacher's Dornier had begun to fall behind, Maassen had turned back and formated on the stricken aircraft. He and his crew had been helpless spectators as Schumacher sank lower and lower and finally ditched. Maassen's radio operator was unable to make contact with the rescue service; there was nothing for it but to leave the survivors, and land as soon as possible to summon help.

His Dornier damaged first over Kenley, then during Harry Newton's attack, Guenther Unger was also in difficulty. One of his engines had stopped and the other gradually lost power and he too was forced to alight on the sea. Again there was the violent arrival, as the aircraft hit the water. 'The water pressure smashed in the glass nose and I received a blow in the face that shook me. I held my breath and opened my eyes, but I couldn't see anything because of the air bubbles in the swirling water. Now I had to release myself quickly, because I was already submerged. I felt for the buckle to release my straps but I could not get to it: the control column was jammed hard against my stomach and I was unable to push it forwards.' The pilot strained against it with every muscle, but the control column refused to budge. Slowly the tail of the Dornier rose and the machine slid under the waves, taking the struggling Unger with it. A sudden, numbing fear of death swept over him. Then it passed and he found he was able to think with great clarity and calmness. 'I was still holding my breath, I had not swallowed a single drop of water. I kept thinking to myself "Open your mouth and swallow the water, and it will soon be over." But before I could act on these thoughts, the control column suddenly became free and moved forwards by itself.' At last Unger was able to reach the harness buckle and release his straps. By now the Dornier was sinking fast, in water so dark that he could make out only a vague outline of the cabin around him. He groped his way to the escape hatch, pushed himself out, and inflated his life jacket. In a flurry of bubbles he rose rapidly towards the lighter water above, like a cork out of a champagne bottle.

Unger's crew had already given up their pilot for lost when there was a commotion in the water about 30 yards away. They were amazed to see his body suddenly lift clear of the waves, then flop back. He was alive! The men paddled towards each other and Unger learned that the dinghy had failed to inflate: one of the crewmen, operating the unfamiliar valve mechanism in the stress of the moment, had allowed the compressed gas to escape from the bottle. The men tried to inflate the dinghy using the hand bellows pump but this operation, so simple when they had tried it under training on land, proved almost impossible at sea. Each time a wave hit them the dinghy was knocked away and they found that they were pumping in more water than air. Finally, reluctantly, they gave up the unequal struggle.

Unger and his crew had survived their ordeals by fire and water; now they faced death from exposure. Unless they were picked up within the next two or three hours they were condemned to a slow, numbing death from the elements. And, because Harry Newton had wrecked the Dornier's radio and nobody had seen it ditch, the German rescue service had no idea where they were.

The first of the 9th Staffel Dorniers to reach safety was Wilhelm Raab's. He landed at Amiens, where the badly wounded navigator was carefully lifted out of the aircraft and carried to the waiting ambulance. Once this had been done, he and the other crewmen examined their aircraft for signs of damage: what had been inside those mysterious smoke trails, which had so nearly ensnared their aircraft over Kenley? One thing that bothered Raab was that his radio operator, facing rearwards, had seen no red balls or trails of smoke, only a line of small parachutes hanging in the sky. 'We went round our brave Dornier 17 and counted 26 hits; one could recognise the corresponding exit holes by their greater size. My crew had felt the jerk of our hitting something, but had not taken it seriously. It worried me. I had to find a flak hit, or some other sign, that could be linked with the columns of smoke.' Before he took off again to return to his base at Cormeilles-en-Vexin, Raab had to be sure that his aircraft had not suffered some serious, if less obvious, form of damage. After a second, more detailed, inspection of the Dornier it was clear that there were no holes from anything heavier than machine gun rounds. 'My clear sight of the fiery balls, and the small parachutes the radio operator mentioned seeing, had to be linked in some way. Perhaps it was a special device to counter low-flying aircraft, a wire or net or something similar. But I had never heard of such a thing.' Raab climbed on top of the wing and carefully examined the leading edge for signs of damage and, lo and behold, just outside the port engine, he found dents and rippling of the skin. 'It looked just as if a strong cable had been dragged forcibly across the paintwork,' he remembered.

The second Dornier to land was Maassen's, at an airfield near Boulogne, with the report that Schumacher's aircraft had ditched a few miles offshore. Maassen himself took off soon afterwards, flying as observer in a Fiesler Storch spotter aircraft searching for his comrades.

Otto Stephani only just made it back across the Channel, on two battered engines. To lighten the aircraft everything moveable had been jettisoned, including the body of the dead flight engineer. Stephani was almost out of height when he finally reached the French coast. 'I wanted to make an emergency landing on the sand but at the last moment I caught sight of a three-storey building beyond the beach which made that impossible. I allowed the aircraft to drift slightly to the left and tried to bring it up over the dunes,' he later wrote. By pulling up the nose, Stephani was able to ease the aircraft close over the sand dunes, but he lost so much of his precious speed in the process that the Dornier thumped down on the ground on the other side. 'There was a great bang inside the machine and everything was thrown into confusion. Bits of the aircraft were knocked off and strewn around the sand, but she landed quite well and eventually came to rest.' The pilot and radio operator, both with gunshot wounds, were rushed to hospital where the radio operator died soon afterwards. The navigator, Unteroffizier Groemmer, who alone in the crew had escaped unscathed, later walked round the Dornier counting the bullet holes; when he reached two hundred he gave up.

Feldwebel Reichel flew his Dornier back to France on one engine, straining the whole time to hold it on a straight heading. Soon after reaching the coast he developed cramp in his arm, however, and was forced to crash-land the aircraft near Abbeville. 'I heard the corn scraping against the machine. Or was it only the wind whistling past the stopped motor? I closed my eyes. A crash! Was that all? Then came a feeling of drifting, a mad crash, a creaking and a grinding. I was knocked down as if by a giant fist,' wrote war photographer Rolf von Pebal, on board the Dornier. 'For a moment every-thing was deathly still, then we all scrambled for the escape hatch. But it obstinately refused to open. The machine might catch fire at any moment! Desperately the three of us hurled ourselves against the hatch in the cabin roof, and finally it gave way. In an instant we clambered out.' The Dornier's flight engineer, wounded in both knees, was carefully but quickly lifted out of the aircraft, but there was no fire. Afterwards the men counted 110 hits on the bomber.

The last aircraft of the 9th Staffel to land was that brought back by the navigator, Wilhelm Illg, after his pilot had been hit. Illg regained the French coast and, after three baulked attempts, on the fourth succeeded in making a wheels-down landing on the airfield at St Omer. Oberleutnant Magin, the wounded pilot, never regained consciousness and died on his way to hospital. There were over a hundred bullet holes in the Dornier.

As the raiding forces were streaming back across Kent, 29-year-old Ober-leutnant Wolfgang Ewald led the sixteen Messerschmitt 109s of the Ist Gruppe of Fighter Geschwader 52 out over the Straits of Dover to cover the German withdrawal. This duty performed without meeting the enemy, Ewald's fighters had plenty of fuel left so he led them northwards over Kent looking for trouble.

At about the same time Flight Lieutenant Dennis Armitage, 26, leading the eleven Spitfires of No 266 Squadron, received orders to land at Manston to refuel and re-arm. Once down the Spitfires taxied to one side of the landing ground and the pilots shut down their engines. Normally they would have dispersed their fighters over a large area, so as not to present the enemy with an attractive target; but the landing ground at Manston was pock-marked with so many bomb craters from earlier attacks that such a dispersal would have made a rapid scramble take-off impossible. Accordingly No 266 Squadron's Spitfires were drawn up close together for refuelling.

High above, Wolfgang Ewald had watched the Spitfires landing at Manston. He had taken part in a strafing attack on the airfield a couple of days earlier and now the sight of the fighters bunched together neatly looked too inviting a target to pass by. He ordered the ten Messerschmitts of the 3rd Staffel to stay high and give him top cover, while he led the six aircraft of the 2nd Staffel in to attack.

As Dennis Armitage later recalled, his squadron had no warning of the Messerschmitts' approach. The first thing he knew was the sound of gunfire and exploding cannon shells. Then he looked round and saw the German fighters sweeping over the airfield fast and low, wings and fuselages blinking as they fired. Dust clouds began to spurt up round the Spitfires about a hundred yards away, as he and the pilots with him hurled themselves to the ground.

Worst off were the pilots of the final section to land. No sooner had they shut down their engines than the Messerschmitts struck. 'They hit us soon

after I taxied in,' remembered Sergeant Don Kingaby. 'There was no warning, just the roar of their engines. I glanced round and found myself looking
along the nose of a Messerschmitt coming straight for me.' As Kingaby
galloped away from his Spitfire the shooting started. He stumbled and fell
then, for a few breathless seconds, rolled over and over on the ground out of
the way of the rapidly advancing line of spurts of earth thrown up by the
enemy bullets. A bullet nicked one of his fingers, otherwise he escaped
unharmed. Still wearing his parachute, Dick Trousdale could not run or even
lie flat. He simply dropped down on his knees, pointed his rear end and the
parachute pack to the enemy, and huddled on the ground. Dennis Armitage
remembered that he looked 'just like a Mohammedan at prayer'. Miraculously, Trousdale escaped injury from the bullets striking all around him.

The Spitfire pilots were helpless to defend themselves, but others on
the airfield did fight back. Private Joseph Lister, 23, of the 6th
Battalion of the Border Regiment, was manning a Bren gun on a tripod
mounting on the south side of the runway. As the Messerschmitts ran in he
stood up and fired burst after burst at them. Then one of the attackers curved
round and opened fire at his position. 'The bullets were striking the ground
around me, like hailstones,' he recalled. 'Then they caught me. I was hit on
the left shoulder, the left arm and ear, on the left thigh and the right knee.'
Lister collapsed in a heap beside his gun.

The Messerschmitts made two firing runs on Manston, then sped away
out to sea. They left behind two Spitfires of 266 Squadron ablaze and six
more damaged. 'It's amazing how fiercely an aluminium aircraft will burn if
it once gets going,' Dennis Armitage explained. Another fighter which had
landed at Manston to refuel, a Hurricane of No 17 Squadron, was also
destroyed. Joseph Lister was rushed to hospital, where later his right leg was
amputated above the knee.

After about an hour on the ground at Amiens, off-loading his wounded
navigator and checking his Dornier for damage, Wilhelm Raab of the
low-flying 9th Staffel took off to return to his base at Cormeilles-en-Vexin.
The flight took about twenty minutes and as he circled his base before
landing, he was amazed to see not a single aircraft in his Staffel dispersal
area: in spite of the hour's delay at Amiens, his was the first aircraft back! He
set the Dornier down and taxied over to where the ground crewmen were
waiting for him. Even before the motors had stopped turning, a staff car
skidded to a halt in front of the aircraft and one of the unit's officers,
Oberleutnant Andres, jumped out. 'The hatch was opened and out we
climbed. Without formality the officer's questions rained down on me:
Raab, what has happened? Where are the others? Why has it taken you so
long to get back?' Before Raab could give any but the briefest of answers, he
was ordered to get in the staff car. He was rushed to the Geschwader
headquarters in the nearby chateau, to deliver his report to the commander
in person. Still in his sweat-drenched flying suit, the young Feldwebel was
ushered into the presence of Generalmajor Froehlich and his staff. At his
commander's bidding, Raab outlined the attack as he had seen it: the

approach flight that had gone exactly according to plan, the terrifying reception from the ground defences at the target, the skirmish with the British fighters after leaving Kenley, and how his navigator had been hit by ground fire. He told the attentive officers that when he started back across the Channel there had been two other Dorniers with him, and of his amazement that he should have been the first to arrive at Cormeilles – considering he had spent about an hour on the ground at Amiens. Raab then went on to describe the mysterious secret weapon that had been set off in front of him at the target. He described the fire balls, the columns of smoke, the jerk he had felt on his aircraft, the little parachutes his radio operator had seen and the cable dents now running along the wing of his Dornier. 'At the end of my explanation I was greeted with a chorus of incredulity,' the German pilot remembered. 'Raab, you're crackers!' 'Obviously this attack has demanded too much from you!'

In the meantime, Mathius Maassen and his crew had also landed at Cormeilles, but they were unable to shed any further light on the mystery of the fire balls and smoke trails seen over Kenley. Maassen's search for his comrades in the water had been successful: he had spotted the three survivors from Schumacher's Dornier in their dinghy and a German navy minesweeper was on its way to pick them up.

Of the nine Dorniers of the 9th Staffel that had set out for the low-altitude attack on Kenley four had been destroyed, two suffered serious damage and the remaining three suffered minor damage. Of the forty men on board the aircraft eight had been killed, five taken prisoner, three returned with wounds and seven were now floating in the cold waters of the English Channel hoping for rescue. The Staffel's officer casualties had been particularly severe: seven had flown on the mission and of these three had been killed, three had been taken prisoner, wounded, and the remaining one had returned seriously wounded.

From the start, the low-altitude attack on a target deep in England had been a calculated risk. By putting in the dive-bombing and high-altitude attacks on Kenley first, however, and using the well-proven low-altitude approach tactics to sneak in unobserved, the Geschwader planners had hoped to destroy Kenley as an operational fighter base without incurring heavy casualties. In the event, cloud over the Pas-de-Calais had delayed the first two attacks and sent the plan awry. Afterwards, survivors of the 9th Staffel blamed their chance meeting with the Royal Navy patrol boats off Beachy Head for their loss of surprise at the target. The defences of Britain rested on surer foundations that day, however, and the Observer Corps posts had passed a continuous stream of plots on the raiders as they came in, giving the Kenley defenders plenty of time to prepare their reception. Robbed both of support from other units and the element of surprise, the 9th Staffel had suffered accordingly. It was a sombre case-history of what must be expected if low-flying aircraft have to meet alerted ground defences.

With four aircraft destroyed and five damaged, out of nine engaged, the 9th Staffel of Bomber Geschwader 76 suffered the highest proportional loss of any of the German units involved in the attack. Altogether, the raiding force lost 9 bombers destroyed and 10 damaged, and 12 fighters destroyed and 3 damaged.

The hardest-hit British unit was No 501 Squadron, which lost 6 fighters during the engagement; one pilot was killed and three wounded. Altogether, Fighter Command lost 17 fighters destroyed and 8 damaged during the air action; and 8 destroyed and 10 damaged on the ground. Four British pilots were killed and seven wounded.

So ended the lunchtime action. Yet even before the last bombers of Air Fleet 2 had left the coast of England, those assigned to the next big raid were airborne and assembled in attack formation: Air Fleet 3 was about to launch its major effort of the day.

CHAPTER 3

The Stukas Strike

If bloody slaughter is a distressing sight,
then that is a reason for paying greater respect to war.
VON CLAUSEWITZ

During the morning of 18 August Generalfeldmarschall Hugo Sperrle's Air Fleet 3, based in France to the west of the Seine, had taken scarcely any part in the fighting. The sole offensive act by the entire Air Fleet had been committed by the single Focke-Wulf Condor four-engined bomber which had taken off from Bordeaux shortly after 6 am that morning. Nearly seven hours later, at 12.45 pm, as the bombers of Air Fleet 2 had been moving across the Channel to attack Kenley and Biggin Hill, about 100 miles off the north-western tip of Ireland the Condor came upon the 1,900 ton Norwegian freighter *Sveinjarl* straggling behind its westbound convoy. The bomber carried out repeated bombing and strafing runs on the ship, expending six 550-pound bombs and 256 rounds of 20-mm ammunition. *Sveinjarl*, damaged and trailing oil, turned back for Londonderry. The Condor, having expended almost all its offensive armament, resumed its northerly heading and continued with the reconnaissance part of its mission.

Along the coasts of Sussex, Hampshire and Dorset the morning had passed quietly. The only excitement for the defences had come from the occasional German reconnaissance aircraft darting in to photograph targets or observe the weather, and leaving as soon as it had done so. From time to time fighters were scrambled to intercept the intruders, but without success.

Only one of these reconnaissance missions over Britain deserves further mention: that which passed over Portsmouth, heading north-westwards, at 1.25 pm. This high-flying aircraft left a ruler-straight condensation trail across the clear blue sky. It was a sight so beautiful that 22-year-old Alexander McKee, an air enthusiast waiting to join the Royal Air Force, photographed it from the garden of his grandmother's house beside the main Fareham to Porchester road.

That a reconnaissance aircraft should leave a condensation trail was unusual: flying alone, the survival of their crews depended on an ability to sneak in, get the photographs or information they had come for, and leave with a minimum of fuss. They avoided condensation trails, like the plague. Such a blatant flaunting of presence, especially over one of the most heavily defended areas in Britain, was normally out of character. Nor, usually, was it necessary: since condensation trails form only in a comparatively narrow band of altitudes, it was a relatively simple matter to climb or descend to a height where the trails ceased. A further twist to the mystery is that the records of Air Fleet 3, which have survived in some detail and in whose operational area Portsmouth lay, make no mention of any reconnaissance mission which can be linked with the one McKee saw.

There is, however, one explanation that fits the known facts. The Luftwaffe High Command's special reconnaissance Gruppe operated without regard to Air Fleet boundaries. And the crews of the Junkers 86Ps, flying at altitudes around 38,000 feet, knew that provided they stayed there they were safe from the defences even if they did announce their presence with a condensation trail. Almost certainly it was one of these aircraft that McKee had photographed.

The lone high-flyer, designated 'Raid 47' by the Fighter Command filter room, was tracked on radar as it came in. But on aircraft above 30,000 feet the altitude readings were unreliable, and the operators had no inkling of the true height of the intruder. Observer Corps posts reported the aircraft flying inland as far as the airfield at Middle Wallop, then it turned round for home. No 43 Squadron at Tangmere was ordered to send up a Flight to intercept, but the Hurricane was quite unsuitable for such an enterprise and could get nowhere near this quarry. It is doubtful whether the German crew even noticed the feeble attempt to interfere with their mission.

By mid-day, however, Air Fleet 3's airfields in Normandy and Brittany were alive with the sound of aircraft engines. Generalmajor Baron Wolfram von Richthofen, 45, cousin of the famous 'Red Baron' of the First World War and commander of the VIIIth Flying Corps with almost half of Sperrle's bombers, was positioning his forces. The attack was to involve the largest concentration of Junkers 87 'Stuka' dive-bombers yet employed: four Gruppen, with a total of 109 aircraft, were to hit the airfields at Gosport, Ford and Thorney Island, and the radar station at Poling near Littlehampton. Reconnaissance photographs had shown that all three of the airfields were active. But, because the photographs had been taken from high altitude and therefore lacked the necessary resolution, the types of the aircraft seen on the ground could not be identified. Thus, although the German Intelligence service presumed all three airfields to be in use by Fighter Command, in fact none of them was. Gosport housed a torpedo development unit. Thorney Island was the base of two Coastal Command Blenheim squadrons, No 59 with bombers and No 235 with fighters. Ford, HMS *Peregrine*, was a naval air station and the base of No 829 Squadron which was working up with the Fairey Albacore, the newest carrier-borne torpedo-bomber to enter service; the airfield was also the home of the naval air observers' training school.

For the attack the whole of Dive Bomber Geschwader 77 was to be committed: Ist Gruppe, with 28 Stukas, to attack Thorney Island; IInd Gruppe, 28 Stukas, to attack Ford; and IIIrd Gruppe, 31 Stukas, to attack Poling. The fourth unit to take part, the Ist Gruppe of Dive Bomber Geschwader 3 with 22 Stukas, was to attack Gosport. The dive-bombers were to cross the Channel in one huge formation, supported by no fewer than 157 Messerschmitt 109 fighters: seventy from Fighter Geschwader 27 and thirty-two from Fighter Geschwader 53 acting as close escort; and fifty-five from Fighter Geschwader 2 from Le Havre flying independently, mounting a sweep over the Portsmouth area to flush out the British fighters.

The dive-bombers were based round Caen, the fighters of the close escort round Caen and Rennes. In each case the distance from the bases to the targets was close to, or beyond, the effective radii of action of the aircraft. Accordingly, around noon, the fighter and Stuka Gruppen moved up to forward landing grounds round Cherbourg. There fuel tanks were topped up and bombs loaded, while the crews had lunch and received their final briefings.

By 1.29 pm the Stukas were ready: one Gruppe to each landing ground, drawn up in line abreast along the downwind side, engines turning. One minute later each of the four Gruppe leaders, in the aircraft in the far left of each line, opened his throttle wide and his Stuka bumped across the grass, slowly gathering speed. Before he was airborne the next aircraft in the line was accelerating after him, then the next, then the next. Once off the ground, each Gruppe circled the airfield until its Stukas were in position in formation, then moved to over the city of Cherbourg to join up with the other Gruppen.

One man not disconcerted by the 85-mile sea crossing ahead was 32-year-old Major Helmut Bode, in the leading Stuka. Before the war he had been a reconnaissance seaplane pilot accustomed to nine-hour oversea flights covering over a thousand miles; compared with that, this crossing was a mere hop. The target for Bode's Gruppe, IIIrd of Dive Bomber Geschwader 77, was the radar station at Poling. He himself knew nothing about the technicalities of his target; he had been briefed to attack the *Funkstation* (radio station) near Littlehampton.

By 1.45 pm the Stukas had assembled in formation and Bode led the force first eastwards to Cape Barfleur, then almost due northwards towards the targets. A few hundred yards behind and to the left of Bode's Gruppe came Hauptmann Alfons Orthofer's IInd Gruppe, bound for Ford; after them and further to the left came the Ist Gruppe, led by Hauptmann Herbert Meisel and bound for Thorney Island; and finally, in the rear and still further to the left, came the Ist Gruppe of Dive Bomber Geschwader 3 led by Hauptman Walther Siegel and bound for Gosport. 'The formation was a magnificent sight,' wrote 25-year-old Leutnant Kurt Scheffel, piloting one of the Stukas. 'Cherbourg lay in the sunshine below us, with the breakers visible along the coast. The sky had a light blue tint while over the Channel there was a light haze.'

Each laden with a 550-pound bomb under the fuselage, and four 110-pounders under the wings, the Stukas climbed slowly away to the north, leaving Cape Barfleur lighthouse behind them.

While the dive-bombers had been assembling into formation, the fighters which were to escort them remained on the ground. Ahead lay a long sea crossing and the climbing Stukas were flying at only 120 mph. There would be plenty of time to catch up with them along the route to the target. Not until the bombers were over the sea did the fighters begin taking off and heading after them.

During the next few minutes the fighters, even flying at their most economical climbing speed, rapidly overhauled the dive-bombers. Shortly after 2 pm Helmut Bode caught sight of the escorting Messerschmitts moving reassuringly into position round him, one Gruppe of fighters to each Gruppe of Stukas. On arrival, each fighter Gruppe split into three Staffeln, one of which continued climbing into position to act as top cover, while the other two took position one on each side of each dive-bomber Gruppe.

At 1.59 pm the radar station at Poling picked up the first echoes from the incoming Stuka formation, soon being reported as '80 plus', to the north of Cherbourg; smaller forces with '20 plus', '12 plus' and '9 plus' (the fighters) were moving up with it. Also, coming in from Le Havre, was a force of '10 plus' aircraft (Fighter Geschwader 2 moving up for its sweep of the Portsmouth area). Altogether, the radar operators estimated, the incoming force comprised about 150 aircraft; it was an underestimation by almost half. Within minutes these plots had passed through the Fighter Command filter room and thence to the operations rooms of the Groups concerned with the defence of the south coast: No 11 at Uxbridge and No 10 at Box in Wiltshire.

From the initial indications it seemed that the raiders were moving towards the Solent: it looked like a repetition of the attack on Tangmere two days earlier, when Stukas had devastated much of the airfield. To meet the threat, the two fighter Group controllers now disposed their squadrons. One of these, No 601 with eleven Hurricanes, was already airborne and patrolling over its base at Tangmere. During the next few minutes five squadrons of Spitfires and Hurricanes took off to reinforce them: one each from Tangmere and Westhampnett in the No 11 Group area, and Exeter, Warmwell and Middle Wallop in the No 10 Group area. No 43 Squadron, with 9 Hurricanes, was to patrol over the airfield at Thorney Island; No 602, with 12 Spitfires, was to patrol over its base at Westhampnett; No 152 Squadron, with 11 Spitfires, was to patrol over Portsmouth; No 234, with 11 Spitfires, was to move out to the south of the Isle of Wight to meet the attackers; and No 213 Squadron, with 12 Hurricanes, from Exeter to move 80 miles to the east and patrol over St Catherine's point. No 609 Squadron, with 12 Spitfires, was to remain in reserve on the ground at Middle Wallop.

In addition, two Hurricanes took off to intercept flown by pilots of the Fighter Interceptor Unit from Tangmere. Formed to conduct trials with the new and highly secret airborne radar sets, the FIU had lost all its Blenheim night fighters during the attack on Tangmere two days earlier. While waiting for new aircraft the unit had borrowed a couple of Hurricanes from the airfield's resident fighter squadrons and its pilots now went into action in these. Also, at the Coastal Command airfield at Thorney Island, No 235 Squadron prepared to send up a Flight of Blenheim fighters to assist in the defence.

Altogether there was a total of 68 Spitfires and Hurricanes moving to contest the incursion: a ratio of one British fighter to just over two German ones, or one British fighter to every four German fighters and bombers. Even had the British fighter controllers known the true size of the attacking force, there was little more they could have done. Almost all of the fighters in the area were now airborne. Those at the bases round London were returning to their airfields in ones and twos after the attacks on Kenley and Biggin Hill and had to be refuelled and re-armed; they could not reach the threatened sectors in time to assist with the defence.

Of the fighter squadrons ordered off one, No 602 at Westhampnett, had been released from operations for the afternoon: it was the first chance for the pilots to rest after five days almost continuously at readiness for 16 hours per day; it was a chance, too, for the ground crews to carry out much-needed maintenance work on the aircraft. The pilots had adjourned to their messes. 'I sat down with some relish to a pint of beer,' recalled 24-year-old Flight Lieutenant Dunlop Urie, temporarily in command, 'I had taken two sips when the telephone went: we were to take off as soon as possible.' The pilots galloped the quarter mile back to their aircraft. But as Urie breathlessly arrived at his Spitfire he found it up on jacks, the wheels being changed. Urie looked round desperately: he was supposed to lead the Squadron, he had to have an aircraft. Then his eyes fell on a Spitfire delivered only that morning, so new that its guns had not yet been harmonised with the sight. It would have to do. He grabbed his parachute and helmet, sprinted over to it, strapped in and started up. Belatedly, No 602 Squadron roared into the air.

During the morning the sirens along the south coast had sounded from time to time, though no attack had materialised. The frequency of the warnings is borne out by the yo-yo-like antics of the Portsmouth balloon barrage: at 10.52 am it had been raised to 4,500 feet; at 11.36 it was lowered to 1,000 feet; at 1.02 pm, up to 4,500 feet; and 1.49 it was lowered to 1,000 feet; and at 2.09 it was raised to 4,500 feet.

Nineteen-year-old Midshipman Dick Dearman, a trainee Naval air observer at Ford, 20 miles to the east, remembered the morning as one continual series of alerts. Whenever the sirens sounded he and other trainee observers had had to make their way to the station armoury, draw Vickers machine guns, and mount them on spigots fitted to specially modified Bedford trucks. The trucks were intended to serve as mobile machine gun posts in the event of an air or a land attack. Just before 2 pm, however, a local all-clear was issued for the Naval air station at Ford. Dearman and his comrades dismounted the guns and handed them back to the armoury, then cleaned themselves up and made their way to the mess hall for lunch.

Four miles to the south-west, alone on sentry duty on the esplanade at Bognor, stood 28-year-old Private Arthur Sindall of the Royal Army Service Corps. Looking out to sea, to his left was the pier with a neat twenty-yard gap in its centre to prevent enemy ships discharging troops; to his right was the deserted promenade, sparsely garnished with concertina wire. He later commented that it was his fervent hope 'that the Fuehrer would not discover that Britain's sole defence against the might of the Wehrmacht for this particular two hundred yards of coastline was a roll of barbed wire – and me!' One of the few advantages of Sindall's post, however, was that he would be privileged to have a ringside view of the fight about to begin.

Seven miles to the east, 29-year-old Leading Aircraftman Ernie Clarke was just getting out of bed. He had been on duty at the radar station at Poling during the night. Now, at the rented house in Walders Road, Rustington, where he lived with his wife and young son, he planned to spend the rest of the day relaxing with his family.

It was 2.15 pm and through the thin haze Helmut Bode at the head of the Stuka formation could see the Isle of Wight, about 15 miles away to his left. A similar distance in front lay the distinctive promontory of Selsey Bill, the point he was making for. Looking down through the window cut in the floor of his aircraft Bode could see the streaks of the 'white horses' on the surface of the sea: the wind was blowing from the south-west. To bomb accurately, the Stukas had to attack from dead into wind. Bode made a mental note that he would have to lead his Gruppe in to attack from the north-east of the target. A few minutes later part of the Stuka formation broke away and headed off to the north-west with its escorting fighters: it was Hauptmann Siegel and his Gruppe, making for Gosport. Four minutes later the formation reached Selsey Bill and another Gruppe split away: Hauptmann Meisel with the force to attack Thorney Island. With the remaining two Gruppen Bode swung on a north-easterly heading, for Poling and Ford. Fussing round the dive-bombers, the escorting Messerschmitts now began accelerating to fighting speed, zig-zagging at regular intervals to maintain position on their charges.

In the operations room at Tangmere Squadron Leader David Lloyd, the senior controller, could see that the main weight of the German attack was coming in over Selsey Bill and ordered No 601 Squadron to move there.

From his vantage point, Arthur Sindall gazed up in awe at the German formation passing above: 'Their immaculate formation, wing-tip to wing-tip, a kind of airborne Trooping of the Colour, engendered a grudging admiration. Their black and white crosses were all too clearly visible on the underside of the wings.' It was a sight magnificent or sinister, depending on the eye of the beholder.

Through his floor window Helmut Bode watched the Bognor seafront moving underneath his aircraft. As he passed the coast Hauptmann Orthofer and his Gruppe peeled away to the left, for Ford. Bode led his Gruppe straight ahead over Littlehampton, then round in a wide sweeping turn over Angmering woods to the north-east of the town. He levelled out on a south-westerly heading, straight into wind, the cluster of buildings at Poling radar station sliding underneath his floor window. Calmly he completed his final checks in preparation for the dive: engine cooling gills closed, propeller in coarse pitch, bomb sight switched on, bomb release mechanism switches on and bomb fusing switches on. In the dive-bomber on either side of him the pilots completed their checks, then watched expectantly for their leader to begin his dive. In most Stuka units, the aircraft made their diving attacks individually in line astern; but in Bode's Gruppe the aircraft attacked in threes, to split the defensive anti-aircraft fire.

In Rustington, Ernie Clarke was summoned to the garden to watch the
formation passing over. It was a beautiful display, he remembered, 'Just like
a Hendon air pageant.' The people living next door were watching also.
'What are they, Mr Clarke?' they asked. Because he was in the Royal Air
Force they expected him to know everything about aircraft. Pride would not
let him admit that he had been in the Service only two months, and had spent
those at a radar station away from any airfield. Trying to look knowledge-
able, Clarke replied that they were Spitfires coming back from a patrol. His
son Terry, not yet 3 but mad keen on aircraft, interjected 'They're dive-
bombers!' 'No, Terry,' Clarke replied with fatherly sternness, 'they're
Spitfires.' 'They're Junkers 87s!' the young boy snapped back defiantly.
Ernie Clarke was just thinking of some suitably crushing reply to terminate
this embarrassing conversation, when the three aircraft at the head of the
formation suddenly pushed over into near-vertical dives, followed three-
by-three by the aircraft behind. Then the Bofors guns positioned round
Poling began banging away. Obviously the aircraft were not Spitfires! The
Clarkes and their neighbours dashed for cover.

Arthur Sindall, too, watched the leader begin his dive, 'the sun catching
his perspex cockpit cover in a sudden flash of light, so bright that it was
almost as if he'd fired a Very pistol as a signal for the attack to start.'

As soon as Helmut Bode had established his Stuka in its 80-degree dive,
close to the vertical, he concentrated on positioning the illuminated graticule
of the reflector sight over the target building. To keep the defenders' heads
down, Bode opened fire with his two machine guns. It was an odd feeling,
going down hanging against his chest and lap straps, but one Bode had
experienced many times before. Even though his throttle was back, the
speed built up gradually until the aircraft reached its terminal velocity at just
under 300 mph. The dive, starting from 13,000 feet (4,000 m), lasted about
half a minute. Shortly before the Stuka reached 4,500 feet, an electrical horn
sounded in the cockpit: four seconds to bomb release. At 2,275 feet (700 m),
the horn ceased. Bode pressed the bomb release button on his control stick
and the bombs fell away from his fuselage and wings. At the same instant the
automatic pull-out system came into operation to haul up the nose of the
aircraft until it was pointing at the horizon, the centrifugal forces pressing
the pilot and radio operator hard down into their seats. As his Stuka levelled
out Bode retracted the dive brakes, re-trimmed the aircraft and opened his
throttle for the getaway. On either side of Bode the Stukas were still in
position, their pilots going through the same drills. And in the rear of each
Stuka the radio operator sprayed the target with his machine gun, to cover
the aircraft attacking behind.

At Poling 24-year-old WAAF Corporal Joan Avis Hearn was working at
the telephone switchboard, passing plots on the formations to the filter room
at Stanmore Park, from Poling and the neighbouring radar stations along the
coast. When the order came to take cover, the plots were coming in so
rapidly that she felt she could not simply get up and walk away. Then, from
the radar station at Truleigh Hill ten miles to the east, came an urgent voice:
'Poling, do you realise that what we've given you is right on top of your

station?' By then Avis Hearn could hear the diving aircraft plainly, the whistles of the bombs and the explosions. The Stanmore operator asked 'Are you all right Poling?' Then the doors blew in, the lines went dead and the telephone switchboard became alive with lights popping and bells ringing.

In his home in the middle of Ham Manor golf course, which his father owned, 12-year-old Michael Wilcox sat huddled with his mother and cousin, all wearing saucepans on their heads for protection. The house was less than a mile to the south-east of the Poling radar station and outside they could hear the howl of engines as the Stukas pulled out of their dives, the whistles and crumps of the exploding bombs, the crackle of machine gun fire and the banging of the Bofors guns.

At Ford Naval air station, four miles to the south-west, Dick Dearman was on his way to lunch with other midshipmen when he stopped and, following the gaze of those around him, looked up at the aircraft wheeling in the sky high above. Somebody joked that it seemed the air force was playing around again. One of the watchers thought the aircraft were Hurricanes, another suggested Defiants. Dearman, more interested in aircraft than most, knew they were not. 'Balls!' he declared. 'They're Junkers 87s!' The men watched fascinated as the aircraft turned into line astern, seemingly jockeying for position, then began their dives. Still some thought they were Hurricanes. After all, the local all-clear at Ford was still in force. Then Dearman shouted 'They're Stukas!' and dashed for cover, hotly pursued by the rest. He sprinted into his hut, nearby. 'Even before I could dive under my bed I could hear the scream of the first bomb coming down, followed by that of the second. Soon there was a series of shrieks of various cadences coming down at us.' Then came the explosions and the clatter of machine gun bullets striking the ground. Protected from above only by the hut's thin wooden roof and a horsehair mattress, Dearman heard the windows shatter in the blast and the whole hut seemed to lift off its foundations.

At Ford some men died facing the enemy. Instructor Lieutenant Commander Michael de Courcy was last seen outside the wardroom firing his revolver at the German dive-bombers. It was the final, despairingly futile, act of a courageous man. Afterwards his dismembered body was found, his right hand still grasping the revolver.

There were only six Lewis guns manned at Ford to engage the dive-bombers, and the latter attacked with great precision. Bombs rained down on the barrack huts, the hangars, and amongst the aircraft drawn up close together for maintenance. Early on bombs struck the airfield's fuel storage compounds; the blaze rapidly took hold, sending up a huge pillar of black smoke.

As Ford was undergoing its ordeal by fire, Hauptmann Siegel was leading his Gruppe against Gosport. On the way up the Solent the Messerschmitt 109s giving top cover came under attack, and lost three of their number in rapid succession. The attackers were the eleven Spitfires of No 234 Squadron, led by Squadron Leader Joe O'Brien. O'Brien himself fired at one of the Messerschmitts and saw it turn slowly on to its back and go

The opposing forces at 2.30 p.m.

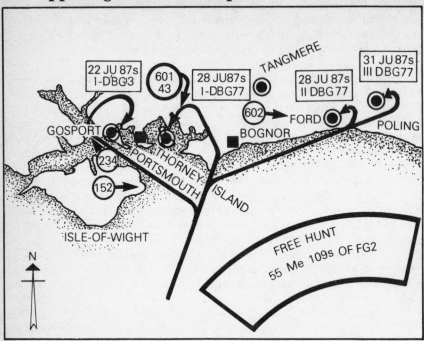

Approximate position of the opposing forces at 2.30 pm. The 31 Junkers 87s of IIIrd Gruppe of Dive Bomber Geschwader 77 are bombing the radar station at Poling, escorted by Messerschmitt 109s of the Ist Gruppe of Fighter Geschwader 53; 28 Junkers 87s of IInd Gruppe of D.B.G. 77 are bombing the airfield at Ford, escorted by Messerschmitt 109s of IIIrd Gruppe of F.G. 27; 28 Junkers 87s of Ist Gruppe of D.B.G. 77 have started their attack on the airfield at Thorney Island but both they and their escorting Messerschmitt 109s, from IInd Gruppe of F.G. 27, are hotly engaged by the Hurricanes of Nos 43 and 601 Squadrons; 22 Junkers 87s of Ist Gruppe of Dive Bomber Geschwader 3 are moving into position to begin their attack on the airfield at Gosport, their escort of Messerschmitt 109s from Ist Gruppe of Fighter Geschwader 27 under attack from the Spitfires of No 234 Squadron. From Le Havre, 55 Messerschmitt 109s from Fighter Geschwader 2 are moving in on a free-hunting patrol. The Spitfires of No 602 Squadron have sighted the Junkers 87s attacking Ford and are moving in to attack. The Spitfires of No 152 Squadron are moving across the Isle of Wight to engage the raiders on their withdrawal.

down, but could not watch it further because his own aircraft came under attack. Sergeant Alan Harker chased one of the German fighters down to sea level, firing off two bursts at it. Petrol streamed back over his windscreen, forcing him to break off the attack. The Messerschmitt burst into flames, then plunged into the sea. Pilot Officer Edward Mortimer-Rose manoeuvred in behind two Messerschmitts and fired at one of them, setting the port wing on fire. Just before it hit the sea the second Messerschmitt came in to attack; Mortimer-Rose pulled hard round and succeeded in getting on its tail and closing to within 20 yards, but after three short bursts he ran out of ammunition and had to break away.

Major Eduard Neumann, the commander of the Ist Gruppe of Fighter Geschwader 27 which was escorting the Gosport raiders, could hear scraps over the radio which indicated that there was a hard fight going on above, but radio conditions were poor and the picture was confused. In any case Neumann, flying with the 3rd Staffel, had to remain in position covering the vulnerable dive-bombers. Hauptmann Karl-Wolfgang Redlich, commanding the top-covering force and at 25 one of Neumann's most experienced Staffel commanders, would have to fight alone. Keeping a wary eye for the British fighters he knew must be somewhere about in the patchy haze, Neumann snatched the odd glance at the Stukas as they curved round into position on the north-eastern side of their target and began their dives.

For the dive-bombers the attack on Gosport was straightforward, and made with minimal interference from the enemy. From his vantage point 2½ miles north of the target, Alexander McKee also watched the Stukas swooping down almost vertically. 'They came down with a horrible vicious certainty and efficiency, tearing through the yellow flame of bursting shells,' he later wrote in his diary. 'Smoke rose at once from the aerodrome. The vivid yellow flashes of bursting bombs leapt above the hangars and the trees. Then the Stukas were gone and only fading puffs of shell smoke drifted in the heights.'

Three of the four dive-bomber Gruppen, those attacking Poling, Ford and Gosport, had been able to reach their targets and complete their attacks without interference from enemy fighters. The fourth, the 28 Stukas of Ist Gruppe of Dive Bomber Geschwader 77 on their way to Thorney Island, was not so lucky. As the Gruppe's Stukas passed Selsey Bill, the Messerschmitts of IInd Gruppe of Fighter Geschwader 27 kept a wary eye open for the expected British fighters. Twenty-three-year-old Oberleutnant Julius Neumann was leading the ten aircraft of the 6th Staffel, giving top cover to the force. Just after he passed the coast, Neumann picked out small specks emerging from the patchy haze to the north of him: British fighters! He alerted his Staffel, then swung round to engage.

Kurt Scheffel, flying one of the leading Stukas in the Gruppe, glanced up and saw the British fighters coming down from his right, guns blazing. He shouted a warning over the radio and at the same time his radio operator, Otto Binner, opened fire in reply. Scheffel could see the rearwards-facing guns of the other Stukas in the leading element firing back also.

Nos 43 and 601 Squadrons, with a total of 18 Hurricanes, smashed into the Stuka formation as the German pilots were manoeuvring into line astern formation in preparation for their dives. Twenty-eight-year-old Flight Lieutenant Frank Carey led No 43 Squadron in to the attack; he fired a long burst into one of the dive-bombers and saw it go down in flames. Sergeant Herbert Hallowes flew down a line of five Stukas, firing at each one in turn; he saw the crews bale out of two of them.

One of the first dive-bombers to go down was that piloted by Unteroffizier August Dann of the 3rd Staffel. His Stuka plunged vertically more than two miles and smashed into the ground at West Broyle, immediately to the north-west of Chichester, killing both men on board. A local cameraman photographed the Stuka during its final moments and the picture would later become one of the classics of the Battle of Britain.

Twenty-five-year-old Flight Sergeant Bill Pond of No 601 Squadron saw a couple of Messerschmitts curving round to protect the dive-bombers. But they were still some way away and he determined to get in his attack first. Pond singled out one of the Stukas and opened fire at it, starting from the side and working round to the rear. As he closed in he could see the rear gunner in the Stuka determinedly firing back. With only one gun to Pond's eight, the British pilot thought his opponent 'was a very brave man'. Pond saw his rounds hitting the Junkers, which started to trail smoke. Then, next thing he knew, the German gunner's rounds started hitting his Hurricane and the windscreen suddenly went black with splashes of oil from his engine. Pond recalled the pair of Messerschmitts he had seen earlier: if they came in and attacked him now he would be helpless. He rolled his aircraft on to its back and dived away.

By pulling his Stuka round in a tight turn Feldwebel Guenther Meyer-Bothling, 24, succeeded in avoiding the attack from one Hurricane. Then the shouted warning from his radio operator that a second fighter was coming in was cut short by a final scream and the sound of tearing metal, as bullets slashed into the dive-bomber. Meyer-Bothling pressed himself back against his armoured seat and watched the instrument panel in front of him suddenly dissolve into an unrecognisable mass of twisted metal and broken glass. One round grazed his skull, another ripped across his thigh tearing away the lower strap of his parachute harness. Bleeding profusely and with a dead radio operator, the German pilot was helpless if anyone further attacked him. He pushed down the nose of the Stuka and dived away from the mêlée; as he did so he tried to jettison his bombs, but part of the mechanism had been shot away and the two under the port wing remained firmly in place. Going down almost vertically, Meyer-Bothling tore off his blood-saturated helmet and pressed a bunched neckerchief against his head wound.

Frank Carey was lining up to attack a second Stuka when he felt a sharp blow on his right knee, as though somebody had struck it with a hammer: an almost-spent bullet, whether fired by friend or foe he never knew, had lodged under his kneecap. 'If the bullet had been anything but spent, I shouldn't have had a knee left!' he later explained. Carey handed over control of the Squadron, then dived away from the fight. 'I didn't feel too bright. My knee seemed to be locked, which made things a bit awkward. Although one did not use the rudder all that much in the Hurricane, there were times when one needed to waggle it a bit.' Carey called Tangmere and said he was going back to land. He was told: 'Don't do that. There are a lot of bombers heading this way and it looks as if they are going to give us another thumping!' The injured Hurricane pilot headed off to the north, resolving to keep out of everyone's way.

Oberleutnant Johannes Wilhelm, 24, had heard the warning of fighters over his radio, but he concentrated on holding his position in the Stuka formation. He could see the A-shaped pattern of runways at Thorney Island moving back across his floor window. Not long to go now before the Gruppe leader's tail flipped up and the aircraft followed him in succession into their dives; and once it was in its dive the Stuka was, temporarily, relatively safe from fighter attack. In the rear of the Stuka Wilhelm's radio operator, 22-year-old Unteroffizier Anton Woerner, also heard the warning of approaching fighters and now he squinted into the bright sun behind looking for them. Where on earth were they? Then, appearing as if from nowhere and with guns belching fire, the Hurricanes came flashing up through the German formation so close that Woerner found it difficult to fire at them without endangering the Stukas round him. Through the corner of his eye Wilhelm caught a glimpse of three or four British fighters roaring past; he also noticed a Stuka burst into flames and disappear out of view, going down. Still he concentrated on holding his position in the formation, ready to begin his dive at any moment. Then, suddenly, there was a loud crash from the Stuka's engine and the aircraft began to shudder. Great gulps of oil came streaming back over the cabin, blotting out everything outside. Yet more disconcerting, the cockpit began to fill with smoke: the aircraft was on fire! Wilhelm turned the Stuka on to its back and shouted '*Raus!*' (Get out!) to Woerner. The pilot slid back his canopy and immediately a gout of hot engine oil struck him in the face, almost blinding him. One after the other the two men released their straps and fell clear of the stricken dive-bomber, and their parachutes opened.

Pilot Officer Clifford Gray of No 43 Squadron attacked one Stuka from a range of 250 yards and saw a fire start on the underside of the fuselage. The dive-bomber continued on, however, so he closed in to short range and gave it a 5-second burst, causing an internal explosion. The victim fell away into a steep dive and continued all the way down, until it plunged into the ground just to the east of Nutbourne.

Julius Neumann could see the British fighters streaming in to hit the dive-bombers, but his Staffel of Messerschmitts was also under attack and could not go down to help. Desperately he tried to edge the dog fight lower and lower, to try to give the Stukas some protection, but without success.

With a bullet lodged in his right knee, Frank Carey was beginning to feel sick and faint with shock. He had to get his Hurricane down somewhere: if he passed out in the air, that would be the end of him. By now he was approaching Pulborough, about 15 miles to the north-east of Tangmere, and below him he noticed rather a nice-looking field. 'I did a low fly-past and it looked perfect. There were none of the anti-glider poles that obstructed so many of the fields around,' he recalled. 'I should have guessed that there would have been something . . .' Carey came in for what he felt was, under the circumstances, quite a good wheels-down landing. He had just touched down and was thinking to himself 'Phew, that wasn't too bad', when suddenly he felt himself being thrown forward against his straps. The nose of the Hurricane plunged down and stopped as if it had run into a brick wall; the tail lifted and continued relentlessly on under its own momentum, slamming the aircraft down on its back. Carey passed out. To prevent enemy aircraft using the field, men from the nearby Observer Corps post had dug a trench across it and covered it with turf. The 'aircraft trap' was quite invisible from the air, and had caught the landing Hurricane exactly as intended.

Bill Pond did not ask for permission to land his damaged Hurricane back at Tangmere, he simply went in and did so. Opening his hood so that he could see round his oil-spattered windscreen, he dived towards the airfield. As he approached to land he glanced down at his instruments and saw that his oil pressure gauge was reading zero and the engine temperature was almost at the danger mark; the redoubtable Merlin engine kept going, however. Pond lowered his flaps and undercarriage and went straight in to land. Then, just before he crossed the airfield boundary, the motor did cut. His speed fell away and the Hurricane was almost stalled as he passed over the fence. Unable to see ahead, Pond plonked the aircraft down so hard that he sheared off the undercarriage legs and the machine skidded along on its belly until it came to rest with its nose dug into the ground. Two days earlier Pond had seen a good friend suffer fatal burns following a similar crash-landing and had no wish to share this fate. 'People who watched said they had never seen anyone get out of an aeroplane so quickly,' he recalled.

Kurt Scheffel had lined his Stuka on the target and was almost in position to begin to dive, when his aircraft shook under machine gun hits and he felt a hefty blow against his left shoulder. The cabin window to the left of him shattered and he felt a stinging pain in the thumb of his right hand; a metal splinter more than an inch long was embedded in it. The reflector sight in front of him was smashed to smithereens and glass splinters from it had slashed into his face; fortunately for him he was wearing sun glasses, or he would probably have lost his sight. As Scheffel recovered from the shock and collected his thoughts, he saw that he had fallen slightly away from the formation: the Stukas of the 1st Staffel, which had been behind him, were now passing overhead. The German pilot looked back and saw that his radio operator was slumped lifelessly over his machine gun. Then Scheffel saw the aircraft of the 1st Staffel flipping over into their dives; he pushed down his nose and went after them. Once he was established in the dive, Scheffel saw the airfield at Thorney Island spread out in front of him. He could even see aircraft taking off: Blenheim fighters of No 235 Squadron, rising to defend their base. Scheffel aimed his bombs using his metal auxiliary sight, pressed the release button, and as the aircraft pulled itself out of the dive he headed low over the sea, to the south.

At Inlands Lane, Nutbourne, just over a mile to the north-east of the airfield and right underneath the Stukas' approach path, 36-year-old Amelia Sopp sat under the stairs of her home calmly eating her Sunday lunch; from outside she could hear the whine of diving aircraft, the clatter of machine gun fire and the bangs of exploding shells and bombs, yet she felt quite safe. Then her ear caught a different sound, that of people shouting. Cautiously she made her way to the kitchen window to see what was going on, and burst out laughing at the scene that met her eyes: her next door neighbour's 8-year-old son was standing on top of the garden shed cheering on the British fighters, while on the ground below his mother was shrieking at him to come down and get into the house; to give protection from the shell fragments, cartridge cases and spent rounds raining down from above, the mother held a large white apron over her head!

Twenty-three-year-old Oberleutnant Otto Schmidt released his bombs on one of the hangars at Thorney Island and pulled out of his dive. Then something caught his eye coming in from behind: a fighter looming large, bent on his destruction. Schmidt glanced back to see why his radio operator was not firing: the poor man was collapsed in his seat, his gun pointing uselessly upwards. In concentrating on his attack, the pilot had not even noticed that his aircraft had come under attack. Schmidt put the Stuka into a screaming side-slip and the fighter shot past.

From the upstairs bedroom of his home at Batchmere Estate, Birdham, four miles to the south-east of Thorney Island, 15-year-old Norman McCarthy watched the aircraft milling around above the airfield. Then he saw the dive-bombers following each other down to attack, the smoke rising from the exploding bombs then, after a delay of nearly a third of a minute, he heard the 'crump' of the detonations. Pulling out their dives, the Stukas streaked southwards low over Chichester Harbour to make their escape. With the eye of a young expert he noted that the German tactics were almost exactly the same as those he had witnessed during the attack on Tangmere, two days earlier.

Dunlop Urie had got the twelve Spitfires of No 602 Squadron off from Westhampnett after the impromptu scramble. Now, in position over Tangmere at 2,000 feet, he suddenly caught sight of a succession of Stukas swooping down on Ford airfield, five miles to the east. Urie gave a quick call 'Villa Squadron, Tally Ho!' and led his squadron round to engage the bombers as they pulled out of their dives and passed low over the streets of Middleton-on-Sea and Bognor. Urie himself fired bursts at five of the Stukas before he ran out of ammunition. Sergeant Basil Whall, 21, singled out one of the dive-bombers, made four deliberate attacks on it and saw his tracers striking home. The Stuka curved round towards the coast and Whall watched it go down and make a gentle landing on open ground behind Rustington, not far from the Poling radar station.

It was 2.32 pm, just ten hectic minutes after Helmut Bode had led the dive-bombers in past Selsey Bill. Gone were the stately formations of Stukas which had crossed the coast; now the survivors were streaming southwards as fast as they could go, like a receding tidal wave. 'In a minute or two it was all over and there they were away, lickety-split for home, no longer in impeccable line but in any old style and the Devil take the hindmost,' Arthur Sindall observed from Bognor esplanade. 'But even in that short time the RAF were after them and whilst fingers of black smoke from Ford poked upwards to the sky we watched the Spitfires take their toll over the sea.' Now, along the 25-mile strip of coastline from Bognor in the east to Gosport in the west, the sky was a turmoil of over 300 aircraft, twisting and turning to bring guns to bear or to avoid guns being brought to bear.

For one Stuka pilot, 24-year-old Oberleutnant Karl Henze, 'as fast as he could go' was not very fast at all. As he pulled out of his dive after bombing

Thorney Island he found to his horror that his hydraulic system had been hit and the dive brakes would not retract. They worked very efficiently, limiting his speed to a little over 100 mph. He found himself being overtaken by everyone, a sitting duck for the first British fighter that came along. One soon did. As his radio operator engaged the attacker Henze took the Stuka just a few feet above the sea and turned across the nose of the fighter to give it the most difficult shot possible. But there was a loud bang as the fighter's rounds struck home and the German pilot felt a hefty blow against the back of his head. His grip on the control column relaxed for an instant, but that was long enough to precipitate disaster. The Stuka descended a few feet and the unyieldingly strong undercarriage legs touched the water. Nine times out of ten such a lapse would have ended with the aircraft digging in to the sea and flipping over on to its back in an explosion of white foam. But on this occasion providence was watching over Henze: the Stuka bounded back into the air. The pilot regained control and glanced anxiously behind, expecting to see the fighter curving in for the coup de grâce. But it had gone, probably having run out of ammunition.

Coming in from the west, over the Isle of Wight, Flight Lieutenant Derek Boitel-Gill ordered the eleven Spitfires of No 152 Squadron into line astern, then led them down to join the mêlée. He picked a small gaggle of dive-bombers making their way southwards and, after a 4-second burst at one of them, saw it go straight into the sea. He then shifted his attack to three others, but had to break off when the German escorts came sweeping down to protect their charges. 'We dived after them and they went down to 100 feet above the water,' wrote 19-year-old Pilot Officer Eric Marrs. 'Then followed a running chase out to sea. The evasive action they took was to throttle back and do steep turns to right and left so that we would not be able to follow them and would overshoot. There were, however, so many of them that if one was shaken off the tail of one there was always another to sit on.' Marrs fired at six of the Stukas and saw one of them strike the sea, streaming burning petrol from its port wing. 'When I had finished my ammunition I turned away and found an Me 109 sitting on my tail. As I turned it fired a burst in front of me. I could see the tracer and seemed to fly straight through it. I was not hit, however, and ran for home as it was senseless staying without ammunition.'

Otto Schmidt saw a British fighter coming in to attack and again he put his Stuka into a crabbing side-slip; once again the fighter overshot before the pilot could correct his aim. To one side Schmidt saw a dive-bomber plunge straight into the sea; and a second hit the surface, bounce off, then disappear for good. There was little time to worry about the fate of his comrades, however, for yet another fighter came in to attack him and, yet again, Schmidt side-slipped to avoid its tracer.

Unteroffizier Heinz Sellhorn, 23, radio operator on board one of the Stukas which had attacked Thorney Island, remembered: 'There were burning Stukas all over the place. I fired and fired, and saw the muzzle flashes from the attacking fighters. We radio operators felt as though we were human armour plate – armour plate to protect the pilot sitting behind us!'

Away on the eastern side of the engagement Basil Whall had seen 'his' Stuka set down gently beside the radar station at Poling. Then he opened his throttle and swung his Spitfire round to chase after the fleeing dive-bombers, like a hound after hares. He rapidly overhauled Helmut Bode's Gruppe moving away from Poling and, picking out one of the Stukas, closed in to 50 yards through accurate return fire and put a burst into it. The dive-bomber burst into flames and crashed into the sea. Whall's Spitfire was also hit, however, and started to trail smoke. Losing height, he hauled the wounded fighter round towards the shore.

Kurt Scheffel was straining every last ounce of speed out of his battered Stuka, as he picked his way through the 'witch's cauldron' of tracer rounds, plunging aircraft and floating parachutes to the south of Thorney Island. He managed to thread his way to the front of one of the depleted Staffel formations; with his own radio operator dead, he needed some protection from behind. A Blenheim passed right across his nose, holding an almost vertical bank as its pilot yanked it round in pursuit of another of the dive-bombers. It was one of the Coastal Command fighters from No 235 Squadron, that had stormed vengefully after the Stukas which had attacked their base.

Meanwhile, the Messerschmitt 109s of the escorting Gruppen counter-attacked again and again, doing their utmost to break up the murderous attacks on their charges. No 602 Squadron, engaging the Stukas pulling away from Ford, had four Spitfires hit in quick succession. Flying Officer Ian Ferguson had just attacked his third Stuka, when his Spitfire shuddered under the impact of cannon shells from a Messerschmitt diving on him from above. One blew a hole in his port wing, another cut away part of his elevator and a third ruptured his petrol tank. Ferguson banked round towards the shore and was about to bale out when he saw the streets of Littlehampton passing immediately below. He decided to stay with the aircraft. On his way to open ground to the north of the town, overhead power lines seemed suddenly to appear in front of him. There was a flash as his propeller slashed through four of the six 33,000 volt conductors; the Spitfire continued on, to crash-land beside the cemetery at Toddington. The encounter added little to the damage already sustained by the Spitfire, but it cut the electricity supply to Littlehampton for some hours.

Pilot Officer Harry Moody had seen his rounds entering one of the Stukas, which then rolled on to its back and plunged into the sea. Then his Spitfire was hit by a cannon shell and he broke away, hotly pursued by four Messerschmitts. He managed to shake them off and set down his damaged aircraft on the landing ground at Ford, its buildings now well ablaze follow-ing the attack a couple of minutes earlier. One of the Spitfire's tyres had been shot through, and it came to rest standing on its nose.

Having exhausted his ammunition against the Stukas coming away from Ford, Dunlop Urie was heading back to Westhampnett. 'There was a machine on my tail which I assumed was my No 2. It wasn't,' he later recalled. The mistake was nearly his last. The next thing Urie knew was a series of loud bangs as cannon shells exploded along the rear fuselage of his

Spitfire and metal splinters gouged their way into his legs. Other splinters rammed into the parachute pack he was sitting on, pushing the front of it forwards over the lip of the bucket seat with Urie perched uncomfortably on top. As he tried to struggle back into the seat the Messerschmitt attacked again and the Spitfire received further hits. Then, mercifully, the German fighter broke away. Urie knew that his aircraft was badly damaged about the rear end and, for all he knew, the control wires to the rudder or elevators might part at any moment. But he was flying at only 500 feet and, his legs gradually becoming numb with pain, he felt it would be more risky to bale out than to stay with the aircraft. Using the controls as little as possible, Urie gingerly eased the Spitfire back to Westhampnett. He lowered his undercarriage but the flaps refused to budge, forcing him to make a fast approach. As the fighter touched down it slewed round to the right, the tyre on that side having been shot to pieces. Urie's guardian angel was watching over him, however: after a painful ride over grass that seemed as hard as cobblestones, the Spitfire came to a halt right way up. With immense relief, Urie switched off the engine. Already help was converging on him from all sides: the organ-like musical note, caused by the wind whistling through the shell holes in his fuselage, had alerted the groundcrewmen to his plight. In great pain, Urie was helped out of the cockpit. The inside of the fuselage, behind the armoured seat back which saved his life, was a shambles of twisted metal: the back of the aircraft was broken and it would never fly again. Spitfire X 4110, delivered to the Squadron only that morning, had had an operational life of just 24 minutes.

Flying Officer 'Mickey' Mount also had his Spitfire damaged during the German counter-attack, but he too managed to land back at Westhampnett.

No 602 Squadron's assailants had come from the IIIrd Gruppe of Fighter Geschwader 27, covering the Stukas attacking Ford. Twenty-two-year-old Oberleutnant Baron Erbo von Kageneck claimed a Spitfire shot down, as did Oberfeldwebel Franz Blazytko and Unteroffizier Karl Born.

Diving his Messerschmitt after a Spitfire towards the west of the mêlée, Julius Neumann had long since lost his wing-man. He pursued his quarry as it picked its way through the bedlam of aircraft, then low over the Isle of Wight twisting and turning in a deadly game of tag. Whenever the German pilot could bring his sights to bear he loosed off another burst. With some satisfaction, he saw that the enemy aircraft was beginning to trail smoke. Now he had him! Neumann threw a quick glance over his shoulder to check that no British fighter was trying to sneak up from behind, and noticed that there were two trails, a black one and a white one. He jerked his head to the front: there was only one black trail coming from the Spitfire. The white trail was coming from his Messerschmitt: a glycol leak! A glance at the engine temperature gauge confirmed his fears: the needle was hard against the upper stop, and he suddenly realised that the cockpit was getting uncomfortably hot. He broke off the chase. With the nearest friendly territory some 70 miles away, Neumann had no chance of getting home. The motor began to run rough and then, as he was trying to gain height to bale out, it packed up completely and flames started to leak back from a joint in the cowling.

Above Pilots of No 501 Squadron, believed to have been taken on 16 August. Left to right: standing, Flying Officer S. Witorzene. Flight Lieutenant G. Stoney, Sergeant F. Kozlowski; sitting, Sergeant R. Dafforn, Sergeant P. Farnes, Pilot Officer Kenneth Lee, Flight Lieutenant J. Gibson and Sergeant H. Adams. During the action on 18 August Lee and Kozlowski were shot down by Gerhard Schoepfel: both were wounded. Dafforn was shot down soon afterwards but baled out unhurt. Stoney was shot down and killed during the late afternoon action. Witorzenc and Farnes both took part in the destruction of German aircraft that day. (Central Press) **Centre**: Oberleutnant Gerhard Schoepfel of IIIrd Gruppe of Fighter Geschwader 26, who shot down four Hurricanes of No 501 Squadron in rapid succession soon after 1pm on 18 August. (Schoepfel) **Bottom** The four victory bars on the tail of Gerhard Schoepfel's Messerschmitt after the 18 August action. (Schoepfel)

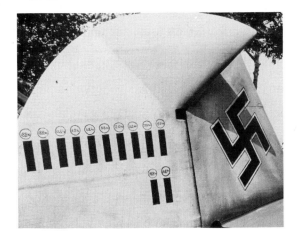

Above Smoke rising from fires at Kenley seen from Coulsdon, 2 miles to the north-west of the airfield at about 2pm on 18 August. In the foreground is St Andrew's Church. The smoke cloud could be seen from Brighton, 34 miles away. (via Flint) **Below** Hurricane of No 615 Squadron damaged by flying debris during the attack on Kenley. (Fisher)

Above Pilot Officer 'Dutch' Hugo of No 615 Squadron and . . . (Samson) **Below left** Flight Lieutenant 'Hump' Russell of No 32 Squadron were both shot down during action near Kenley and were lucky to escape with their lives. (Russell) Squadron Leader Don MacDonell led No 64 Squadron during the engagement over Kenley, and shot down the Messerschmitt 110 piloted by Ruediger Proske. (MacDonnell)

Above Biggin Hill airfield under attack from Heinkel 111s of Bomber Geschwader 1. at about 1.30pm on 18 August. The weight of the attack fell on the landing ground and on the open ground to the east of it, and there was little damage to buildings. **Inset** Sergeant Elizabeth Mortimer assisted in making safe several of the unexploded bombs at Biggin Hill after the attack, for which she later received the Military Medal. (Mortimer)

Raiders which did not return after the lunchtime engagement: **Left** The Messerschmitt 109 piloted by Oberleutnant Tiedmann of Fighter Geschwader 3 suffered damage to its glycol system in combat with British fighters, and he was forced to crash land at Leeds near Maidstone. His aircraft was camouflaged with straw to prevent it being destroyed before British Intelligence officers could examine it. Tiedmann walked away from his aircraft and was at liberty for about 12 hours before he was captured.

Above The Messerschmitt 110 piloted by Leutnant Kaestner of Destroyer Geschwader 26, crash landed near Newchurch after being damaged in combat near Kenley. Both crewmen were taken prisoner. **Below** Messer-schmitt 110 of Destroyer Geschwader 26 which crashed at Bonnington, after being shot down by Flight Lieutenant Weaver of No 56 Squadron. Both crewmen were killed.

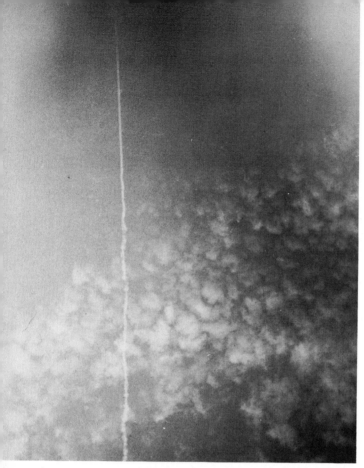

Left: Condensation trail of a German aircraft photographed by Alexander McKee near Portsmouth about 1.30pm on 18 August. (McKee) **Below**: Almost certainly the aircraft was a Junkers 86P high-altitude reconnaissance machine, powered by double-supercharged diesel engines and with a pressurised cabin for the crew. (via Schliephake)

Above: Junkers 87 Stuka of Dive Bomber Geschwader 77 being prepared for a mission at a forward landing ground. (Scheffel) **Below**: Major Helmut Bode led the mass attack by 109 Stukas on 18 August. (Bode) **Right** : Oberleutnant Julius Neumann of Fighter Geschwader 27, photographed at about 1pm on 18 August, immediately before he took off for the mission during which he was shot down. (Neumann)

Three British pilots who made victory claims during the air action near Portsmouth on 18 August. **Above** Pilot Officer Bob Doe of No 234 Squadron. (via Saunders) **Below** Squadron Leader Derek Boitel-Gill, who led No 152 Squadron. **Right** Sergeant Herbert Hallowes of No 43 Squadron. (Hallowes)

Above Dense smoke rising from the blazing fuel tanks at Ford. (via Wood) **Below** Station personnel emerging from their slit trenches at Ford, immediately after the airfield had been dive-bombed. (via Wood)

Above German reconnaissance photograph, showing the fires at Ford **Left** Police Constable Jack Hamblin of the Sussex Constabulary was the first outsider to reach Ford after the attack. (Hamblin)

Top left The final moments of a Stuka of 1st Gruppe of Dive Bomber Geschwader 77, before it crashed at West Broyle near Chichester. The crew, Unteroffizier August Dann and Unteroffizier Erich Kohl were both killed. (via Saunders) **Top right** The wreckage of the Stuka burning on the ground. (via Saunders) **Right**: Hauptmann Herbert Meisel, the commander of the ill-fated 1st Gruppe, who was killed during the attack on Thorney Island. (via Sellhorn)

Above left: Sergeant Basil Whall of No 602 Squadron. (Whall via Saunders) **Above right**: Part of the ammunition belt taken from the rear gun of the Stuka below. One of Whall's rounds had smashed through the cartridge on the left, without detonating it. (Wilcock)

Below. Stuka of the IInd Gruppe. Dive Bomber Geschwader 77, forced down by Sergeant Whall on Ham Manor Golf Course with both crewmen wounded; the radio operator later died of his wounds. (via Saunders)

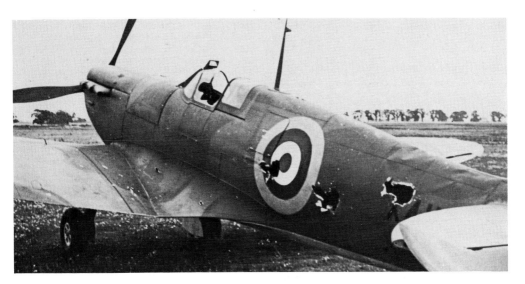

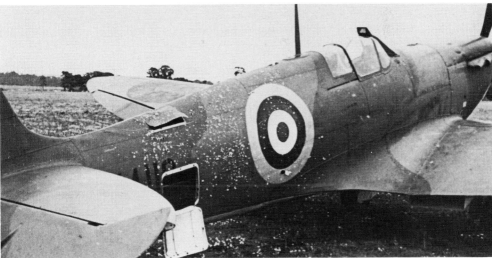

Above Spitfire X4110 had a service life of just 25 minutes! Delievered to No 602 Squadron at Westhampnett on the morning of 18 August, it was flown by Flight Lieutenant Dunlop Urie during the afternoon action over Bognor and severely damaged. The crinkling of the skin along the top of the rear fuselage shows that the aircraft's back had been broken: it never flew again. (Urie)

Right Dunlop Urie, his injured feet bound up, waiting to go to hospital (Urie)

Left 'Like a fiery blob of water running down a windowpane' was how Alexander McKee described the sight of barrage balloons going down in flames near Portsmouth after being shot up by German fighters on the afternoon of 18 August. He took this photograph at the time. To the right of the house can be seen smoke from the fires at Gosport. (McKee)

Below Johannes Wilhelm, of 1st Gruppe of Dive Bomber Geschwader 77. A photograph of him being taken to Chichester station appeared on the front page of the *Daily Telegraph*. (by permission of the Editor)

Daily Telegraph

and Morning Post

UST 21, 1940 BROADCASTING—Page Two

U.S. READY TO CO-OPERATE ON DEFENCE

Mr. Roosevelt On Discussions

HASTENING SALE OF DESTROYERS

Joint Use Of Bases Likely

FROM OUR OWN CORRESPONDENT
NEW YORK, Tuesday.

Mr. Churchill's announcement that Britain had decided to offer the United States air and naval bases struck a sympathetic note in this country.

Sentiment in favour of the sale to Britain of over-age destroyers is already strong, and nothing is more calculated to overcome the

JUNKERS PILOT WHO BALED OUT

The pilot of a Junkers 87 who baled out when his aircraft was shot down during a recent raid, arriving under escort at a railway station in South-East England on his way to a

HOW

FIRST FIGH

Daily T

The our force hold the

The defend, w penetrate river bed The defer the hills, between

It wa force so

Right Unteroffizier Karl Maier, of the same unit, was the luckiest man on 18 August; hit eight times on his body by machine-gun bullets, he escaped serious injury. (Sellhorn)

Two successful German fighter pilots, who lost their lives late on the afternoon of 18 August. **Left** Haumptmann Horst Tietzen of Fighter Geschwader 51, the fourth highest scoring German ace, who was shot down during an action with Hurricanes of No 501 Squadron. (via Ring)

Right Oberleutnant Gerhard Mueller-Duhe of Fighter Geschwader 26, photographed beside a Spitfire shot down over France a few days earlier. He was shot down by Flight Lieutenant Peter Brothers and Pilot Officer Boleslaw Wlasnowolski of No 32 Squadron. (via Cornwell)

Yesterday's enemies meet in friendship: **Left** Ex-members of the 9th Staffel of Bomber Geschwader 76 return to Kenley in August 1978, to meet some of the people they tried to kill, 38 years earlier. From left to right: Mathius Maassen, Reg Sheldrake, Guenther Unger. Air Commodore Thomas Prickman (the station commander in 1940). Franz Bergmann, Clifford Kenyon, Peggy Bray (née Jones) and Max Schumann. In the background is the old Sector operations building.

Left Alan Eckford (right) at the Battle of Britain Museum at Hendon with Wilhelm Lautersack whom he shot down on 18 August.

Below Harry Newton (centre) relives the action in which he was shot down on 18 August, with his opponents Guenther Unger (left) and Franz Bergmann.

Neumann jettisoned his canopy but, with only about a hundred feet between himself and the ground, he was far too low to jump. He called his leader, Oberleutnant Ernst Duellberg: 'Pine Tree leader, this is Pine Tree 7: my motor is on fire and I've got to go down.' Back came the reply 'Where are you?' What did that matter? For a few moments Neumann considered a final radio call which would be suitable to the occasion. 'Long live the Fuehrer!' sounded too pretentious. 'Goodbye to my wife and children' would have been better; but he had no wife, nor any children that he knew about. So he left the final call unsaid and concentrated on getting the Messerschmitt down in one piece. There seemed to be no good fields within gliding range on the hilly part of the Isle of Wight below him, so Neumann selected the least bad and side-slipped into it. The left wing struck the ground and took the force of the landing, then the aircraft spun round and slithered to a halt. Though he was tightly strapped in, the German pilot's head was jerked violently to one side as the aircraft swung and he took a hefty blow from the heavy metal frame of the windscreen. It took Neumann a few seconds to recover his wits and scramble clear of the Messerschmitt in case it exploded into flames. It did not. Now the fighter lay smouldering slowly, embarrassingly intact on the ground, a gift for the enemy. The pilot walked back to the cockpit and pulled out the signal pistol, then fired a couple of flares into the radio to prevent the British learning the tactical frequencies used by his Gruppe ('As if they did not know them already,' he later commented). Then, as Neumann walked clear of his aircraft which was now beginning to burn nicely, he could see his comrades heading southwards for home. Suddenly he felt very lonely. There seemed nothing else to do but light up a cigarette and await developments.

As the main body of the attacking force withdrew southwards, a few Messerschmitts with ammunition still to spare gave vent to their feelings by shooting up barrage balloons flying above Portsmouth and the surrounding area. Alexander McKee noted in his diary: 'A lull: then the sounds of invisible aeroplanes, of cannon and machine guns. Three or four fighters were diving at the Porchester balloons. One balloon blazed, fell slowly, gleaming red and orange, with a black plume of death above it. Like sharks the flight of black Messerschmitts rolled and plunged amongst the balloons. Over the dockyard another gas bag flamed immediately, and trickled down the sky like a fiery blob of water running down a window pane.' He continued, 'Funny how balloons wriggle down like worms, ever so slowly, twisting and writhing from side to side, lurching in slow motion to their doom. The banning of firework displays on Guy Fawkes Day won't be noticed – if the supply of balloons holds out.'

Twenty-year-old Pilot Officer Bob Doe, flying a Spitfire of No 234 Squadron, also saw the Messerschmitts shooting up the balloons. He picked out one of the enemy fighters, rammed his throttle wide open and went after it: 'He saw me, put down his nose and went dead straight for France. He did not do any turns at all. He went down to about 100 feet and just kept on going, with me gaining on him very slowly.' After a lengthy chase and a few experimental bursts, Doe was within range and saw his rounds striking the enemy fighter. The Messerschmitt began to lose speed and Doe saw its canopy fly away. 'I flew alongside him, to his right, about 30 or 40 yards away. It was most odd, the first time I had ever seen a German in the air. The impression of him has stuck with me to this day: a big man with fair hair and a round face. As he went down I looked back and saw him splash into the sea,' Doe recalled. The long chase out to sea had left the Spitfire low on fuel and Doe could not wait to see whether his victim had survived; he pulled the Spitfire round and headed northwards for base.

Just as the engagement was drawing to its close, the twelve Hurricanes of No 213 Squadron arrived on the scene after their long approach flight from Exeter. Pilot Officer Harold Atkinson pounced on a lone Messerschmitt heading southwards for home at low altitude, and shot it down off Ventnor.

From his vantage point at a searchlight site on the coast to the east of Middleton-on-Sea, 23-year-old Lance Bombardier John Smith had watched the dramatic fight overhead and the German withdrawal. Then he caught sight of a single aircraft about a mile out to sea, flying west. It turned towards the coast, descending the whole time, then turned again and flew eastwards along the shore line. By now Smith could see that it was a Spitfire, its propeller blades almost stopped and smoke trailing from the engine; the flaps were lowered but the undercarriage was up. Obviously the pilot was bent on setting it down in shallow water. With a splash the aircraft alighted, then the starboard wing struck a submerged groyne. The aircraft leapt back into the air, spun horizontally through a semi-circle, and flopped into the sea going backwards. Smith sprinted down the beach and waded out to the Spitfire, which had come to rest about 20 yards out in waist-deep water. He scrambled on to the wing, to see the dazed pilot still in his cockpit: 'I could not release the canopy from the outside but in no time at all the pilot opened up, unstrapped himself and with very little assistance from me (in fact I was in his way, if anything) climbed out.' Sergeant Basil Whall of No 602 Squadron, having accounted for two Stukas and had his Spitfire shot up in the process, was safely down.

Silence had returned to Ham Manor Golf Course after the attack on Poling when Michael Wilcox's father, Frederick, came dashing noisily into the house to grab his Smith and Wesson revolver: he shouted that a German plane had come down next to the golf course and he was off to capture the crew. Young Michael followed him out, and was immediately appalled to see the vast pall of black smoke rising from the blazing fuel dumps and buildings at Ford: 'In broad sunlight the sky had become one large red ball of fire of immense proportions, and quite unforgettable. I had seen the Crystal Palace fire before the war but that was nothing by comparison and I felt that nothing on earth would extinguish it.' Along the 16th fairway Michael Wilcox saw the wheelmarks left by the landing aircraft and there, in front of him just beyond the tee, sat the Stuka Basil Whall had hit and seen go down near Poling. 'Father arrived first and I saw him brandishing his revolver at the rear gunner who was still sitting behind his machine gun,' Michael Wilcox remembered. 'The aircraft was quite intact except for slight damage to the perspex canopy and a very small petrol leak which was dripping on the ground.' The two Germans eased themselves slowly and painfully out of the Stuka, the pilot bleeding from the leg and the radio operator with a neck wound. Shortly afterwards the Wilcox's gamekeeper arrived on the scene and helped bind up the Germans' wounds.

As the bombing ceased, 33-year-old railway signalman Charles Allaston grabbed his rifle and emerged from his home on the northern edge of Littlehampton, mid-way between Ford and Poling. He had been on duty with the Home Guard that morning and still wore his uniform. Once outside, he recalled, 'The sight that met my eyes was heartbreaking, a great pall of black smoke was drifting over us from Ford aerodrome.' Allaston made his way to the nearby railway level crossing, where he joined a Home Guard colleague. From there the two men watched a Spitfire to the east of them, flying low down, descending behind a row of trees. When the aircraft failed to reappear on the other side the men guessed that it must have landed so they ran along the railway line in its direction, past the concealing trees. 'We observed the fighter in a small field south of the railway line and apparently undamaged,' Allaston remembered. 'We found the pilot standing by his aircraft, quite young and in a great state of excitement. We were unable to converse as he was obviously not English and we felt at the time that he might have been Polish. The humour in all this was that whilst he could not converse with us, he certainly had made a point of learning English swear words. I thought as a fairly broadminded person that I had heard most of them, but he seemed to know some that I did not.' The greater humour of the story is that the pilot was not Polish, but Scottish: Flying Officer Ian Ferguson, who had crash-landed his Spitfire after cutting through the 33,000-volt overhead power cables running along the north of Littlehampton. Ferguson's comrades remember him as being normally a quiet, mild-mannered man: his hair-raising experience had brought about a complete, if temporary, change of character.

It was not long before Julius Neumann's Messerschmitt, burning in a field just to the west of Shanklin, summoned attention. A pair of rather elderly Home Guardsmen appeared over the brow of the hill and advanced cautiously, their rifles with fixed bayonets levelled at the German pilot. Neumann waved his arms in the air and shouted in his schoolboy English that he was unarmed. Once the Home Guardsmen established that this was indeed the case, the mood became more relaxed. 'Have you any souvenirs?' the pilot was asked. Neumann said he had nothing. 'You must have a souvenir' one of the captors stated, his tone more demanding. Neumann reached into his pocket, pulled out his Luftwaffe-issue flying sunglasses and offered these. No, there had to be two souvenirs, one each. Neumann wondered what to do next, then he had an idea: he snapped the sunglasses into two and handed a piece to each of his captors. They were delighted.

For almost the entire air action Johannes Wilhelm had been dangling, oil-bespattered, on the end of his parachute after jumping from his Stuka. His descent from about 12,000 feet lasted twelve minutes, and before he reached the ground the last of the returning raiders was well past the Isle of Wight on its way home. It was then that Air Raid Warden Bill Prestridge, 38,

patrolling Stockbridge Road on the south of Chichester, noticed the parachute blowing slowly towards him from the south-west. He ran towards the
anticipated landing point and arrived, breathlessly, in time to help Wilhelm
to his feet and get out of his parachute. 'He looked as if he had been under a
fountain of clean, brown, oil,' Prestridge remembered, 'so much of it was
running down his flying suit.' Within minutes the field had errupted with
civilians, police and Home Guardsmen, and Wilhelm was ushered into a car
and driven to the local police station.

Wilhelm's radio operator, Anton Woerner, had reached the ground
some time earlier. During the fighter attack his parachute pack had been hit
and some of the rigging lines had been shot through. When Woerner pulled
the ripcord the parachute opened, but the canopy did not develop fully. As a
result he came down very fast but, to his great good fortune, he landed on a
hay stack. He survived, though with severe concussion.

Frank Carey was helped out of his battered Hurricane, lying on its back
after being caught in the 'aircraft trap' at Pulborough. Two ladies from the
local farm came over and bound up his wound. 'They were very disappointed
in finding only one bullet hole in me,' he remembered; 'I think they thought
I was malingering or something!' Carey was taken to the Royal West
Sussex Hospital at Chichester, where the bullet was removed from his
knee.

Leutnant Gerhard Mitsdoerffer of Ist Gruppe of Fighter Geschwader
27, shot down by one of the Spitfires of No 234 Squadron, had baled out of
his Messerschmitt into the sea just off the Isle of Wight. Spencer's Boatyard
at Ventnor sent out a boat to pick him up and later received a government
award of £2, the standard sum for doing so.

Twenty-two-year-old Police Constable Jack Hamblin had watched the
Stukas attacking Ford and Poling, from the top of Arundel High Street. He
rushed to his station to report what he had seen, and was immediately
ordered to go to Ford as Incident Officer. Hamblin kicked his motor cycle
into life, then he was away. 'The road from Arundel to Ford is approximately
three miles long and almost absolutely straight, and I rode at maximum
speed,' he later wrote. 'My steel helmet had slipped to the back of my head
and was being held on by the chinstrap round my throat, which was nearly
choking me due to the force of the slipstream building up inside the helmet.'

As Hamblin neared the airfield he, too, was shaken by the size of the
cloud of dense black smoke rising from the fires, and the scene of death and
destruction that unfolded before him. Beside the entrance to the station he
came upon the body of a young woman aged about 20. Most of her clothing
had been torn away by the blast from a nearby explosion, but she bore only
superficial marks of injury. There was no information as to her identity and,
as she was obviously a civilian and the naval personnel had problems of their
own, she was his responsibility. He covered the body with a blanket then,
resolving to deal with the matter later, made a rapid reconnaissance of the
camp so that he could report back.

As Hamblin toured Ford the magnitude of the carnage and destruction became clear. There were mutilated bodies and wrecked buildings all over the place. 'I think the scene that horrified me most was a partially demolished nissen hut which had been used for showers and bathrooms. Lying in the bottom of one of the baths was the naked body of a naval youth,' he recalled. 'Obviously he had been caught in the raid whilst taking a bath and his body, lying in its own blood, was almost severed in the middle. The walls, such as were still standing, were spattered with blood.'

Ambulances and first-aid parties were soon converging on the station from all round, assisting the naval personnel to rescue and remove the injured. Both of the airfield's fuel storage compounds had been hit and set well ablaze, as had the lubrication oil store and several of the aircraft drawn up by the hangars. The station fire-fighting teams were in action, soon assisted by the Littlehampton, Bognor and Arundel Fire Brigades. The oil fires were treated with foam, the others using water. The station's main water pipe had been fractured, but by using trailer pumps the firemen were able to draw water from the static water tanks and also from a trench flooded by water from the burst main. As the water in the static tanks started to run out, serpentine hose lengths were run to the River Arun, 400 yards away, and the tanks refilled from there.

There were numerous acts of bravery at Ford that afternoon. Leading Wren Steward Nina Marsh, though wounded in the back and elbow, insisted on tending the wounded in her shelter trench and refused attention for herself until the others had all been evacuated. Wren Cook Irene Marriott, though wounded, moved everyone else out of the kitchen where she worked, then returned to put out the fires. Surgeon Lieutenant K. Scott, though severely shaken after being blown into a shelter trench by the blast from an exploding bomb, insisted on tending casualties in a clearing station he had established in an undamaged barrack hut. Chief Petty Officer P. Cahalane had a hut blown in on top of him but, though injured, he worked hard moving casualties and had to be ordered to leave to get his own wounds dressed.

Due to the lack of warning, Ford suffered heavier casualties that day than all the other targets put together: 28 killed and 75 wounded. Of the aircraft in and around the hangars, fourteen were wrecked or damaged beyond repair: 5 Blackburn Sharks, 5 Fairey Swordfish and 2 Fairey Albacore torpedo-bombers, and a Percival Proctor communications aircraft, were wrecked or damaged beyond repair; a further 26 aircraft were damaged but repairable. As well as the petrol and oil storage installations, two aircraft hangars, the motor transport hangar, two stores buildings, the ratings' and petty officers' canteens and numerous accommodation buildings were wrecked.

Having telephoned his report to the police station at Arundel, and seen that the fire and rescue services were functioning properly, Jack Hamblin returned to the dead girl beside the main gate. The guard told him that she had been seen entering the gates as the raid began, and from this Hamblin deduced that she might have been visiting somebody on the station. He asked around if anyone had been expecting a visitor fitting her description, and eventually one of the sailors identified her: she was his girlfriend over from County Mayo in Ireland.

The village hall at Ford was commandeered as a temporary mortuary, and the bodies taken there. Hamblin's final memory of Ford that day was the scene inside that hall just before he left: a long line of coffins each draped with the Union Jack and, at the far end, one lonely coffin containing the girl from Ireland, draped with a white sheet.

At Poling the bombs had fallen in a neat cluster round the receiver section, and one had struck one of the 240-foot-high wooden receiver towers and knocked off the top section. The building housing the receiver itself, and the operations room with the switchboard which Avis Hearn had served, had a blast wall which protected it from major damage. The station's long-range early-warning radar, the Chain Home, was now inoperative until repairs could be carried out to the damaged tower. The station's shorter-ranging Chain Home Low set, for plotting low-flying aircraft, was unharmed and continued in use. The sole casualties at Poling were one man suffering from shock and another with slight injuries.

Due to the disruptive attacks by the Hurricanes of Nos 43 and 601 Squadrons, the damage inflicted by the Stukas on Thorney Island was not so concentrated as elsewhere. Nevertheless two hangars and some buildings were wrecked. Three aircraft were destroyed: a Blenheim, an Anson and a Magister; one Wellington was damaged. The only casualties were five civilians working on the camp, slightly injured when their shelter was hit by a 110-pound bomb.

At Gosport there was considerable destruction, with several buildings wrecked and two hangars damaged. Four aircraft were destroyed and five damaged. There were no casualties.

Throughout, the Stukas' attacks had been discriminate and precise: hardly a single bomb had fallen outside the areas of the military targets assigned to the Gruppen.

In the Portsmouth area ten barrage balloons were shot down in flames; bullets punctured two more, which had to be hauled down and deflated for repair.

To Kurt Scheffel, his injured right hand dripping blood and throbbing excruciatingly from the metal splinter embedded in his thumb, his left arm lacking any feeling at all, the flight in the battered Stuka over the 120 terrible miles back to Caen seemed to last for ever. When he finally reached his base, he had to reach painfully across with his right hand to operate the flap lever on the left side of the cockpit. As he eased the Stuka into the landing pattern he saw that three others had already landed. Weakly he nudged the dive-bomber on to the ground until a violent, jarring, shudder from the undercarriage revealed that his tyres had been shot to pieces. At the end of the landing run Scheffel's engine cut and he was left sitting at the end of the airfield, too weak from loss of blood to get out of the Stuka, behind him a dead radio operator. It was some minutes before help arrived and he was lifted gently out of the blood-stained cockpit.

Examined by a doctor, Scheffel was found to have one large metal splinter embedded in his lung, two more in his shoulder blades, and about a dozen smaller ones in his neck, in addition to the one in his thumb. One of the bullets from the attacking fighter had slashed across the broad shoulder strap of his parachute harness, severing it clean through. Scheffel's Stuka had 84 hits, some 50 of them on the fuselage.

Otto Schmidt landed his dive-bomber back at Caen with almost exactly similar damage: 80 hits on the aircraft, the tyres shot through and a mortally wounded radio operator.

Streaming blood from his head wound, Guenther Meyer-Bothling brought his Stuka across the Channel with a dead radio operator, scarcely any instruments, his trim controls and part of the rudder shot away, no compass, his cabin awash with engine oil and two 110-pound bombs jammed under his port wing. His battered Jumo engine kept going until he reached the French coast then, as though it felt it had done its duty, finally seized up. Gliding down to land on the beach he tried to lower his flaps, but these refused to budge. Instead he kicked on what was left of the rudder to push the crippled dive-bomber into a side-slip, to ease off some of his speed. As the aircraft hit the sand the legs of the fixed undercarriage, cut to pieces by the machine gun bullets, broke away and the Stuka slid along on its belly. Some infantrymen who had been bathing in the sea came running towards him, then stopped in their tracks as they noticed the bombs under the wing. Only after Meyer-Bothling's shouted assurance that the bombs were safe did they clamber on to the wing and help him out of the cockpit. Later, ground crewmen counted a total of 160 hits on the dive-bomber.

The last Stuka to regain the coast of France, about twenty minutes after everyone else, was that flown by Karl Henze: he had had to make the return flight with his dive-brakes jammed in the extended position. An agonising headache did not help matters. Just after Henze crossed the French coast, the hydraulic pipe in front of him suddenly burst, showering him with oil. He had left the dive-brake operating lever in the 'in' position when they had failed to retract, and the pressure in the hydraulic system had gradually built up against the jammed actuator until something had to give. With the alcohol from the hydraulic oil stinging his eyes and almost blinding him, Henze set the Stuka down heavily in a meadow. Later, in hospital, it was found that a bullet had ricocheted off the aircraft structure before lodging in thin flesh against his skull: no wonder he had had such a terrible headache!

Twenty-seven-year-old Oberleutnant Helmut Bruck and his radio operator Feldwebel Franz Hettinger landed in France with 130 hits on their Stuka and not a scratch on either of them. But without question the luckiest man of the day was 20-year-old radio operator Unteroffizier Karl Maier who, though hit eight times by machine gun bullets, survived with only flesh wounds.

In spite of the near-miraculous escape by some of its members, however, the Ist Gruppe of Dive Bomber Geschwader 77 had suffered a fearful mauling during the attack on Thorney Island: of the 28 Stukas which had taken off 10 had been shot down, one was damaged beyond repair and 4 others returned with lesser damage. Of the 56 men involved in the attack 17, including the commander, Hauptmann Herbert Meisel, had been killed or mortally wounded; five more were taken prisoner and six returned with wounds. As Generalmajor von Richthofen later commented in his diary: 'A Stuka Gruppe has had its feathers well and truly plucked.'

In contrast, the other three Gruppen had suffered relatively light losses. The IInd Gruppe, which had mounted the devastating attack on Ford, lost 3 Stukas shot down and one damaged beyond repair; 5 of its men were killed or mortally wounded, and one was taken prisoner. The IIIrd Gruppe, attacking Poling, lost one aircraft shot down, one crashed in France and was wrecked, and two returned with damage; 4 men were killed. Thus of the 109 Stukas involved in the four attacks 15 had been destroyed and one damaged beyond repair, a loss of 14 per cent of the aircraft engaged. A further 6 of the dive-bombers returned with repairable damage. Taken over the entire force it was a sharp loss, but hardly a crippling one.

It had been sheer bad luck for the men of Ist Gruppe of Dive Bomber Geschwader 77 that not only had they run into Nos 43 and 601 Squadrons just before the target, and come under attack from the Blenheims of No 235 Squadron after leaving it; but during the mêlée over the sea No 152 Squadron, coming in from the west, had singled out their aircraft for attention.

The German fighter units had done their best but with the patchy haze it had been difficult to block all of the enemy attacks, especially during the confused withdrawal phase. Eight of the escorting Messerschmitt 109s were shot down. Three of the pilots were killed, three taken prisoner and the remaining two were picked up from the sea by the German rescue service. Fighter Command lost five aircraft destroyed and seven damaged; two pilots were killed and three wounded.

On the British side, the magnitude of the success against the Stukas was greatly exaggerated at the time. Altogether the fighter squadrons claimed 34 of the dive-bombers destroyed and anti-aircraft gunners claimed two more. On the radar the attacking force had been estimated at 150 aircraft, and assumed to comprise dive-bombers and escorts in approximately equal numbers. Had these figures been true it would have meant 36 Stukas shot down out of 75 involved, a debilitating loss of almost half. The dive-bomber losses during the action had been bad, but nowhere near so bad as that.

The Stuka attack on Ford drove home a chastening lesson for the Royal Navy, of the vital necessity to tighten its warning procedures to prevent stations being surprised when ample warning existed of the approach of enemy raiders. The airfield was virtually out of use until it was handed over to the RAF in September.

The temporary loss of the long-range warning radar at Poling caused few problems: the Chain Home Low radar there was still working and could see almost as far. Moreover, along the coast to 70 miles on either side of Poling there were six other radar stations providing interlocking cover, so there was no 'hole' through which German aircraft could sneak unseen. Within a couple of days a mobile radar station was erected in Angmering woods to supplement the coverage of the area, until the main set at Poling was repaired.

At Thorney Island and Gosport the airfields continued in use, albeit with reduced facilities.

So ended Air Fleet 3's great effort for the day. As the ambulances moved away from the airfields in Normandy, carrying the dead and wounded from the bullet-torn Stukas, we shall return our attention to events 150 miles to the east.

CHAPTER 4

The Weather the Victor

In war the outcome corresponds to expectations
less than in any other case.
TITUS LIVY

After the second great attack there followed a couple of hours of relative quiet as Nos 10 and 11 Groups of Fighter Command and Air Fleets 2 and 3 of the Luftwaffe, tired after their massive exertions, stopped to draw breath. On both sides of the Channel, unit commanders now phoned round frantically, trying to establish whether missing crews and aircraft were safely down elsewhere. It was a time to remove the dead, tend the wounded and refuel and re-arm the aircraft before the next confrontation.

During this period of quiescence the Royal Air Force made its only incursions over German-occupied Europe during the daylight hours of 18 August. At 2.40 pm two Blenheims of No 114 Squadron, Bomber Command, attacked Fécamp and Dieppe on the north coast of France. The raids, flown at high altitude by single aircraft which hared for home immediately they had released their small loads of bombs, amounted to no more than a gesture of defiance. Neither Blenheim was intercepted. German records mention the Fécamp attack but say no damage was caused. The Dieppe attack appears to have escaped their notice.

As the bombers sped homewards they passed a couple of Spitfires of the Photographic Reconnaissance Unit, going in the opposite direction. These aircraft had been stripped of guns, armour, radios and everything else not essential for the reconnaissance role, fitted with aerial cameras and extra fuel tanks, then carefully polished to give the last ounce of speed. If the normal Spitfire was like a sports car, the stripped-down and polished-up reconnaissance version was like a racing car. These aircraft had a maximum speed of just under 400 mph, faster than anything the Luftwaffe then had in service. The superb turn of speed was not often necessary, however, for if the skies were clear the reconnaissance Spitfires photographed their targets cruising overhead at around 34,000 feet and usually came and went undetected. That afternoon one of the aircraft photographed airfields in the Orléans area while the other covered ports along the Belgian coast looking for possible invasion activity. Both accomplished their missions without interference and returned safely.

Down in the sea off Le Touquet Guenther Unger and the other three members of his crew bobbed in the water, sodden miserable flotsam left over from the lunchtime engagement. At first the men had swapped dirty jokes to keep their spirits up. Then, gradually, the numbing cold brought the stark realisation that death was near and the men turned to prayers to God to save them. Now at 5 pm, nearly three hours after their Dornier had ditched, even that had passed. The insidious effects of exposure had taken their toll and the men, almost past caring what happened to them, had begun to drift apart. At one stage Unger remembers looking up and seeing a seagull seemingly motionless in the air a few feet above him, gazing down with covetous eyes. The German pilot thought to himself: 'Come back in an hour my little one and you can have your supper, but I'm not willing to oblige yet!' Willing or not, there was little he could have done had the creature taken a peck at him. The cold seemed to have congealed the very blood in his veins and he was no longer master of his own body.

Finally, when Unger had almost given up all hope of rescue, a spotter aircraft roared low over his head. He lacked the strength even to wave, but he and his comrades had been seen and the plane turned back and circled over them. At last succour was at hand. But would it arrive in time? Then a wave hoisted Unger and he caught sight of a small ship, a few hundred yards away, coming straight for him. A few minutes later a couple of sailors drew alongside in a boat. Unger's final illogical fear was that after all he had been through, he was now going to be saved from the sea only to go into captivity. In a croaking voice he asked his rescuers whether they were German or English. In German one of the sailors told him not to be stupid; they had come to save him from death and it did not matter which side they were on.

By a remarkable piece of luck, the aircraft which had spotted Unger's crew in the water was working with a German naval minesweeper sent from Boulogne to pick up another 9th Staffel crew in the water: that of Unteroffizier Schumacher, whose dinghy had been sighted during Mathius Maassen's freelance search effort. Unger and his comrades were hauled into the boat and taken to the minesweeper; there they were winched up one at a time and lowered on to the deck, where their dripping bodies looked like so many water-laden sponges. Strong sailors carried them below, stripped off their wet clothing and wrapped the survivors in blankets. 'I was slumped in a bunk opposite my navigator, August Meyer,' Unger later recalled. 'We asked one of the sailors for cigarettes and he lit a couple and gave us one each. But as we tried to smoke them the nervous reaction began to set in and our hands shook uncontrollably. It took a tremendous effort of concentration to get the moving ends of our cigarettes into our mouths!' Unger's flight engineer had suffered worst from the effects of exposure and required immediate medical attention, so the minesweeper returned to Boulogne at full speed. Schumacher's crew, in their dinghy and therefore in less immediate danger, were picked up later.

At about the same time as Guenther Unger was trying to smoke his cigarette Harry Newton, his opponent of a few hours earlier, was regaining consciousness in hospital at Oxted after the operation to save the skin of his face and hands. He came to, to find the fingers of his right hand pegged out on a wooden board to keep them apart. One of his first acts was to be violently sick, as the reaction of the anaesthetic forced him to bring up the lunch he had gulped down at Croydon while waiting at readiness.

As Guenther Unger and Harry Newton took stock of their personal situations and gave thanks for their survival, the next stage of the day's action was beginning to unfold. By 5 pm the radar stations along the coast of Kent were again reporting numerous plots over the Pas-de-Calais area: the second major attack of the day by Air Fleet 2 was about to move off. Early in the afternoon the bombers had hit Kenley and Biggin Hill. Now they were to go for the two next most important fighter airfields in south-eastern England, those at Hornchurch and North Weald. Fifty-eight Dornier 17s of Bomber Geschwader 2 were to attack the former, fifty-one Heinkel 111s of Bomber Geschwader 53 were to attack the latter. The plan called for the two raiding forces to cross the coast of England at about the same time; so the Heinkels attacking North Weald, with further to go to reach the Essex coast north of Foulness, left the Pas-de-Calais about a quarter of an hour ahead of the Dorniers who were to cross near Deal. Covering the two bomber forces was a total of about 140 Messerschmitt 109s and 110s, drawn from Fighter Geschwader 3, 26, 51 and 54 and Destroyer Geschwader 26.

This time the British radar operators' estimate of the strength of the hostile force was almost exactly correct: 250 aircraft. To meet the threat the No 11 Group controller at Uxbridge ordered thirteen squadrons of fighters into the air or to immediate readiness; his No 12 Group counterpart at Watnall passed similar orders to four more. Soon, from the two fighter Groups, there were 47 Spitfires and 96 Hurricanes moving to meet the German attack. This meant approximately one British fighter for every German, or three British fighters for every five German fighters and bombers. Ten of the British fighters now scrambling into the air, nine Spitfires of No 19 Squadron and a Hurricane of No 151 Squadron, were armed with 20-mm cannon.

As an opening gambit the No 11 Group controller ordered four squadrons, Nos 32, 54, 56 and 501 with eleven Spitfires and 33 Hurricanes, to move forwards into the Margate-Canterbury area to engage the enemy formations first. The remaining units were to climb to altitude and wait over or near the threatened fighter airfields, until a clearer picture emerged of the enemy intentions.

Piloting one of the Heinkels at the rear of the force bound for North Weald was 24-year-old Leutnant Walter Leber, a veteran with some 30 operational missions to his credit. Ranged majestically and extending for more than half a mile in front of him were the rest of the fifty bombers in the formation. On either side of the bombers flew the Messerschmitt 110s of the close escort in fours, matching their speed with that of their charges.

In one of the Messerschmitt 110s in front of Leber was Leutnant Joachim Koepsell of Destroyer Geschwader 26. He hated having to fly throttled-back like this, to maintain position on the bombers at their formation cruising speed of only 180 mph. The twin-engined fighter was slow and heavy enough in combat, without the delay of accelerating to fighting speed when the Spitfires and Hurricanes did appear. As the raiding force headed due northwards from Calais, giving the east coast of Kent a wide berth, Koepsell could see cloud building up ahead in the north-west.

The Heinkels making for North Weald continued northwards until they were almost due east of the target, then wheeled round and headed straight for it. As they did so the Dorniers making for Hornchurch left Calais and headed towards the English coast just north of Deal.

The first of the defending fighter squadrons to engage was No 56, with twelve Hurricanes, which clashed with the North Weald raiding force off the Essex coast. Flying Officer Innes Westmacott recalled his first sight of the enemy formation: 'We had to go up through a bit of cloud and suddenly we saw them and I must say I gulped a bit! It looked an enormous raid.' Squadron Leader 'Minnie' Manton, 30, split his force into four and ordered three of the Sections to go for the bombers while he took Red Section and moved out to try and hold off the German escort. Manton closed in fast and loosed off a burst at one of the Messerschmitt 110s, which by now had accelerated to fighting speed and were moving to block the attack. A general mêlée then developed, during which Manton succeeded in getting on the tail of one of the escorts and followed it as it dived away, firing as he did so. He saw his rounds striking the enemy fighter which continued its dive away to the south, streaming white glycol smoke from both of its engines.

While this was happening, Flight Lieutenant Edward Gracie led Blue Section towards the bombers. As he curved in to attack, however, the German escorts came bounding down on him from the right and he was forced to bear away. Gracie attempted a second attack on the bombers but this, too, was foiled. On the third attempt the Hurricanes were able to loose off short bursts at the bombers, then they became embroiled with the Messerschmitt 110s. Innes Westmacott had attacked with Gracie, but during the mêlée he became separated from his comrades. 'There were a lot of Messerschmitt 110s about and they all seemed to be picking on me! Whichever way I turned, there seemed to be one shooting at me,' he recalled. 'I made for the cover of a small cloud. Unfortunately the cloud was too small and I kept on popping out of it, to find the Messerschmitts flying round outside. I had a shower of tracer about my ears and was frequently hit. No friends were in sight and it was clear I had to get away – fast.' Westmacott rolled his Hurricane on to its back, then pulled back on the stick until he was going down almost vertically with full power on. He dived the Hurricane so fast that the rush of air past the canopy almost drowned the noise from the engine, and the controls felt as though they were locked solid. He could see the sea coming up to meet him and his airspeed indicator hovered above the 350 mph mark, equivalent to a true airspeed of over 450 mph. 'I almost blacked-out when I pulled out of the dive, praying that the aircraft would stay in one piece,' he remembered. 'I was as terrified as I have ever been in my life!' The furious dive was enough to shake off Westmacott's pursuers, however.

By keeping the escorts busy, Red and Blue Sections of No 56 Squadron allowed Flying Officer 'Squeak' Weaver to move in with Yellow Section and attack the rear of the bomber formation. Weaver singled out the left-hand

Heinkel at the rear of the formation and fired a 10-second burst into it, before having to break away violently to avoid a Messerschmitt curving round on to his tail.

Weaver's victim was the Heinkel flown by Walter Leber, occupying the left-hand rear position in the formation. Leber himself saw nothing of the attack. First there was the shout from his gunners that fighters were coming in, then the rattle as they opened fire. At the same time he could see tracer streaking back from the guns of the other Heinkels around him. Seconds later the temperature gauge of his right engine began to rise rapidly to the danger mark: the cooling system had been hit. Leber feathered the propeller and shut the engine down, at the same time struggling to keep up with the rest of the formation. It was a losing fight, however, and the Heinkel soon began to drop back.

As the Hurricanes of No 56 Squadron became embroiled with the bombers and their escorts, No 54 Squadron joined the fight. Squadron Leader 'Prof' Leathart took his eleven Spitfires straight into the fray with the Messerschmitts.

Far below, in St Osyth Road, Clacton, newly-married Kathleen Watton had been out on a stroll with her husband John, snatching a few minutes alone with him. The couple had seen the German bomber formation approaching. Then the fight began over their heads and they bolted back to the bride's home in Astley Road. They arrived to find the wedding guests of both families clustered in the hall, husbands clutching wives as everyone looked up at the ceiling, cowed by the menacing drone of the bombers and the rattle of machine-gun fire above.

Pilot Officer Colin Gray, a 25-year-old New Zealander flying a Spitfire of No 54 Squadron, dashed into the middle of the dogfight and fired bursts at a couple of Messerschmitt 110s. Then he was able to swing his sight on to a third Messerschmitt slightly below him and loosed off the rest of his ammunition at it. The German fighter rolled on to its back and dived away, rapidly gaining speed. Gray followed: 'I didn't have any more ammunition and I wanted to see what happened to him. He was going down fast, spiralling slowly as he did so.' The Messerschmitt's speed continued to build up and it drew away from the Spitfire, then Gray lost sight of it against the dark background of houses at Clacton.

Fireman Frank Jeffries, 24, on duty at Clacton fire station, watched the combat with the rest of his shift. 'The visibility was very good and we could see the dogfight going on overhead. Then we saw an aircraft detach itself from the fight and go into a dive. It looked as if it was going to crash right in the middle of the town,' he later recalled.

Bunched fearfully with the rest of her wedding guests in the hall of her home, Kathleen Watton heard a terrible screaming noise emerge from the drone of engines. Gradually it rose to a crescendo, blotting out every other sound. Her father ran to the back door to see what was happening then he returned, white-faced, and shouted to the guests: 'There's an aircraft coming straight down with one wing off!' The howl grew yet louder, seemingly heading unerringly for the house. To the new Mrs Watton it seemed that her first day of marriage might also be her last. Then there was a hollow-sounding thump, and the scream abruptly ceased. Relieved still to be alive, the guests broke into an excited chatter. At the same instant, high above, Colin Gray saw a yellow spurt of flame suddenly appear near the centre of the town. That was one Messerschmitt that would not get home.

Pilot Officer 'John Willie' Hopkin of No 54 Squadron had also engaged the German escorts, and scored hits on one of them before it dived away. Looking around for other enemy aircraft he caught sight of a lone bomber below the main German formation, flying on one engine. It was Walter Leber's Heinkel, limping along behind the others. Hopkin swung his Spitfire round on to the tail of the bomber and closed in rapidly. He opened fire at 250 yards, holding his finger on the button for a long 9-second burst down to 100 yards, and saw his rounds breaking bits off the raider.

Leber's Heinkel was finished. Hopkin's rounds smashed into the bomber's left engine, wrecking that one as well, and the German pilot had to shut it down. Leber's first thought was to glide over land so that the crew could bale out of the crippled Heinkel; but then he learned that the three men in the rear of the aircraft had all been wounded, one of them seriously. There was no alternative but to crash-land the bomber. Leber's navigator, Feldwebel Heinrich Feick, jettisoned the bombs. As the Heinkel went down in its spiral glide, Hopkin followed. 'All the time I was accompanied by the British fighter, which circled with me but did not attack,' Leber remembered. He appreciated the act of chivalry from his enemy, for had there been a further attack the crew of the Heinkel would have been helpless to meet it. The German pilot set down his bomber on Smallgains Farm, on Foulness Island. The crew clambered out and Hopkin circled his victims, waggling his wings in salute to his fallen foe, then levelled out the Spitfire and roared away to the west.

Shortly after Leber crash-landed, a slow-flying Messerschmitt 110 trailing smoke flew low over the landing ground at Eastchurch on the Isle of Sheppey. Almost certainly this was the aircraft 'Minnie' Manton of No 56 Squadron had hit and seen diving away to the south with white glycol vapour trailing from both of its engines. As the damaged Messerschmitt came within range Bofors gunners of the 12th Light Anti-Aircraft Regiment loosed off a dozen rounds at it and saw some of them hit. The German fighter went into a shallow dive and crashed into the ground at Leysdown-on-Sea nearby, killing the pilot. The radio operator, Unteroffizier Theodor Rutters, was thrown clear of the wreck and survived to be taken prisoner.

The fast and furious engagement off the Essex coast could not last long, for one by one the British fighters ran out of ammunition and had to break away. By now, however, the line of advance of the more northerly raiding formation towards North Weald was becoming clear to the British fighter controllers. Orders had gone out to five squadrons, Nos 46, 85, 151, 257 and 310, with 61 Hurricanes, to move into position to intercept the German bombers in front of or over the target. The raiders continued relentlessly on, passing just to the south of Maldon at 5.35 pm.

Meanwhile the more southerly of the German formations, that compris-

The opposing forces at 5.30 p.m.

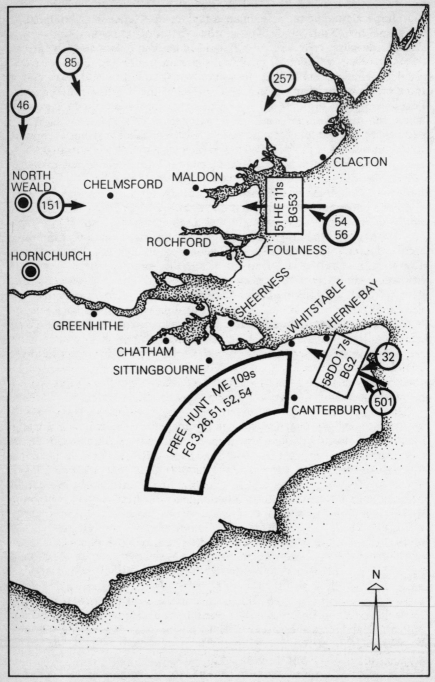

ing 58 Dorniers of Bomber Geschwader 2 and bound for Hornchurch, was over Herne Bay heading straight for its target. Two squadrons of fighters, Nos 32 and 501 with 15 Hurricanes, tried to get through to the bombers but on each occasion they found their way blocked by the escorting Messerschmitt 109s. Flight Lieutenant George Stoney of No 501 Squadron was leading his section towards the Dorniers when the Hurricanes came under attack from the IInd Gruppe of Fighter Geschwader 51. Stoney's comrades became embroiled with the German escorts, but he continued doggedly after his prey. Shortly afterwards, however, he was pounced on by a Messerschmitt piloted by Hauptmann Josef Foezoe, a 27-year-old Viennese. Foezoe later wrote how he had seen the lone Hurricane going in to attack: 'A very brave man, he was the only English fighter in the whole wide area. It was easy to dive down and open fire. He fell like a stone . . .' Stoney's Hurricane plunged into the ground near Chartham, the gallant pilot still on board. Then No 501 Squadron counter-attacked and two of the unit's Polish pilots, Flying Officer Stefan Witorzenc and Pilot Officer Pawel Zenker, each shot down a Messerschmitt 109 into the Thames estuary. Both of the German pilots were killed: one of them was 28-year-old Hauptmann Horst Tietzen, at the time the fourth highest-scoring German fighter pilot credited with seven victories over Spain and twenty more during the Second World War; the other pilot killed was Leutnant Hans-Otto Lessing, the young man who had written such a confident letter to his parents only the day before.

Meanwhile the Hurricanes of No 32 Squadron, led by Squadron Leader Mike Crossley, joined battle with the Messerschmitt 109s of the IIIrd Gruppe of Fighter Geschwader 26 which were also protecting the Dorniers. Flight Lieutenant Peter Brothers watched the Messerschmitts streaking in to attack as his squadron tried to get at the bombers. 'We broke formation as they came in and opened fire and I turned sharply right, on to the tail of an Me 109 as he overtook me,' he later wrote. 'I gave a quick glance behind to ensure that there was not another on my tail, laid my sight on him and fired a short burst. It hit him, another short burst and he caught fire and his dive steepened. I followed him down, he went into a field at a steep angle and a cloud of flame and black smoke erupted.' It seemed that Pilot Officer Boleslaw Wlasnowolski also hit the same Messerschmitt, for he too claimed it. Their victim crashed near Chilham killing the pilot, 22-year-old Leutnant Gerhard Mueller-Duhe.

Approximate position of the opposing forces at 5.30 pm. The 58 Dornier 17s of Bomber Geschwader 2, escorted by some 25 Messerschmitt 109s of Fighter Geschwader 51, are passing Herne Bay on their way to bomb the airfield at Hornchurch; the Hurricanes of Nos 32 and 501 are trying to fight their way through to the bombers, but German fighters block each attack. Meanwhile the 51 Heinkel 111s of Bomber Geschwader 53, escorted by some 25 Messerschmitt 110s of Destroyer Geschwader 26, are just crossing the Essex coast on their way to bomb the airfield at North Weald; they are under attack from the Spitfires of No 54 Squadron and the Hurricanes of No 56 Squadron. About a hundred Messerschmitt 109s of Fighter Geschwader 3, 26, 51, 52 and 54 are moving in across Kent on free-hunting patrols to support the attacks. Nos 46, 85, 151 and 257 Squadrons, with a total of 49 Hurricanes, are moving in to attack the North Weald attacking force.

During the dogfight that then developed, Crossley, Pilot Officer Alan Eckford and Pilot Officer Karol Pniak all made claims. It is likely that all three fired at the same Messerschmitt and saw it go down: that flown by Leutnant Walter Blume, which crashed at Kingston near Canterbury. Blume was picked up severely injured and taken prisoner.

The Messerschmitts then counter-attacked sharply and knocked down three Hurricanes, those of Crossley, Pilot Officer de Grunne and Sergeant Pearce. All three pilots parachuted to safety, de Grunne and Pearce with burns. Of the German pilots involved in the action Leutnant Josef Buerschgens claimed two British fighters shot down, Leutnants Heinz Ebeling and Gustav Sprick claimed one each.

Unmolested, the formation of Dorniers continued westwards past Whitstable and over the Isle of Sheppey. Then, as the bombers neared Sheerness, they came within range of the anti-aircraft gun batteries defending the naval dockyard at Chatham. Along the south of the Thames estuary, between Sittingbourne and Greenhithe, were fifteen gun positions with a total of sixty 4.5-in or 3.7-in heavy guns. These now began engaging the bombers with four-gun salvoes. Wreathed in black shell bursts, the Dorniers opened ranks a little and continued doggedly on.

It was 5.40 pm and so far the two German formations had survived their encounters with the defences with the loss of but a single bomber (Walter Leber's Heinkel). Now, however, the perfidious British summer weather was moving to protect the bombers' targets far more effectively than could any man-made defensive system. Throughout the day low cloud had been drifting south-eastwards across central England, accompanied by some drizzle rain. By 5 pm North Weald was reporting five-tenths stratocumulus cloud at 5,000 feet. During the next half hour the cloud cover became almost complete and its base fell to 3,500 feet. At Hornchurch it was a similar story. For the German formation leaders the implications of this unexpected build-up of cloud ahead were clear enough: the raiders, flying above 12,000 feet, could not put bombs down on targets they could not see; and at this stage of the war the German orders strictly forbade indiscriminate bombing. There was no alternative, and accordingly both formations wheeled round and headed for home.

When the more northerly of the German formations began its turn elements of four British fighter squadrons had it in sight and were about to pounce. Nos 85 and 151 Squadrons and Red Section of No 46 Squadron, with 28 Hurricanes, were manoeuvring into position for a head-on attack. No 256 Squadron, with twelve Hurricanes, was approaching the German formation from behind. The sight of such a large enemy force turning tail and running for home, without a shot having been fired, was like a tonic to the watching British fighter pilots. 'We climbed to 10,000 feet to the east of the aerodrome and had just reached that height below the clouds, when immediately in front of us appeared large formations of enemy bombers,' wrote Flying Officer Richard Milne of No 151 Squadron, which had taken off from North Weald. 'There were other Hurricane squadrons waiting and this sight was too much for them. The complete formation turned to port and commenced heading in the opposite direction.'

On the ground below, at Galleywood just to the south of Chelmsford, 15-year-old Ron Lodge also watched the German formation wheeling round above. 'Forty-five German planes came over, but turned back when 12 fighters met them,' he noted in his diary. To those observing the scene from the ground it seemed that the accounts in the British newspapers, of hoards of German bombers fleeing before a few Spitfires or Hurricanes, really were true. It was, he recalled, 'a most impressive air action'.

Emboldened by the sight of the enemy fleeing in front of them the Hurricane pilots sped after the bombers. Milne was one of the first to attack. 'The bombers were now flying very fast and using full throttle. I encountered fire from the rear gunner but this was not accurate as I kept the rudder of the enemy aircraft between us. I opened fire and after four seconds smoke commenced to come from both motors,' he later wrote. 'I continued firing and was enveloped in the oil and smoke from the enemy aircraft. This got thicker and I could only see the wing tips as I came to the end of my ammunition.' Then Milne had to break away as tracer came flashing past his Hurricane from one of the German escorts. 'I half rolled hard and evaded the rest of his attack. As I glanced behind I saw the Heinkel explode and huge pieces fly off.'

Milne's victim was the Heinkel carrying 34-year-old Major Reinhold Tamm, the commander of the IInd Gruppe of Bomber Geschwader 53. The bomber crashed into the sea just off the coast, taking with it all six men on board.

Wing Commander Victor Beamish, the station commander at North Weald, was flying with No 151 Squadron on this occasion and he plunged into the Heinkels after Milne. Beamish's Hurricane suffered heavily from the German return fire, however, and he had to break away. Also with the squadron was Flight Lieutenant Dick Smith, flying the 'heavy old cow' Hurricane with two 20-mm cannon; he tried to get into position to open fire with his heavy armament, but each attempt was frustrated by the poor performance of his aircraft and the ever-present German escorts.

The Messerschmitts then counter-attacked and shot down two Hurricanes of No 151 Squadron, killing one of the pilots and severely wounding the other.

Next to engage were the twelve Hurricanes of No 257 Squadron, led by Squadron Leader Hill Harkness. The other sections became entangled with the German escorts but Red Section, led by Flight Lieutenant Hugh Beresford, succeeded in getting through to the bombers. Beresford scored hits on one of the Heinkels, then had to break away to avoid an attack from a Messerschmitt 110. Sergeant A. Girdwood, following Beresford, then took up the attack and saw his own rounds striking the bomber. Then, suddenly: 'As I broke away, bullets entered my cockpit which exploded and caught fire. After a struggle I managed to bale out and as I fell I succeeded in pulling the ripcord and in untwisting the lines which wound round my legs,' he later reported. 'After that I was nearly strangled by the lines which got entangled round my neck. A toe of my right foot was fractured by a bolt which was forced into it by a bullet.' Severely shocked, Girdwood landed on Foulness Island not far from Walter Leber's Heinkel. His injuries, mental and physical, must have been more severe than his report suggested for he later succumbed to them.

Flight Lieutenant Alexander Rabagliati led in the three Hurricanes of Red Section of No 46 Squadron, having become separated from the rest of the squadron in the patchy cloud. A further problem was caused by 'jamming from enemy R/T, whose conversations could be plainly heard'. The section entered the dogfight with the German escorts; they would be the only aircraft from No 12 Group to take part in the engagement.

Shortly afterwards thirteen Hurricanes from No 85 Squadron, led by 25-year-old Squadron Leader Peter Townsend, also joined the fight. Townsend's first attempt to lead his force against the bombers was blocked by the Messerschmitt 110 escorts. He fired at one and saw it keel over and spiral away. 'A general engagement was now taking place, enemy aircraft consisting chiefly of Me 110s. The main formation of bombers had now turned east. After a bit of general messing about with Me 110s I encountered four or five Me 109s,' Townsend later reported. The Messerschmitt 109s belonged to the IIIrd Gruppe of Fighter Geschwader 51, providing top cover for the Heinkels.

While the engagement was in full swing the German formation was making its way south-eastwards towards the coast. The fight passed over Rochford, and as they crossed the coast at Shoeburyness several of the Heinkels aimed their bombs at the town's army barracks and railway station.

Around the bombers there were scores of venomous little confrontations, as other British fighter squadrons picked their way through the cloud patches and joined the fray. Sergeant John Etherington of No 17 Squadron became separated from the rest of the Hurricanes of his unit and suddenly found himself in the middle of the fight. 'It was a proper mix-up. I was going in one direction and the other squadrons came from the opposite direction. I attacked a Messerschmitt 110 and almost collided with a British fighter attacking the same aircraft. Someone had a go at me – I saw tracer coming past – I did not hang round to find out who it was,' he recounted. Etherington then attacked one of the German bombers, '. . . and came within inches of colliding with a Hurricane. I had a couple of bursts at a 109, then it was all over. One moment the air was full of aircraft blazing away at each other and the next the sky was empty, almost like a dream.'

Squadron Leader David Pemberton was leading the twelve Hurricanes of No 1 Squadron through cloud layers over Southend, at 21,000 feet, when a similar number of Messerschmitt 109s of Fighter Geschwader 3 dived on them. The Hurricanes easily avoided the attack, then Pemberton was able to pull round on to the tail of one of the Messerschmitts which was straggling behind the others. The German pilot tried to shake off the Hurricane by diving away to the south, but Pemberton followed. The high-speed chase continued across the Thames estuary, then across Kent almost at ground level. 'I gave it a two-second burst from about 260 yards, which made him go down, and the enemy aircraft hedge-hopped through Kent. I withheld my fire for some time in the hope he would go down, but when it started to regain some height I gave him a short burst at 500 feet.' The Messerschmitt burst into flames and crashed into the ground near Staplehurst, killing the pilot.

Joachim Koepsell also found the cloud patches a problem as he and his comrades tried to cover the withdrawal of the bombers. He swung his Messerschmitt 110 round to chase a Hurricane off the tail of a couple of straggling Heinkels, then his radio operator warned him that a second Hurricane was diving on them from the left. Koepsell tried to shake off his assailant, but the more manoeuvrable British fighter slid round easily on to his tail. Koepsell still had a trick up his sleeve, however. He waited until his radio operator called that the Hurricane was opening fire, then he pushed hard on the control column so that the nose of the Messerschmitt went down in a violent bunt which lifted both Germans off their seats and hard against their shoulder straps. From experience Koepsell knew that if the British fighter tried to follow this manoeuvre the Merlin engine's float carburettor would shut off the fuel, the engine would cut out for a few critical seconds and the pursuer would drop back. This was exactly what happened. Determinedly the Hurricane came in for a second attack and Koepsell bunted clear again, diving away. After avoiding four attacks in this way the Messerschmitt and the Hurricane were screaming down almost vertically and the surface of the sea was getting uncomfortably close. The British pilot broke off the chase and Koepsell had to haul back hard on his stick to level the Messerschmitt out a few hundred feet above the waves. His aircraft had taken a few hits, but none was serious. Koepsell looked around but could see no aircraft, friend or foe, so he turned southwards for home.

Thirty-one-year-old Hauptmann Herbert Kaminski, also flying one of the escorting Messerschmitt 110s, was not so fortunate. During his combat with British fighters his left rudder pedal was shot away from under his foot and his right engine was hit and began to trail smoke and lose revolutions. Desperately he tried to manoeuvre out of the fire from his attackers, but to no avail. On the next firing pass there was an explosion from the Messerschmitt's left engine and that one also began to falter. Kaminski pushed the crippled fighter down until it was flying only about 30 feet above the sea, trailing smoke. The British fighter pilots, out of ammunition or else convinced that the Messerschmitt was doomed, broke off the chase.

As the raiding formation pulled further and further away from the coast, the British fighters began to run out of ammunition or were low on fuel and had to break away. Finally only a few Hurricanes of Peter Townsend's squadron, No 85, were left in the fight.

Pilot Officer 'Nigger' Marshall went in so close to a Heinkel after his firing run that he collided with its tail, damaging the wing-tip of his Hurricane in the process. Marshall gingerly pulled away from the dogfight and turned for home, his throttle jammed in the fully-open position.

Flight Lieutenant 'Hammy' Hamilton, a Canadian, threaded his way past the Messerschmitt 110 escorts and succeeded in getting in a 5-second burst at one of the Heinkels. As he broke away he saw the bomber's

The opposing forces at 5.45 p.m.

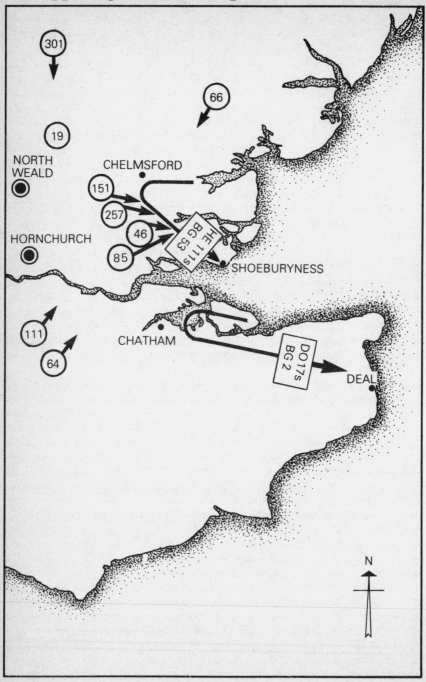

undercarriage flop down and heavy black smoke start to trail backwards from its engines. The Heinkel continued on its easterly heading, steadily losing height. It was the aircraft piloted by Unteroffizier Wilhelm Grasser of the IIIrd Gruppe of Bomber Geschwader 53; Grasser later ditched his Heinkel mid-way between Clacton and Ostend, and the crew took to their dinghy.

The action was not entirely one-sided, however. Pilot Officer 'Paddy' Hemmingway got into a fight with several Messerschmitt 110s and his Hurricane was hit in the engine. He broke off the action and headed for home, but on his way the engine faltered then stopped and he had to bale out into the sea off the Essex coast.

Flight Lieutenant Dick Lee was last seen 30 miles north-east of Margate pursuing three Messerschmitt 109s out to sea. It was an act brave to the point of foolhardiness and Lee, who had fought in France and already been credited with nine victories, should have known better. His body was never found.

In contrast to the northerly raiding force, that to the south was not molested by British fighters after the initial brush near Canterbury. The Dorniers of Bomber Geschwader 2 had turned away in time to avoid contact with the squadrons waiting for them over the eastern outskirts of London, and they cleared the Chatham gun-defended area without loss. As the bombers passed over the coast at Deal three of them pulled out of the formation and aimed their bombs at the Royal Marine Barracks there. Bombardier John Clark, 32, serving with the 75th Heavy Anti-Aircraft Regiment, watched the Dornier formation crossing the coast from his 3.7-in gun position D3, to the north of Dover. 'They appeared in the north-west coming straight at us, then turned east to avoid Dover. We opened on them as did D2 [the position to the east] but the range was extreme and the shooting not good,' he noted in his diary.

At the end of his parachute descent, following his brush with the Messerschmitts, Squadron Leader Mike Crossley of No 32 Squadron landed in an allotment in Gillingham. 'The Home Guard, a bit disappointed that I wasn't a German, took me to the Queen's Arms and got me plastered,' he later wrote.

Leutnant Walter Leber and his crew stood and sat round their battered Heinkel after it had crash-landed on Foulness Island, waiting to be taken prisoner. The pilot and navigator had avoided injury but the other three crew members were wounded, the flight engineer seriously. After a couple of minutes soldiers from the nearby searchlight site arrived on the scene and,

Approximate positions of the opposing forces at 5.45 pm. Both of the German bomber formations have been forced to abandon their attacks by cloud cover at the targets, and have turned round for home. The northerly force is under attack by 40 Hurricanes of Nos 46, 85, 151 and 257 Squadrons. The southerly force has avoided further attack by British fighters. Due to the turn away, Nos 19, 64, 66, 111 and 310 Squadrons, which had been ordered to move into position to block the anticipated line of advance of the German formations, fail to intercept.

having checked that the Germans were unarmed, ordered them to squat down on the grass. Thirty-two-year-old farm worker Bertie Shinn had watched the bomber come down from his home on New Marsh Farm, and ran over to see what he could do. He came upon a soldier standing over Leber who sat alone on the grass, and the captor asked him to keep an eye on the German pilot while he went for help to remove the prisoners. To Leber the change-over looked decidedly sinister: he had heard rumours of German aircrew being beaten up by civilians in England and it seemed that he was now being handed over to the man for this purpose. Squatting down on the grass Leber felt almost defenceless; to ward off the expected blow, he lifted his hand in front of his face. Bertie Shinn had no intention of striking the German pilot, however, and as Leber raised his hand it looked as if he was asking for a cigarette. Shinn reached into his pocket, pulled out a packet, and offered his last one. Leber did not smoke but, relieved at this unexpected turn of events, he thought to himself 'Now Walter, you start!' Gratefully he accepted the cigarette and light and puffed away as courtesy demanded. Shortly afterwards vehicles arrived to take the wounded men to hospital and the others into captivity; later Leber learned that his flight engineer had died soon after reaching hospital.

Flying Officer Innes Westmacott of No 56 Squadron eased his damaged Hurricane back to North Weald and set it down on the grass. He shut down the engine and as he was climbing out one of the ground crewmen called to him 'Come and look at this, Sir.' Just outside the port undercarriage leg an exploding cannon shell had blown out a complete panel from the underside of the wing, leaving a hole large enough for Westmacott to get his head and shoulders inside. On examination the fighter was found to have 26 other hits from machine gun fire. Exactly in the centre of the armour of Westmacott's seat, behind where the small of his back had been, lay embedded the hardened-steel core of a German armour-piercing bullet; had it not passed through one of the metal structural members of the rear fuselage on the way, the round would almost certainly have gone clean through the armour plating and into his body.

Flight Sergeant Taffy Higginson, also of No 56 Squadron, landed at North Weald and was about to taxi to his dispersal when the control column suddenly went limp in his hand: the elevator cable, shot through by an enemy bullet, had somehow held together until he was safely down. 'Thank God I didn't try a victory roll,' he later commented.

Pilot Officer 'Nigger' Marshall of No 85 Squadron returned to Debden with his throttle jammed wide open and the starboard wing of his Hurricane damaged after colliding with the Heinkel. He made a fast approach on the airfield, then shut down the engine and went gliding in. His brakes had been shot away, but skilfully he brought the fighter to a halt without further damage.

Heading for home in his badly damaged Messerschmitt 110, Herbert Kaminski did not get very far. First his right engine packed up, then the revolutions from that on the left slowly fell away. Unable to defy the laws of gravity any longer, the German pilot set the crippled fighter down on the sea.

The Messerschmitt rapidly sank and as the two crewmen struggled clear of it they found that their dinghy had been damaged and refused to inflate. Shortly afterwards a Heinkel 59 rescue floatplane arrived on the scene and circled the survivors, but the sea was too rough for the aircraft to alight. The would-be rescuers dropped another dinghy to the men in the water and, gratefully, Kaminksi and his radio operator inflated and boarded it.

Pilot Officer 'Paddy' Hemmingway of No 85 Squadron had only a life-jacket to support him when he came down in the Thames estuary about 12 miles off Clacton. After an hour and a half in the water, however, he was picked up by a boat from the nearby Barrow Deep lightship.

A couple of minutes after the Messerschmitt 110 hit by Colin Gray struck the ground near the centre of Clacton, fireman Frank Jeffries was on the scene with the local brigade. By a stroke of luck the aircraft had crashed not on houses but on Smith's Sandpits, a strip of waste land. 'The aircraft had just disappeared,' Jeffries recalled. 'There was nothing of the crew, nothing of the aircraft to identify it as a Messerschmitt; only a few unrecognisable pieces of aluminium.' Where the aircraft had plummeted into the ground there was a gaping hole in the sand with a pool of oil-flecked water in the bottom. Slowly the hole was filling in, as saturated sand oozed down the sides and into the water. Soon a large crowd of civilians gathered round the bizarre spectacle, with children hunting for souvenirs.* One who did not go to see it was Kathleen Watton; it was, after all, her wedding day.

After the Heinkels were clear of Shoeburyness and the bombs ceased exploding, 32-year-old air raid warden 'Lordy' Mercer had difficulty opening the door of his shelter in Elm Road; blast from a bomb exploding nearby had jammed it shut. In the end, however, he and the other wardens were able to force the door open and they found a 6-inch long bomb splinter embedded in it. Outside there was a lot of smoke about and the telephone lines running past the wardens' post were hanging down; beside his post ran a row of bomb craters. He and the other three wardens now went their separate ways, to see where the bombs had fallen and whether anyone was injured or trapped.

Altogether, 32 bombs had fallen on the town of Shoeburyness. One had landed beside an Anderson shelter in a garden in West Road, killing the man and his wife inside. Another landed on the signal box at the railway station, killing the signalman. And in a garden off the High Street a bomb had fallen beside an Anderson shelter, injuring five out of the seven people inside; by a grim irony the most seriously injured was the head of the family, a leading conscientious objector in the area. Two houses were damaged beyond repair and twenty more were seriously damaged. Several bombs fell on the War Department gunnery range to the south of the town, though without causing

---

* Later attempts to unearth the wreckage of the Messerschmitt were unsuccessful. Rods pushed down 19 feet into the soft sand failed to locate anything solid. The remains of the aircraft and its crew lie undisturbed to this day, underneath an industrial estate which was later built on the site.

any serious damage or injuries. Some two hundred bombs landed on the mud flats and sandbanks off the foreshore of Shoeburyness; many of these had delayed-action fuses, and would go off at irregular intervals during the hours that followed.

At Deal there were no casualties but some damage, after three of the Dorniers had released 24 bombs on the town. Bombs fell in Gladstone, Ravenscroft and Blenheim Roads, in Victoria Park, and on the evacuated Royal Marine infirmary. Redsull's furniture store in Gladstone Road was hit and burned to the ground, and three houses in Blenheim Road were damaged beyond repair.

During this final major attack on 18 August the raiding force lost four bombers destroyed and two damaged, and ten fighters destroyed and at least one damaged. Fighter Command lost nine aircraft destroyed and five damaged; three pilots were killed and three injured.

During the attacks the raiders had been foiled by cloud which blanketed their targets. This cut short the action and undoubtedly reduced losses on both sides. Of the 165 British fighters sent up to engage the raiders, only 103 were able to intercept. Of the 45 fighters sent from No 12 Group to engage the bombers only three, from No 46 Squadron, went into action. Not one of the ten cannon-armed fighters scrambled succeeded in getting into a firing position on an enemy aircraft.

That evening there was understandable jubilation amongst the defenders, that the large formations of German bombers had been forced to turn back obviously short of their objectives. The real reason for the turn-round is not mentioned in any of the British records, however. Major General Goschen, the General Officer Commanding the Chatham area, went so far as to send a congratulatory telegram to his gunners stating that their anti-aircraft fire 'definitely turned raiders away from their objectives – presumably Chatham dockyard'.

On the evening of 18 August the sun set at 8.16 pm and half an hour later it was almost dark. By this time the situation maps at the various Fighter Command operations rooms were almost clear of plots and the fighter controllers released their squadrons one by one. For the weary pilots, many of whom had been on duty since sunrise and flown three or more operational sorties, there would be time for a beer or two in the mess or the local pub before they flopped into their beds. For the ground crews, working in shifts, night was the time to patch up the aircraft ready for yet another day's fighting. Both the pilots and the aircraft had to be available to stand to at first light the next morning.

As darkness fell Wilhelm Grasser and his four comrades, survivors of the Heinkel 111 shot down by 'Hammy' Hamilton of No 85 Squadron, resignedly settled down to a miserable, cold night aboard their slopping dinghy; the following day they would be picked up and taken prisoner. A few miles away were Herbert Kaminksi and his radio operator, survivors from a Messerschmitt 110 which had ditched after being shot up by British fighters; the two men would have to spend four gruelling days on board their dinghy, before they were finally rescued by the German Navy. In spite of the discomfort, however, those in the dinghies were far better off than those without. When night came all of those in the water without a dinghy were either dead or about to die from exposure. During the weeks that followed the sea would disgorge most of their bodies along the shores on either side of the Channel.

Of the Germans who came down in England only one, Oberleutnant Helmut Tiedmann, was still free at nightfall. He had crash-landed his Messerschmitt 109 in open country at Leeds near Maidstone early in the afternoon, and was well clear before anyone else reached the scene. Able to speak fairly good English, he would have a few more hours' liberty before he was finally apprehended.

With the coming of darkness both sides sent night raiders to harass the enemy. The Luftwaffe sent 92 aircraft, drawn from Bomber Geschwader 1, 2, 3, 27 and 53, to bomb targets at Sheffield, Leeds, Hull, Colchester, Canvey Island, Manningtree and Sealand. British records mention damage only at the last of these, with a scattering of bombs spread widely over rural districts elsewhere.

Meanwhile, 36 Blenheims of Royal Air Force Bomber Command set out in ones and twos to attack over a score of airfields used by the Luftwaffe in France and Holland. Their sole success was at Flushing, attacked by a Blenheim of No 101 Squadron at about 10 pm, where two Messerschmitt 109s of Fighter Geschwader 54 suffered minor damage. At the same time four Whitleys were droning out to attack the Fiat works at Turin in northern Italy, and twenty more were heading for the aluminium works at Rheinfelden in southern Germany; Sunday 18 August would end before either force reached its target.

The final deaths on 18 August had little to do with the contest between Fighter Command and the Luftwaffe. Shortly before midnight a Heinkel 111 of Bomber Geschwader 27, piloted by Oberfeldwebel Alfred Dreher, attacked the flying training school at Windrush in Gloucestershire where night flying was in progress. The Heinkel dropped its bombs and machine-gunned the flare path, then pulled away probably for another strafing run. Suddenly the sky lit up as the bomber collided with an Anson piloted by Sergeant Bruce Hancock, a pupil on one of his first night solo flights. Whether it was a deliberate act of vengeance, or a simple flying accident, will never be known. Locked together the two aircraft fell blazing to the ground at Blackbitch Farm, Aldsworth. All five men on board were killed.

CHAPTER 5

18 August Summed Up

A big butcher's bill is not necessarily evidence of good tactics.
LORD WAVELL

During 18 August the Luftwaffe put up a total of about 970 sorties over England: some 495 by bombers, 460 by fighters and 15 by reconnaissance aircraft. Of these, about 170 of the bomber sorties were flown on the nights of the 17th and 18th; the remainder were flown during the daylight hours on the 18th. Less than half of the serviceable fighters and bombers available to Air Fleets 2 and 3 were involved in the action that day, so it is clear that the Luftwaffe was not greatly extended to provide forces for it. Air Fleet 5 took no part in the fighting, though its reconnaissance aircraft were active over northern England and Scotland.

Altogether the Luftwaffe lost 69 aircraft destroyed or damaged beyond repair as a result of its operations over Britain, during the 24-hour period under review. Of these 59 were lost to certain or probable action by fighters, 2 fell to ground fire, 4 to fighters and ground fire and one collided with a British training aircraft. The remaining three aircraft crashed in German-occupied territory at night due to technical or other failures. Altogether the loss represented about 7 per cent of the force committed. Twenty-nine of the German aircraft, or just under half of those brought down, crashed in England. In the course of the action the Luftwaffe lost 94 aircrew killed, 40 taken prisoner and 25 returned with wounds. Twenty-seven German aircraft returned with repairable damage.

Because of the gross under-estimate of Fighter Command's strength issued to Luftwaffe units, the British reaction was much stronger than expected. In fact, during the 24-hour period, Fighter Command put up a total of 927 sorties or only slightly fewer than the Luftwaffe. Forty-one of the sorties were flown by night, 28 on the 17th/18th and 13 on the 18th/19th. The remaining 886 sorties were flown by day, a number almost exactly equal to the 861 serviceable Spitfire, Hurricane, Defiant and Gladiator day fighters available to the squadrons. This average operational sortie rate of one per serviceable fighter was not spread evenly throughout the Command, however. Nos 12 and 13 Groups in the Midlands and north of Britain, with between them about a third of the serviceable fighters, put up 129 or only 15 per cent of the day sorties and of these only three made contact with the enemy. As is to be expected, No 11 Group in the south-east made by far the greatest effort: with just over a third of the serviceable fighters it put up nearly 600 sorties, or more than two-thirds of the total; on the average, each of its serviceable Spitfires and Hurricanes flew 1.7 operational sorties. And even beyond this there were great variations in squadron effort, with some of No 11 Group's units committed far more often than others: No 43

Squadron, which was worked hardest that day, flew 63 operational sorties or an average of nearly five from each of the 13 Hurricanes serviceable at the beginning of the day.

Surprisingly only 403, or about 45 per cent, of the operational sorties put up by Fighter Command during the daylight hours of 18 August were to counter the three major attacks by the Luftwaffe. A further 56, or just over 6 per cent, were standing patrols to protect shipping off the coast. Most of the remaining 427 sorties, nearly half of the total, were attempts to intercept German reconnaissance aircraft over Britain. Provided there was no more potent threat in the offing, several half-squadrons would be ordered up against each of these difficult targets to chase them away or, hopefully, shoot them down. At first sight the use of so many British fighters against the unarmed reconnaissance aircraft might seem excessive. But, as we have seen, the results were well worth the effort involved. By threatening each incursion and forcing the reconnaissance aircraft to remain high, the fighters prevented the German crews from descending to lower altitudes where they could take high-resolution photographs of the airfields in southern England. And, because the German Intelligence officers could not determine which airfields were used by Fighter Command and which were used by other aircraft, much of the German effort was dissipated against non-fighter airfields (specifically, on 18 August, against Gosport, Ford and Thorney Island).

Of the 403 sorties put up by Fighter Command to meet the major German attacks, 320 of those by Spitfires and Hurricanes made contact with the enemy. Thus 80 per cent of the fighters ordered to intercept the major attacks actually did so, and the proportion would have almost certainly been far higher had not the bombers turned round short of their targets during the last attack. Thirty-one British fighters, or about 10 per cent of those engaging, were destroyed or damaged beyond repair in aerial combat.

Of the 320 fighters involved in the three major actions, 110 were Spitfires and 210 were Hurricanes; this was in almost direct proportion to the number of each type in service in the Fighter Command squadrons. What was the relative effectiveness of each type in combat? Probably 59 German aircraft were destroyed or damaged beyond repair during the day by fighters; of these 29 can be allocated either to Spitfires or Hurricanes acting alone, 10 to Spitfires and 19 to Hurricanes. From this admittedly small sample, the number of victories scored by each type on this day appears to have been in almost direct proportion to the number engaging. In other words, in spite of its lower performance, a Hurricane was as likely to score a 'kill' as was a Spitfire. On the average, during the major actions, one German aircraft was destroyed or damaged beyond repair for every six Spitfires or Hurricanes which engaged or for every seven which took off to engage.

Of the 31 British fighters destroyed or damaged beyond repair 25 fell to enemy fighter action, 2 to return fire from the bombers, one was shot down by British ground fire and the cause of the remaining three losses cannot be established. Twenty-six of the fighters lost were Hurricanes and five were

Spitfires. Allowing for the difference in the numbers present, it can be seen that the Spitfire's better performance meant that it was almost three times more likely to survive contact with the enemy than was the Hurricane.

During the 18 August action ten British fighter pilots were killed and one died of wounds later. Nineteen pilots were wounded, in eleven cases so seriously that they took little or no further part in the Battle of Britain.

During the German attacks on Kenley, Croydon and Manston, Fighter Command lost two Spitfires and six Hurricanes destroyed on the ground. Twenty-eight aircraft of other types were also destroyed on the ground, in the course of attacks on other airfields. Thus, with the 31 fighters destroyed in the air and the Anson lost in the collision, a total of 68 British aircraft were destroyed or damaged beyond repair on 18 August; this was *one less* than the Luftwaffe lost. Of the British aircraft losses, however, 17 were training or other non-operational types.

The action had shown that against low-flying aircraft, if there was warning of their approach, ground fire from light machine guns, Bofors guns and even parachute-and-cable barrages could be lethal. During the day these were primarily responsible for the destruction of two German aircraft, they shared four more with fighters and damaged at least eight others. In a confused tactical situation, however, the ground gunners could be as dangerous to friend as to foe: on 18 August they shot down one Hurricane, possibly shot down a second and damaged a third.

On 18 August the German bombers' intended targets were strictly military in nature; and for the most part their attacks were remarkably discriminate. As a result there were only thirteen deaths in non-military areas. Fifty-one people, service and civilian, were killed during the attacks on military establishments. Of these 28, or over half, died at Ford where the local all-clear was issued prematurely and many were caught unprepared when the dive-bombers attacked.

Of the fighter airfields bombed, Kenley was put out of action but only for about two hours. Biggin Hill continued operating. One of the two radar sets at Poling was heavily damaged, but the other was untouched and continued operating; and along the coast for 70 miles on either side of Poling there were six other radar stations providing interlocking cover, so there was no hole in the radar screen which the Luftwaffe could exploit.

Of the German attacks, the most devastating had been those by the low-flyers and the dive-bombers. The nine Dorniers of the 9th Staffel of Bomber Geschwader 76 carried only about nine tons of bombs between them; a Gruppe of Stukas carried about 13 tons; yet in each case, because of their pin-point bombing accuracy, these units caused considerable damage to their targets. In contrast the attack on Biggin Hill by sixty Heinkels flying at altitudes above 12,000 feet, during which more than 80 tons of bombs were dropped, achieved minimal results.

The laurels for the day's action went to the defenders. The aim of the Luftwaffe was to wear down Fighter Command without suffering excessive losses in the process, and in this it had failed. It had cost the attackers five aircrew killed, wounded, or taken prisoner, for each British pilot casualty. In terms of aircraft, it had cost the Luftwaffe five bombers and fighters for every three Spitfires or Hurricanes destroyed in the air or on the ground. If the battle continued at this rate the Luftwaffe would wreck Fighter Command, but it would come close to wrecking itself in the process.

How well did the German attacks on 18 August fit in with the general aim of destroying Fighter Command as an effective fighting force? It will be remembered that there were four means open to the Luftwaffe to achieve this: to attack targets of such importance that Fighter Command would be drawn into action with the German fighter force; to attack British fighter airfields; to attack the British fighter control system and radar stations; and to attack the British factories producing fighters.

From the viewpoint of target selection, Air Fleet 2 was well used on that day. The targets chosen, Kenley, Biggin Hill, Hornchurch and North Weald, were No.11 Group's four most important airfields for the defence of south-eastern England. Not only would the destruction of the facilities at these airfields have hit the Group hard, but such objectives were certain to draw the defending fighters into action. The attempt at the co-ordinated attack on Kenley by Bomber Geschwader 76 was a risky venture: it depended on accurate navigation and timing by three separate forces and, given the unpredictability of the weather over northern Europe, had only an even chance of success; in the event the plan came unstuck, and the 9th Staffel paid a heavy price. The late afternoon attacks on Hornchurch and North Weald had to be abandoned because of the unexpected cloud, but the German formation leaders never lost control of the situation.

Due to faulty Intelligence, the target selection of Air Fleet 3 was not so good as that of its easterly neighbour. The radar station at Poling was part of the Fighter Command system and so an attack on it could degrade the defensive system. But Ford, Gosport and Thorney Island airfields were not used by Fighter Command and were therefore not relevant to the main battle.

Nor was the tactical handling of Air Fleet 3 good on that day. The attacking force and its escorting fighters were split between four targets on a thirty-mile front. By chance more than half of the defending fighters went into action against one of the four attacking formations, with disastrous results for the Stuka Gruppe concerned. The huge force of Messerschmitts covering the attacks, which outnumbered the defending fighter force in the area by more than two to one, would have been far more effective both in protecting the dive-bombers and shooting down British fighters if the targets had been closer together and the force more concentrated.

Considering the weight of the attack on the airfields very few British fighters – only eight – were destroyed on the ground. This was because the vast majority of the squadrons remained at a high state of readiness during the daylight hours, and the warnings from the radar chain and the Observer Corps usually gave them plenty of time to get into the air before an attack developed. The successful strafing attack on Manston by the Messerschmitt 109s of Fighter Geschwader 52, which destroyed or damaged most of No

266 Squadron's Spitfires and a Hurricane of No 17 Squadron while they were drawn up for rapid refuelling, depended on a combination of circumstances which would not occur often during the battle.

Regarding the direction of the British fighter squadrons, there is little that can be criticised. All three major attacks were engaged by a sizeable proportion of the fighters available in their respective areas. Four-fifths of the fighters sent to intercept these attacks actually did so, a commendable performance by the fighter controllers; and the proportion would certainly have been higher had not the late afternoon raiders turned back short of their targets. The No 11 and No 12 Group controllers worked together well and the latter put up 45 fighters to cover the former's airfields; only three of these went into action but, again, more would certainly have done so had the raiders not turned back short of their targets during the final attack.

Several of those involved in the action on 18 August received decorations. Of these the highest was the Ritterkreuz, the Third Reich's successor to the coveted 'Blue Max' of the First World War; this was awarded to navigator Oberfeldwebel Wilhelm-Friedrich Illg of the 9th Staffel of Bomber Geschwader 76, for bringing back the Dornier after the pilot had been mortally wounded.

For his conspicuous display of courage Lance Sergeant William Button, who had been leading the disposal team which lost most of its members when the delayed-action bomb they were working on exploded, received the Empire Gallantry Medal.

Of the Scots Guardsmen involved in the defence of Kenley, Second Lieutenant J. Hague received the Military Cross and Lance Corporals Gale and Miller received the Military Medal. It was the first time, in the 298-year history of the Regiment, that any of its members had been decorated for gallantry under fire within the British Isles. Private Joseph Lister of the Border Regiment, who suffered the loss of his right leg following his courageous effort to beat off the strafing attack on Manston, also received the Military Medal.

Several servicewomen displayed exemplary conduct that day, at installations under attack. WAAF Sergeant Elizabeth Mortimer received the Military Medal for helping to defuse unexploded bombs on the airfield at Biggin Hill. So did Corporal Joan Avis Hearn, who remained at her post at Poling radar station as the bombs were bursting around her. At Ford Leading Wren Nina Marsh and Wren Irene Marriott both received the British Empire Medal, for devotion to duty after they themselves had suffered wounds.

Apart from Wilhelm-Friedrich Illg, none of the aircrew on either side were decorated solely for what they had done on 18 August. Several of those who played leading parts in the action were later decorated, however. Don MacDonell, Mike Crossley, Colin Gray, Richard Milne, Kenneth Lee, 'Humph' Russell, Frank Carey, 'Squeak' Weaver, Alan Eckford, Peter Brothers, Bob Doe, Eric Marrs, Innes Westmacott and Peter Townsend all received the Distinguished Flying Cross. Basil Whall, Herbert Hallowes and 'Taffy' Higginson received the Distinguished Flying Medal. On the German side Gerhard Schoepfel, Erbo von Kageneck, Karl Henze, Otto Schmidt, Ernst Duellberg, Helmut Bruck, Josef Foezoe, Heinz Ebeling and Helmut Bode all later received the Ritterkreuz. Horst Tietzen, who was killed on 18 August, received the award posthumously.

Having looked at the action on 18 August in some detail, let us now consider its significance within the Battle of Britain as a whole. Why should it deserve the title 'The Hardest Day'? Its claim to this title rests on the fact that on this day both of the main contestants, Fighter Command and the Luftwaffe, suffered a greater number of aircraft destroyed or damaged than on any other day during the Battle of Britain. The Luftwaffe had 100 aircraft put out of action, 69 of them wrecked or damaged beyond repair. Fighter Command had 73 fighters put out of action, 39 of them wrecked or damaged beyond repair. A further 62 British aircraft of other types were destroyed or damaged during the attacks on airfields, 29 of them wrecked or damaged beyond repair. Never before during the battle, nor afterwards, would the two sides suffer such heavy material losses during a single day.

CHAPTER 6

What the Papers Said

*In time of war the nation is always of one mind,
eager to hear something good of themselves, and ill
of the enemy. At this time the task of news-writers
is easy: they have nothing to do but tell that the
battle is expected, and afterwards that a battle has
been fought, in which we and our friends, whether
conquering or conquered, did all, and our enemies
did nothing.*
SAMUEL JOHNSON

Having seen what did happen on Sunday 18 August 1940, how accurately
were the events reported in each side's newspapers immediately afterwards?

In its issue of 19 August, *The Times* carried the headline:

GERMANY'S HEAVIEST AIR DEFEAT
140 Machines Shot Down Out of 600

An initial Air Ministry communiqué on the previous day's fighting was then
given, which stated:

> In the raids upon this country at mid day today bombs were dropped in the
> outer fringe of the South London area, in Kent and in other parts of
> South-Eastern and Southern England. Information so far available shows
> that some civilian casualties were caused in the neighbourhood of Croydon.
> Elsewhere the number of casualties was small and damage was slight.
>
> This evening large formations of enemy aircraft again crossed the
> South-East coast near Dover and North Foreland. These formations
> attempted to penetrate the London defences along both sides of the
> Thames Estuary but were broken up by our attacking fighters and were
> driven back over Kent and Essex . . .

As further reports came in, the defenders' claim of the number of enemy
aircraft destroyed rose still higher, until the final communiqué on the day's
fighting which announced:

> Latest reports show that 144 German bombers and fighters were destroyed
> during Sunday's engagement, of which 13 were brought down by anti-
> aircraft guns and two by Lewis gun crews at searchlight posts. Twenty-two
> British fighters were lost. Twelve of the pilots are now known to be safe.

In the narrowest sense, the headline in *The Times* was correct: 18 August
had indeed seen the heaviest aircraft casualties for the Luftwaffe during the
attacks on England. However the Fighter Command estimate of 650 enemy
aircraft involved in the three major attacks had somehow dropped to 600 in
the communiqué; this served to make the proportion claimed destroyed

seem all the larger. The figure of 144 enemy aircraft claimed destroyed by the defences, an overclaim of more than two to one, was broken down as follows: to Fighter Command 126; to Coastal Command (the Blenheim fighters at Thorney Island) 2; in collision with a British aircraft (the Anson at Windrush) 1; to ground fire 15. These figures were identical to those issued by the various military commands, and were not 'doctored' before their issue to the press.

Looking at Fighter Command's actual losses, it is difficult to reconcile these with the 22 aircraft admitted lost in the communiqué: during the day ten fighter pilots were killed in their aircraft, 17 more abandoned them in flight, 4 fighters returned too badly damaged for repair and 8 more were destroyed on the ground during the attacks on airfields. There was no mention of the 28 other aircraft which were destroyed on the ground, nor of any damage at the airfields which came under attack.

So much for the reliability of the British official communiqués. What about those of the Germans? The official communiqué issued by the Wehrmacht High Command on 19 August, and used as the basis for reports in the German newspapers, stated:

> The Luftwaffe, as partially reported in previous special announcements, has had new successes on 18 August. Formations of German aircraft have attacked militarily important targets in southern and central England, such as industrial works, railways, anti-aircraft gun positions and above all airfields around London and in the counties of Kent and Hampshire, with considerable effect ... The enemy losses yesterday amounted to 147 aircraft. Of these 124 fell in aerial combat and 23 were destroyed on the ground or were brought down by Flak. In addition, 33 barrage balloons were destroyed. Thirty-six German aircraft did not return.

Once again the number of enemy aircraft claimed destroyed was in exaggeration by more than two to one; and the figures issued by the Luftwaffe seemed high enough and were not inflated by Dr Goebbels's propaganda service before they were issued to the press. The reference to aircraft brought down by Flak concerned a single Blenheim claimed by gunners in France on the night of the 18th; British records mention no such loss. As in the case of the British reports, the main area for 'doctoring' was in the Germans' own admitted losses. The term 'failed to return' was used by both sides and could, and frequently did, conceal a host of losses; it meant that aircraft that reached friendly territory in whatever state, even if they crashed or landed beyond hope of repair, were not included in the loss total. Sixty German aircraft 'failed to return' on 18 August; the communiqué admitted 36 of these, just over half.

Looking at both side's figures for the day, actual and released, one finds certain similarities in the way they were distorted to present the required picture. In the case of the losses claimed to have been inflicted on the enemy, both air forces reported figures so impressively large that the propagandists felt that they could safely be issued to the press without further adjustment. The reasons for overclaiming during an air combat are well known, and the reader has seen specific instances of this during the 18 August action; for the most part the aircrews' claims were honestly made though, as survivors readily admit, it was easy to be mistaken in the heat of combat. In the case of each side's admitted losses, these were reduced in two distinct stages. First there was the play on words, to reduce the number of aircraft lost without seeming to do so: the British by mentioning only those Fighter Command aircraft destroyed in air combat, and quietly ignoring everything else; the Germans by mentioning only those aircraft that 'failed to return'. The resultant figure was then reduced by nearly half, in each case, before release to the public.

For the 18 August action there is a certain touching symmetry in the figures each side's propagandists thought the public would swallow. The British communiqué claimed 144 German aircraft destroyed whereas in fact there were 69 and the Germans admitted 36; the German communiqué claimed 147 British aircraft destroyed, whereas in fact there were 68 and the British admitted 23. As Dean Acheson once remarked, propaganda is that branch of the art of lying which consists in very nearly deceiving your friends, without quite deceiving your enemies.

CHAPTER 7

With Hindsight

History is written for schoolmasters and armchair
strategists. Statesmen and warriors pick their way
through the dark
LORD ESHER

It now remains to assess the importance of the 18 August action within the context of the Battle of Britain, and the Battle of Britain within the context of the Second World War.

Although the action on 18 August resulted in the two sides having more aircraft put out of action than during any other day's engagement fought over England, the action was not in itself decisive. Rather it was just one action, albeit a particularly costly one, in a protracted battle of attrition. Those who took part in or were affected by the day's fighting remember it only as it involved them personally; for many of those at Ford, or at or around Kenley, or who had something particularly frightening happen to them in the air, 18 August is remembered as 'the hardest day'. Others, elsewhere, have different dates they remember as being the hardest.

The only major effect of the 18 August action on the course of the Battle of Britain was that after it the bulk of the Junkers 87 dive-bomber units, the Stukas, were withdrawn from the action. Thereafter this type was used over England only rarely, and in small numbers. Since they represented the only really effective anti-shipping force available to the Luftwaffe at that time, the Stukas had to be conserved to support the planned invasion.

On 19 August the weather broke and for five days large-scale air operations were not possible. When the onslaught against Fighter Command's airfields was resumed, on the 24th, the two sides fought with renewed vigour but with somewhat greater circumspection.

Considering the Battle of Britain as a whole, what were the chances of the Luftwaffe succeeding in its aim of smashing Fighter Command as an effective fighting force? Given the German resources, how effective were the four methods of attack open to the Luftwaffe: destruction of the British fighters in the air by forcing them into action with German fighters and bombers; destruction of the Fighter Command airfields; destruction of the British fighter control system; and destruction of the British factories building fighters?

Certainly the bomber attacks on militarily important targets in south-eastern England did succeed in their aim of bringing Fighter Command into action. But the Luftwaffe fighter force did not enjoy a sufficiently great quantitative or qualitative advantage over the defenders to enable it to inflict the desired heavy losses. Moreover, because most of the pilots and crewmen

who were shot down landed in England, these actions resulted in dispropor-
tionately high losses to the Luftwaffe in trained personnel.

Nor were the attacks on the airfields particularly effective, even when
they did hit those used by Fighter Command. During the action on 18
August the Luftwaffe mounted heavy attacks on two major Fighter Command airfields, Kenley and Biggin Hill. Kenley was put out of action for two
hours; Biggin Hill was not out of action on that day or any other, in spite
of repeated attacks. Against airfields the Luftwaffe would employ forces of
about fifty twin-engined bombers, carrying between 60 and 85 tons of
bombs. In fact, as has been borne out during numerous later conflicts, many
hundreds of tons of bombs are needed and attacks have to be repeated at
frequent intervals, if airfields are to be kept out of action. It was a relatively
simple matter to fill bomb craters in the landing grounds with rubble and roll
them flat; once this had been done the fighters could operate again. At
fighter airfields most of the buildings were desirable rather than essential: if
barracks and messes were hit, the men and women could be billeted in the
surrounding towns and villages; if the hangars and workshops were hit,
engineering work could take place in the open in the blast pens (it was, after
all, high summer). And even if, as a result of repeated heavy attacks, some of
the fighter airfields in south-eastern England had to be abandoned, there
were literally scores of actual or potential landing grounds in the area that
could have been used in their place. Almost any firm, flat piece of ground
700 yards long and 100 yards wide could have been used to operate Spitfires
or Hurricanes. So the most the Luftwaffe could have achieved by a protracted offensive against the Fighter Command airfields was to force the
British squadrons to operate off improvised field landing grounds – which
was exactly what a large part of the Luftwaffe was doing in France. All of this
leads to the general conclusion that, given the size of the bomb loads and the
number of bombers available in the summer of 1940, the Luftwaffe could
not have knocked out sufficient of Fighter Command's airfields for long
enough to seriously reduce the latter's effectiveness. The effect of the
attacks on the British fighter airfields could be likened to a father whose
chest is being pummelled by his nine-year-old son's fists: the blows were
uncomfortable, at times they were painful; but they were never going to be
lethal to the system as a whole.

Nor did the radar stations or the system of fighter control represent an
easy target for the Luftwaffe to attack. In each case the radar stations were
small, pin-point targets, virtually impossible to hit except by dive-bombers
or low-flying attackers; and during the action on 18 August both of the latter
were shown to be vulnerable to fighter and gun defences. Not only were the
radar stations difficult to hit, but when they were damaged equipment could
be replaced quickly; rarely were stations out of action for more than a couple
of days. Moreover, Fighter Command possessed a reserve of mobile radar
sets which could be erected near stations knocked out, to fill gaps in the radar
chain. Of the fighter control rooms, those at the Group Headquarters were
deep underground and invulnerable. Some of the Sector operations buildings, like that at Tangmere, were in concrete bunkers; others, like those at

Kenley or Biggin Hill, were in unhardened brick buildings. But in either case these were small pin-point targets, difficult to hit even if the Germans had known where they were – and they did not. Cutting the land lines which linked the various operations rooms with the fighter squadrons, the radar stations and the Observer Corps posts could and did slow the operation of the defences. But the buried cables were invisible from the air; when Sector operations buildings or land lines were damaged by bombing it was by stray bombs intended for other, more conspicuous, targets.

Finally, as a means of reducing Fighter Command, the Luftwaffe could attack the factories which produced the British fighters. Production of the most important types was concentrated at eight centres: at Woolston, Itchen and Eastleigh near Southampton, and Castle Bromwich near Birmingham, producing Spitfires; and at Langley, Brooklands and Kingston in Surrey, and Brockworth near Gloucester, producing Hurricanes. Merlin engines for the two fighter types were built at the Rolls-Royce factories at Derby, Crewe and Glasgow. Of these plants, however, only the Supermarine factories round Southampton and the Hawker factories in Surrey were within range of the Messerschmitt 109; and only large-scale escorted attacks, mounted by day, were accurate and powerful enough to destroy such targets without the raiders suffering severe losses. Later in the Battle of Britain, on 26 September, the Spitfire factories at Woolston and Itchen were hit and seriously damaged by the Luftwaffe during a heavy attack by day. Yet although the buildings were seriously damaged, few of the all-important machine tools and jigs inside suffered. Afterwards the production of components continued, in many cases under canvas, until the production facilities could be dispersed to thirty-five smaller factories located within a radius of 45 miles of Southampton; the move took six weeks to complete. Because many of the components were also built by sub-contractors, the loss in long-term output was remarkably small; probably it was no more than thirty aircraft, or less than a week's production. Once production had been dispersed between a large number of small factories it became almost invulnerable to air attack (the same pattern would be repeated in Germany four years later, when aircraft production reached its highest levels at a time when the Allied air forces were mounting powerful attacks on the factories). The destruction of aircraft production facilities, though easy to state in theory, proved extremely difficult in practice.

To sum up: none of the methods of attack open to the Luftwaffe, either singly or collectively, was likely to achieve the subjugation of Fighter Command without the Luftwaffe suffering similarly heavy losses in the process.

It is a truism that myths die hard. If they did not, they would probably not have survived long enough to become myths in the first place. One of the most enduring myths of the Battle of Britain is that the Luftwaffe lost it because of Goering's blunder in switching the weight of the attack from the Fighter Command airfields to London, early in September 1940. The truth of the matter, borne out by the events of 18 August, is more prosaic: neither by attacking the airfields, nor by attacking London, was the Luftwaffe likely to destroy Fighter Command. Given the size of the British fighter force and the general high quality of its equipment, training and morale, the Luftwaffe could have achieved no more than a Pyrrhic victory. During the action on 18 August it had cost the Luftwaffe five trained aircrewmen killed, wounded or taken prisoner, for each British fighter pilot killed or wounded; the ratio was similar on other days in the battle. And this ratio of 5:1 was very close to that between the number of German aircrew involved in the battle, and those in Fighter Command. In other words the two sides were suffering almost the same losses in trained aircrew, in proportion to their overall strengths. Thus, in trying to smash Fighter Command, the Luftwaffe was likely to smash itself also. And knocking out both sides in the contest would have amounted to a defeat for the Germans; for without massive air superiority over the Channel, to redress the overwhelming strength of the Royal Navy, any attempt to invade England would have been doomed to bloody failure.

This is clear from an examination of the records, coupled with the benefit of hindsight; it was considerably less clear at the time to those who lacked this powerful aid to decision-making. Factors such as the state of morale and the individual bravery of the participants, and the relative quality of the training and equipment, are impossible to prove or disprove without the acid test of war. The Luftwaffe battering-ram had to smash itself many times against the Fighter Command door, before it was clear whether the force was irresistible or the object immovable. Nevertheless the fact remains that, barring some gross and irreversible error by Dowding and his senior commanders, the Luftwaffe could not have won the battle. And it does no discredit to 'The Few' to say so.

In the Battle of Britain, for the first time during the Second World War, the German war machine had set itself a major task which it had patently failed to achieve; and in failing, it demonstrated that it was not invincible. In stiffening the morale of those determined to resist Hitler, the battle was an important turning point in the conflict.

What are the feelings of those who took part in the action on 18 August 1940, the hardest-fought day of the Battle of Britain? What memories remain, almost forty years later?

Squadron Leader Anthony Norman, Fighter Controller at Kenley: 'We felt we had won a great victory – the Germans had obviously tried very hard to wreck Kenley but we had survived. And by the late afternoon we were back in business again. If one had spoken to anyone on Kenley that afternoon, one would have found them in the highest of spirits. Nobody in the front line worried too much about the wrecked hangars. Nor the wrecked aircraft; it was merely a case of asking for some more and they would arrive – and they did. So long as the people and the system survived, that was all that mattered. Equipment could be replaced and buildings could be repaired.'

Feldwebel Wilhelm Raab, who flew a Dornier 17 of the 9th Staffel of Bomber Geschwader 76 during the low-altitude attack on Kenley: 'Afterwards I discussed the attack with my comrades. We agreed that if there were a couple more like that one, we should all end up with grey hair.'

Aircraftwoman Peggy Jones, fighter plotter at Kenley: 'Before the 18 August attack the men at Kenley did not know how we girls would cope if we came under fire. Some of them seemed to think that we would all fall about the place having hysterics. After the attack, when we had shown what we could do, the men's attitudes changed completely and they were wonderful to us.'

Oberfeldwebel Wilhelm Lautersack, flight engineer on a Dornier 17 of Bomber Geschwader 76: 'In Poland and France it had been easy to bomb our targets, but over England it was quite different. The British fighter pilots fought back hard, but always with chivalry.'

Pilot Officer Kenneth Lee, who flew a Hurricane with No 501 Squadron: 'I have no hard feelings towards Gerhard Schoepfel [who shot him down on 18 August]. He was just doing his job. I should have done exactly the same thing to him if I had the chance – that was what we were there for.'

Oberleutnant Julius Neumann, who flew a Messerschmitt 109 with Fighter Geschwader 27: 'We had the highest respect for the British fighter pilots. They were well trained and they knew what they were fighting for.'

Squadron Leader 'Minnie' Manton, who flew a Hurricane with No 56 Squadron: 'I don't think any of us (and I was older than most) really appreciated the seriousness of the situation. When we could be scared to death five or six times a day and yet find ourselves drinking in the local pub before closing time on a summer evening, it all seemed unreal – rather like another Annual Air Exercise but with live ammunition.'

How This Book Came to be Written

*Of the events of the war, I have not ventured to
speak from any chance information, nor according
to any notion of my own; I have described nothing
but what I either saw myself, or learned from others
of whom I made the most careful and particular
inquiry. The task was a laborious one.*
THUCYDIDES: *HISTORY OF THE PELOPONNESIAN WAR*

This book did not result from any single conscious decision on my part.
Rather it was the outcome of a series of fortuitous events, which in the end
developed a momentum which proved irresistible.

If there was a starting point it was in May 1975, when I attended the
grand reunion of the German Bomber Crews Comrades' Association
(*Gemeinschaft der Kampfflieger*). On the thirtieth anniversary of the end of
the war some 1,500 former aircrew and their wives and friends came
together at the German Army airfield at Celle. After a flying display we
moved into one of the hangars which had been suitably decorated for the
occasion. Each Geschwader had its own long table bearing the unit's em-
blem, around which the former members were gathered.

For the historian such as myself, interested in the Second World War
period, the hangar full of wartime aircrew was like an Aladdin's Cave full of
treasure. I was able to make several interesting contacts, which I followed up
later. One line of inquiry I wished to investigate concerned the low-altitude
attack by the 9th Staffel of Bomber Geschwader 76 on Kenley on 18 August
1940. I have always had a soft spot for Kenley, ever since the day in 1950
when, as a young Air Training Corps cadet, I had taken off from that airfield
to make my very first air-experience flight. Was it possible that one of those
in the hangar had taken part in the attack on Kenley? I started at one end of
the Geschwader table and asked each knot of men in turn if any had been
involved in the action. Half an hour later I reached the other end, having
drawn a blank. I was wondering what to do next when out of the corner of my
eye I noticed a figure making his way purposefully towards me from the
other side of the hangar.

It was Guenther Unger. Was I the young man someone had told him was
asking about the attack on Kenley on 18 August 1940? He told me he had
served in the 9th Staffel and remembered the attack clearly: 'Come and
meet some of the other comrades,' he said, and took me to meet Wilhelm
Raab and Franz Bergmann. On the following morning I taped a long
interview with Guenther Unger, during which he described his terrible
experiences of the day almost 35 years earlier. Soon after my return to

England I received from Wilhelm Raab eight closely-typed pages in which he set down his recollections of the day.

Towards the end of the year Guenther and his wife Ilse visited my home. Did I know, he asked, that 18 August was such a hard-fought day that immediately afterwards the commander of his Air Corps had ordered a book to be produced of the personal experiences of aircrewmen on that day? My ears pricked up but I dared not hope too much; surely no copy still survived? 'I've brought my copy for you to see,' he continued, and handed it to me. There, between the battered black cardboard covers of a standard Luftwaffe spring folder, was a half-inch-thick wad of duplicated pages describing in detail the experiences of several aircrew from Bomber Geschwader 1 and 76 on that day, including no fewer than fifteen separate accounts from members of the 9th Staffel who had attacked Kenley. Here was treasure indeed!

Guenther kindly left the prized book with me. I delved into the British records at the Public Record Office and it soon became clear that only one unit, No 111 Squadron from Croydon, had engaged the 9th Staffel's Dorniers. One of the combat reports, from Sergeant H.S. Newton, stated that after being hit while attacking a Dornier at very low altitude: 'My aeroplane caught fire. I managed to climb to 700 feet and turn on my back and bale out.' Almost certainly this was the Hurricane which Guenther Unger had seen going down.

I located Harry Newton and taped an interview with him. There was now no doubt that his was the Hurricane which Unger's gunner, Franz Bergmann, had shot down. Certainly the doctors at Oxted had done a magnificent job in repairing the terrible burns Newton had suffered during the action: I did not notice he had been burnt, until he told me. A few months later Guenther and Ilse Unger were in England again and they called on Harry and Rona Newton; the two families have been firm friends ever since.

Now I had some excellent material on the attacks on Kenley and Biggin Hill on 18 August 1940. But what should I do with it? Could it form the basis of a book on the day's events, as seen from both sides?

At first my reaction to this notion was in the negative. The events of 18 August went far beyond those two attacks. Moreover there had already been more than twenty books written on the Battle of Britain; was there enough that was both new and interesting still to be said? A glance through the previous books on the subject revealed, however, that every serious one had tried to cover the battle as a whole and none had devoted more than a few pages to the events of 18 August. Perhaps there was room for the sort of story I had in mind, provided I could find the material from both sides to assemble it properly.

As I reviewed the material I had, I felt sure that the main problem would be in putting together the German side of the rest of the actions. So far I had been lucky; would that luck continue? I had no similar doubts regarding the British side of the action: the documents in the Public Record Office at Kew are comprehensive and their general layout was well known to me; moreover I was confident that given hard work, patience and time, I could locate the Battle of Britain pilots of Fighter Command I needed to tell their side of the story.

I broadcast a call for help, and many good friends responded. Peter Cornwell, who has assembled probably the most accurate day-to-day records of the actions during the Battle of Britain period, gave me detailed lists of the German and Fighter Command aircraft lost on 18 August with, in many cases, their causes. Andy Saunders gave me a lot of detailed information on the German aircraft which came down along the south coast on that day. Cliff Vincent gave me the present addresses of several of the German ex-aircrew I was trying to track down. Derek Wood, co-author of the book *The Narrow Margin*, gave me free run of his files and photographs; so did Robert Wright. My old friend Karl-Hermann Millahn, leader of the Bomber Geschwader 76 Comrades' Association, put me in touch with Theodor Rehm, the Geschwader historian, who questioned several members on my behalf and relayed their answers to me. One gentleman, who has asked to remain nameless, presented me with an almost complete list of the names of the men on board each German aircraft lost on that day, together with a wealth of information on where many of the aircraft came down. The *Deutsche Dienstelle* in Berlin provided further information on specific German losses.

Next I had to concentrate my search on finding ex-members of Dive Bomber Geschwader 77, the unit which had suffered so heavily during the attacks on the Portsmouth area. I tracked down Otto Schmid to Celle and interviewed him there. He put me into contact with Helmut Bode at Bielefeld. I visited Johannes Wilhelm at his home outside Hanover where he showed me, on the wall of his drawing room, a framed photograph of the front page of the *Daily Telegraph* for 21 August 1940 bearing the picture of himself being marched off to captivity. Wilhelm passed me to his old friend Kurt Scheffel who kindly presented me with a copy of his unpublished autobiography, which included a very detailed account of the fate of his Gruppe during the 18 August action. He went on to question his comrades on my behalf. Also at this time I made contact with Eduard and Julius Neumann, both ex-members of Fighter Geschwader 27 which had escorted the Stukas, who gave me useful information on the day's events as they saw them.

While I was in Germany I visited the Bundesarchiv Militaerarchiv at Freiburg where Herr Noack, the curator, helped me to discover some useful tit-bits amongst the few official Luftwaffe records which survived the general order for their destruction at the end of the war. Of these the most significant was the detailed break-down of the entire strength of the Luftwaffe on 17 August 1940, Gruppe by Gruppe, giving the type of aircraft in each case and the numbers available and serviceable; this list forms the basis of Appendix C in this book.

By now it was the late summer of 1977 and I began an intensive search for documents and witnesses to put together the British side of the action. From the Meteorological Office at Bracknell I received a detailed account of the changing weather conditions on that day. I went through the Public

Record Office at Kew with a fine-toothed comb and took photocopies of every document, squadron record and combat report I could find which was relevant to the 18 August action; Mr F. Lambert, a member of the search department staff, pointed out several useful documents I would otherwise have missed. I visited the Royal Artillery Museum at Woolwich, where Brigadier Lewendon and his staff proved similarly helpful; the detailed records kept by the anti-aircraft gunners provided useful confirmatory evidence on the positions and times of air combats taking place above. At the Documents Section of the Imperial War Museum at Lambeth I found microfilmed copies of the original Luftwaffe loss reports for the action. Some further points of detail required clarification and Group Captain E. Haslam and the staff of the Air Historical Branch in London helped with these. And at the Royal Air Force College Library at Cranwell Mrs King and her staff allowed me full use of the books and material in their keeping.

I located Anthony Norman at Antibes on the French Riviera, visited him there and taped an interview. Squadron Leader Howard Duart and Wing Commander Norman Hancock gave me invaluable help in contacting specific Fighter Command pilots who had fought on 18 August; as a result of their help I was able to make contact with more than a score of them.

During the autumn of 1977 letters appealing for help had been published in *Air Mail* and *Jagerblatt* (the magazine of the German fighter pilots' association); and my good friend Ralph Barker, who lives at Caterham near Kenley, began questioning people in the area for me. As a result several useful new contacts were made. Particularly significant amongst these was Peter Flint, who had done a lot of original research of his own into the Kenley attacks which he kindly made available to me.

By the close of 1977 I had no doubt that I had on my hands the essentials of an exciting and worth-while book. So now work began in earnest on the first draft. Still I needed many more eye-witness accounts. Letters requesting help published in the *Daily Telegraph*, *Flight*, the *Southend News*, *Chichester Observer*, *Deal Mercury* and *Croydon Advertiser* drew more than 140 replies which provided exactly the leavening of human interest stories I was looking for. Particularly interesting were accounts written at the time: Jack Hamblin sent me a copy of the Police report he had written on the bomb damage at Ford; Alexander McKee (author of *Strike from the Sky*), Peggy Marsh, Pamela Rust and Ron Lodge had all witnessed parts of the action and sent me copies of their diary entries. Observer Commander Ballington wrote to further newspapers on my behalf and Gwen Wilcox gave invaluable help in replying to the resultant correspondence.

In February 1978 I was in Dublin and called on Kenneth Lee. By then I was also in contact with Gerhard Schoepfel who had shot him down. I asked Lee whether he would like to be put into contact with the German ace. 'Oh yes,' he replied, 'he did it so neatly I never knew what hit me!' Some time later I interviewed Gerhard Schoepfel and he showed me his superb photograph collection. One of the pictures depicted the four victory bars on his Messerschmitt after the 18 August action. Lee now has a copy of the photograph, showing how his enemy had recorded shooting down his

Hurricane; few pilots can have such an unusual memento. Lee and Schoepfel are now exchanging friendly letters and I hope they will meet before long.

During the spring of 1978 information and contacts came in thick and fast. Cliff Vincent passed me the addresses of Joachim Koepsell, Rudi Ahrens, Walter Leber and Ruediger Proske, all of whom proved excellent witnesses. Theodore Rehm found and questioned Wilhelm Lautersack; and Alan Killen found Alan Eckford who shot down his Dornier. David Irving made available to me material in his files on the whereabouts of Adolf Hitler and other German leaders on 18 August. Just before his tragic death Roger Parkinson gave me similar information on Winston Churchill. John Dunn passed me the results of his own very detailed research into the 9th Staffel attack on Kenley. Alan Prosper, Derek Johnson and Alan Jasper very kindly conducted interviews for me in the Whyteleafe, Clacton and Foulness areas and sent me the tapes or transcripts. Via Jack Foreman I received Josef Foezoe's account of the late afternoon action. Mr J. Tomankiewicz gave information on Poles involved in the action. Visitors came from near and far to let me have their stories: David Lloyd drove over from his home only 8 miles away; Colin Gray called during a visit from New Zealand.

On Friday 18 August 1978 Guenther Unger was in England yet again, this time with several ex-members of his Geschwader: Wilhelm Raab, Franz Bergmann, Mathius Maassen, Max Schuemann and Wilhelm Lautersack. On the 38th anniversary of the action I took them to see the underground operations room of No 11 Group, now restored, at Uxbridge. Afterwards several national newspapers carried photographs of Vera Shaw (née Saies), who had been a WAAF plotter there in 1940, explaining the working of the operations room to her one-time enemies. That evening, at a dinner in the Royal Air Force Club in Piccadilly, Harry Newton presented Guenther Unger with a painting he had commissioned depicting their air combat.

On the following day the party visited the Battle of Britain museum at Hendon. Alan Killen brought the actual swastika cut from the tail of Joachim Roth's Dornier after it had crash-landed at Leaves Green, and presented it to the museum. Also Alan Eckford met Wilhelm Lautersack, whom he had so nearly killed during the 18 August action. Lautersack told his assailant: 'When you shot me down and had me taken prisoner you probably saved my life; so many of my Geschwader comrades later fell in Russia . . .' It was a fair comment: all of the ex-Luftwaffe men in the party probably owed their survival to the fact that they, too, had been taken prisoner early in the war. On the next day the Germans were taken to Kenley, where time and neglect have achieved what German bombs failed to do.

The local branch of the Royal Air Force Association laid on a superb tea and the visitors came face to face with some of their previous enemies: Air Commodore Thomas Prickman (the station commander in 1940), Peggy Bray (née Jones), Clifford Kenyon and Reg Sheldrake. Air Commodore Prickman commented, as he shook hands with Guenther Unger, 'Don't worry, I'm not going to present you with a bill for the damage!' After the meeting, Andy Saunders and I took Wilhelm Lautersack to Warren Road, Hurst Green near Oxted, to the point where his Dornier crashed beside

Doris Addison's house. The building has been repaired and Doris Addison is still living in it; she was expecting us and had invited round some of the neighbours who remembered the Dornier crash, to meet the German crewman.

By the summer of 1978 there were only a few loose ends to tie up. Heinrich Weiss passed me copies of some useful German documents on the action, including the Luftwaffe Intelligence appreciation for 17 August. Hans Ring was similarly helpful, and passed me a copy of the moving last letter from Hans-Otto Lessing to his parents. Winfried Bock gave me a list of German victory claims for 18 August. Werner Held provided much help with photographs. So did Alec Lumsden, who copied the many from private collections.

Two of the most difficult sections in the book to compile were those dealing with the British and German losses and their causes, given in Appendices D and E. It appears that in 1940 *no* official list was ever compiled showing all of the Royal Air Force and Royal Navy aircraft destroyed and damaged on 18 August; my own list, compiled after a careful collation of information from several different sources, goes far beyond anything previously published. The list of German losses was based on the Luftwaffe Quartermaster General's loss reports, the originals of which are in the Bundesarchiv Militaerarchiv at Freiburg (there is a microfilmed copy at the Imperial War Museum in London). Even this highly detailed official source contained some errors, however. Due to a bureaucratic mistake, the three aircraft casualties of Bomber Geschwader 27 were mentioned twice. Otto Schmid's Stuka was listed as having been wrecked but from the interview with him it is clear that the machine, though battered, was repairable. And there is ample evidence that Herbert Kaminski's Messerschmitt 110 did not return damaged, as the German record stated, but ditched in the sea off the Essex coast.

An even greater problem faced me when I began work to determine the cause of each individual German loss. If one disregards the nine German aircraft which crashed in France or returned damaged beyond repair, there were sixty aircraft to share out between the various British claimants; since British sources reported 144 German aircraft destroyed on 18 August, more than 80 of the claims were either incorrect or involved double-claiming. Only by considering each claim against the minutely detailed information resulting from three years of careful research into British and German records on a single day, coupled with interviews with many of the aircrew involved, has it been possible to state with reasonable accuracy the causes of most, though not all, of the German losses. There was no easy way to determine the causes accurately; again and again prima facie evidence was subsequently proved misleading.

At the end of my research I had a pile of documents, letters and interview transcripts over twelve inches high on the events of 18 August 1940. I am deeply grateful to the ladies and gentlemen mentioned in this chapter and the list of witnesses, and the scores of others who helped in so many ways, for making this possible. With such excellent material, the book almost wrote itself.

The Witnesses

George Adams, schoolboy, Balcombe
Doris Addison, housewife, Hurst Green near Oxted
Leutnant Rudolf Ahrens, He 111 pilot, Ist Gruppe Bomber Geschwader 1,
    Montdidier
Charles Allaston, railwayman and Home Guardsman, Littlehampton
Flight Lieutenant Dennis Armitage, Spitfire pilot, No 266 Squadron,
    Hornchurch
Leading Aircraftman Fred Bailey, Operations room plotter, Kenley
Aircraftman Laurence Bell, groundcrewman, No 64 Squadron, Kenley
Unteroffizier Franz Bergmann, Do 17 radio operator, 9th Staffel Bomber
    Geschwader 76, Cormeilles-en-Vexin
Margaret Birch, housewife, Lewes
Oberleutnant Hans-Ekkehard Bob, Me 109 pilot, IIIrd Gruppe Fighter
    Geschwader 54, Guines
Major Helmut Bode, Ju 87 pilot, IIIrd Gruppe Dive Bomber Geschwader
    77, Caen
Oberleutnant Rudolf Braun, Ju 87 pilot, Ist Gruppe Dive Bomber
    Geschwader 3, Caen
Muriel Brayfoot, housewife, visiting Burgess Hill
Flight Lieutenant Peter Brothers, Hurricane pilot, No 32 Squadron, Biggin
    Hill
Aircraftman Herbert Brotherton, groundcrewman, No 64 Squadron,
    Kenley
Leutnant Josef Buerschgens, Me 109 pilot, IIIrd Gruppe Fighter
    Geschwader 26, Caffiers
Brian Cane, schoolboy, Croydon
Flight Lieutenant Frank Carey, Hurricane pilot, No 43 Squadron,
    Tangmere
Bombardier John Clark, 75th Heavy Anti-Aircraft Regiment, Dover
Lilian Clark, housewife, Whyteleafe
Leading Aircraftman Ernie Clarke, radar operator, Poling
Squadron Leader Mike Crossley, Hurricane pilot, No 32 Squadron, Biggin
    Hill
Sub-Officer Leo Dawe, Auxiliary Fire Service, Coulsdon
Sergeant Harry Deacon, Hurricane pilot, No 111 Squadron, Croydon
Midshipman Dick Dearman, trainee Naval air observer, Ford
Pilot Officer Bob Doe, Spitfire pilot, No 234 Squadron, Middle Wallop
Pilot Officer Alan Eckford, Hurricane pilot, No 32 Squadron, Biggin Hill
Gunner Peter Erwood, 75th Heavy Anti-Aircraft Regiment, Dover
Sergeant John Etherington, Hurricane pilot, No 17 Squadron, Martlesham
    Heath

Oberleutnant Wolfgang Ewald, Me 109 pilot, Ist Gruppe Fighter
    Geschwader 52, Coquelles
Aircraftman Bill Fisher, groundcrewman, No 615 Squadron, Kenley
Pilot Òfficer David Glaser, Spitfire pilot, No 65 Squadron, Rochford
Pilot Officer Colin Gray, Spitfire pilot, No 54 Squadron, Hornchurch
Sergeant 'Sticks' Gregory, Blenheim gunner, No 29 Squadron, Digby
John Grohmann, schoolboy, Caterham
Hauptmann Max Gruber, He 111 navigator, IInd Gruppe of Bomber
    Geschwader 53, Lille
Sergeant Herbert Hallowes, Hurricane pilot, No 43 Squadron, Tangmere
Jack Hamblin, police constable, Arundel
Lance-Bombardier Wally Hatcher, 327th Searchlight Company,
    Bletchingly
Oberleutnant Richard Hausmann, Me 109 pilot, IIIrd Gruppe Fighter
    Geschwader 54, Guines
Flying Officer Jack Hill, fighter controller, Kenley
Jim Hosman, railwayman and Home Guardsman, visiting Harrietsham
Fireman Frank Jeffries, Clacton
Aircraftwoman Peggy Jones, Operations room plotter, Kenley
Aircraftman Clifford Kenyon, Operations room plotter, Kenley
Maretta King, ambulance attendant, Sanderstead
Sergeant Don Kingaby, Spitfire pilot, No 266 Squadron, Hornchurch
Leutnant Joachim Koepsell, Me 110 pilot, Ist Gruppe Destroyer
    Geschwader 26, St Omer
Oberleutnant Heinz Lange, Me 109 pilot, Fighter Geschwader 54,
    Campagne
Oberfeldwebel Wilhelm Lautersack, Do 17 flight engineer, Ist Gruppe
    Bomber Geschwader 76, Beauvais
Leutnant Walter Leber, He 111 pilot, IIIrd Gruppe Bomber Geschwader
    53, Lille
Pilot Officer Kenneth Lee, Hurricane pilot, No 501 Squadron, Gravesend
William Lee, police sergeant, Kenley
Private Joseph Lister, infantryman, the Border Regiment, Manston
Squadron Leader David Lloyd, Senior Fighter Controller, Tangmere
Ron Lodge, schoolboy, Galleywood near Chelmsford
Unteroffizier Mathius Maassen, Do 17 pilot, 9th Staffel Bomber
    Geschwader 76, Cormeilles-en-Vexin
Squadron Leader Don MacDonell, Spitfire pilot, No 64 Squadron, Kenley
Squadron Leader 'Minnie' Manton, Hurricane pilot, No 56 Squadron,
    North Weald
Peggy Marsh, schoolgirl, Ashford
Norman McCarthy, schoolboy, Birdham
Alexander McKee, waiting to join the Royal Air Force, Fareham
'Lordy' Mercer, air raid warden, Shoeburyness
Feldwebel Guenther Meyer-Bothling, Ju 87 pilot, IIIrd Gruppe Dive
    Bomber Geschwader 77, Caen
Sergeant (WAAF) Elizabeth Mortimer, armourer, Biggin Hill

Major Eduard Neumann, Me 109 pilot, Ist Gruppe Fighter Geschwader 27, Plumetot

Oberleutnant Julius Neumann, Me 109 pilot, IInd Gruppe Fighter Geschwader 27, Crépon

Sergeant Harry Newton, Hurricane pilot, No 111 Squadron, Croydon

Squadron Leader Anthony Norman, Senior Fighter Controller, Kenley

Pilot Officer Bob Oxspring, Spitfire pilot, No 66 Squadron, Coltishall

Flight Sergeant Bill Pond, Hurricane pilot, No 601 Squadron, Tangmere

Bill Prestridge, air raid warden, Chichester

Wing Commander Thomas Prickman, Station Commander, Kenley

Oberleutnant Ruediger Proske, Me 110 pilot, Ist Gruppe Destroyer Geschwader 26, St Omer

Bryan Prosper, apprentice motor mechanic, Whyteleafe

Feldwebel Wilhelm Raab, Do 17 pilot, 9th Staffel Bomber Geschwader 76, Cormeilles-en-Vexin

Kathleen Rhodes, nurse, Kenley

Kathleen Rose, Post Office telegraphist, Coulsdon

Flight Lieutenant 'Humph' Russell, Hurricane pilot, No 32 Squadron, Biggin Hill

Aircraftwoman Pamela Rust, Operations room plotter, Kenley

Aircraftwoman Vera Saies, No 11 Group Headquarters, Uxbridge

Aircraftman 'Sammy' Samson, groundcrewman, No 615 Squadron, Kenley

Leutnant Kurt Scheffel, Ju 87 pilot, Ist Gruppe Dive Bomber Geschwader 77, Caen

Oberleutnant Otto Schmidt, Ju 87 pilot, Ist Gruppe Dive Bomber Geschwader 77, Caen

Leutnant Winfried Schmidt, Me 109 pilot, IIIrd Gruppe Fighter Geschwader 3, Desvres

Oberleutnant Gerhard Schoepfel, Me 109 pilot, IIIrd Gruppe Fighter Geschwader 26, Caffiers

Feldwebel Max Schuemann, Do 17 radio operator, 9th Staffel Bomber Geschwader 76, Cormeilles-en-Vexin

Unteroffizier Heinz Sellhorn, Ju 87 radio operator, Ist Gruppe Dive Bomber Geschwader 77, Caen

Flight Sergeant Reg Sheldrake, Station Fire NCO, Kenley

Bertie Shinn, farm worker, New Marsh Farm, Foulness

Pilot Officer Peter Simpson, Hurricane pilot, No 111 Squadron, Croydon

Private Arthur Sindall, Royal Army Service Corps, Bognor

Flight Lieutenant Dick Smith, Hurricane pilot, No 151 Squadron, North Weald

Lance Bombardier John Smith, Royal Artillery, Middleton-on-Sea

Amelia Sopp, housewife, Nutbourne

Len Spain, electrical contractor, Deal

Flight Lieutenant Bob Stanford-Tuck, Spitfire pilot, No 92 Squadron, Pembrey

Leslie Stevens, bank clerk, Selsdon

Hauptmann Hannes Trautloft, Me 109 pilot, IIIrd Gruppe Fighter
    Geschwader 51, St Omer
Unteroffizier Guenther Unger, Do 17 pilot, 9th Staffel Bomber
    Geschwader 76, Cormeilles-en-Vexin
Flight Lieutenant Dunlop Urie, Spitfire pilot, No 602 Squadron,
    Westhampnett
Kathleen Venn (Watton), shop assistant, Clacton
Ned Walsh, schoolboy, Morden
Corporal Lesley Webber, groundcrewman, Biggin Hill
Flying Officer Innes Westmacott, Hurricane pilot, No 56 Squadron, North
    Weald
Michael Wilcox, schoolboy, Ham Manor near Angmering
Oberleutnant Johannes Wilhelm, Ju 87 pilot, Ist Gruppe Dive Bomber
    Geschwader 77, Caen
Wing Commander Lord Willoughby de Broke, Senior Fighter Controller,
    No 11 Group Headquarters, Uxbridge
Flying Officer Donald Wiseman, No 11 Group Headquarters, Uxbridge

Bibliography

Air Ministry: *Signals Vol IV, Radar in Raid Reporting* (unpublished)
   The Air Defence of the United Kingdom (unpublished)
   The Rise and Fall of the German Air Force (unpublished)
Dennis Armitage 'Battle of Britain', article in autumn 1958 issue '*Elevator*'
E.C.R. Barker: *The Fighter Aces of the R.A.F.*, William Kimber, London
Katherine Bentley-Beauman: *Partners in Blue*, Hutchinson, London
Georg Brütting: *Das Waren die Deutschen Kampfflieger Asse 1939–1945*,
   Motorbuch Verlag, Stuttgart
   Das Waren die Deutschen Stuka Asse 1939–1945, Motorbuch Verlag, Stuttgart
Basil Collier: *Leader of the Few*, Jarrolds, London
   The Defence of the United Kingdom, HMSO, London
Richard Collier: *Eagle Day*, Hodder and Stoughton, London
Len Deighton: *Fighter*, Jonathan Cape, London
Larry Forrester: *Fly For Your Life*, Frederick Muller, London
Adolf Galland: *The First and the Last*, Methuen, London
Werner Girbig: *Jagdgeschwader 27*, Motorbuch Verlag, Stuttgart
William Green: *Warplanes of the Third Reich*, Macdonald and Jane's, London
David Irving: *Hitler's War*, Hodder and Stoughton, London
Sandy Johnstone: *Enemy in the Sky*, William Kimber, London
Francis Mason: *Battle over Britain*, McWhirter Twins, London
Eric Marrs: '152 Squadron: A Personal Diary of the Battle of Britain', published in
   The Aeroplane, 14 September 1945
Alexander McKee: *Strike from the Sky*, Souvenir Press, London
Ernst Obermaier: *Die Ritterkreuzträger der Luftwaffe, Jagdflieger 1939–45*, Verlag
   Dieter Hoffmann, Mainz
Alfred Price: *Blitz on Britain*, Ian Allan, Shepperton
   Luftwaffe Handbook, Ian Allan, Shepperton
   The Bomber in World War II, Macdonald and Jane's, London
   World War II Fighter Conflict, Macdonald and Jane's, London
Joseph Priller: *Geschichte eines Jagdgeschwaders*, Kurt Vowinckel Verlag, Heidelberg
John Rawlings: *Fighter Squadrons of the R.A.F.*, Macdonald and Jane's, London
Christopher Shores and Clive Williams, *Aces High*, Neville Spearman, London
J.R. Smith, Anthony Kay: *German Aircraft of the Second World War*, Putnam,
   London
Kurt Scheffel: *Meine Erlebnisse bei der I. Gruppe Sturzkampfgeschwader 77*
   (unpublished)
Peter Townsend: *Duel of Eagles*, Weidenfeld and Nicolson, London
Graham Wallace: *R.A.F. Biggin Hill*, Putnam, London
Derek Wood and Derek Dempster: *The Narrow Margin*, Hutchinson, London
Robert Wright: *Dowding and the Battle of Britain*, Macdonald and Jane's, London
Various: *Ein Heldenlied deutschen Fliegergeistes: Tagesbericht 18-8-40,
   Grosseinsatz des I. Fliegerkorps* (unpublished)
   Battle of Britain issue, *Icare*, Paris
Luftwaffe Quartermaster General's loss reports; originals at the Bundesarchiv
   Militaerarchiv at Freiburg, microfilm held at the Documents Section,
   Imperial War Museum, London

Equivalent Ranks

Royal Air Force	Luftwaffe
Marshal of the Royal Air Force	Generalfeldmarschall
Air Chief Marshal	Generaloberst
Air Marshal	General
Air Vice-Marshal	Generalleutnant
Air Commodore	Generalmajor
Group Captain	Oberst
Wing Commander	Oberstleutnant
Squadron Leader	Major
Flight Lieutenant	Hauptmann
Flying Officer	Oberleutnant
Pilot Officer	Leutnant
Warrant Officer	Stabsfeldwebel
Flight Sergeant	Oberfeldwebel
Sergeant	Feldwebel
Corporal	Unteroffizier
Leading Aircraftman	Obergefreiter
Aircraftman First Class	Gefreiter
Aircraftman Second Class	Flieger

Aircraft Strengths and Locations of Units of Air Fleets 2, 3 and 5 and the Luftwaffe High Command Reconnaissance Gruppe, 17 August 1940

First figure, aircraft serviceable; in brackets, aircraft unserviceable

AIR FLEET 2. HEADQUARTERS BRUSSELS

Long Range Bombers

Bomber Geschwader 1

Staff	Heinkel 111	5	(0)	Rosiéres-en-Santerre
I Gruppe	Heinkel 111	23	(5)	Montdidier
II Gruppe	Heinkel 111	25	(5)	Montdidier
III Gruppe	Heinkel 111	19	(9)	Rosiéres-en-Santerre

Bomber Geschwader 2

Staff	Dornier 17	4	(1)	Arras
I Gruppe	Dornier 17	21	(7)	Epinoy
II Gruppe	Dornier 17	31	(3)	Arras
III Gruppe	Dornier 17	24	(5)	Cambrai

Bomber Geschwader 3

Staff	Dornier 17	5	(1)	Le Culot
I Gruppe	Dornier 17	24	(10)	Le Culot
II Gruppe	Dornier 17	27	(7)	Antwerp/Deurne
III Gruppe	Dornier 17	29	(5)	St Trond

Bomber Geschwader 4

Staff	Heinkel 111	6	(0)	Soesterberg
I Gruppe	Heinkel 111	20	(10)	Soesterberg
II Gruppe	Heinkel 111	23	(7)	Eindhoven
III Gruppe	Junkers 88	25	(10)	Amsterdam/Schiphol

Bomber Geschwader 53

Staff	Heinkel 111	3	(2)	Lille
I Gruppe	Heinkel 111	17	(2)	Lille
II Gruppe	Heinkel 111	20	(1)	Lille
III Gruppe	Heinkel 111	21	(5)	Lille

Bomber Geschwader 76

Staff	Dornier 17	3	(2)	Cormeilles-en-Vexin
I Gruppe	Dornier 17	26	(3)	Beauvais
II Gruppe	Junkers 88	29	(8)	Creil
III Gruppe	Dornier 17	23	(7)	Cormeilles-en-Vexin

Bomber Gruppe 126

	Heinkel 111	16	(13)	Marx

Dive Bombers

Dive Bomber Geschwader 1

II Gruppe	Junkers 87	26	(10)	Pas-de-Calais

Tactical Development Geschwader (Lehrgeschwader) 1

IV Gruppe	Junkers 87	16	(10)	Tramecourt

Fighter-Bombers

Trials Gruppe 210	Messerschmitt 110	15	(15)	Calais-Marck

Tactical Development Geschwader 2

II Gruppe	Messerschmitt 109	34	(5)	St Omer

Single-engined Fighters

Fighter Geschwader 3

Staff	Messerschmitt 109	2	(0)	Samer
I Gruppe	Messerschmitt 109	24	(6)	Samer
II Gruppe	Messerschmitt 109	30	(4)	Samer
III Gruppe	Messerschmitt 109	25	(9)	Desvres

Fighter Geschwader 26

Staff	Messerschmitt 109	2	(2)	Audembert
I Gruppe	Messerschmitt 109	24	(10)	Audembert
II Gruppe	Messerschmitt 109	29	(6)	Marquise
III Gruppe	Messerschmitt 109	33	(6)	Caffiers

Fighter Geschwader 51

Staff	Messerschmitt 109	2	(2)	Wissant
I Gruppe	Messerschmitt 109	23	(6)	Wissant
II Gruppe	Messerschmitt 109	25	(0)	Wissant
III Gruppe	Messerschmitt 109	39	(0)	St Omer

Fighter Geschwader 52

Staff	Messerschmitt 109	1	(1)	Coquelles
I Gruppe	Messerschmitt 109	36	(9)	Coquelles
II Gruppe	Messerschmitt 109	23	(12)	Peuplingues

Fighter Geschwader 54

Staff	Messerschmitt 109	3	(1)	Campagne
I Gruppe	Messerschmitt 109	24	(10)	Guines
II Gruppe	Messerschmitt 109	36	(2)	Hermelinghen
III Gruppe	Messerschmitt 109	29	(7)	Guines

Tactical Development Geschwader 2

I Gruppe	Messerschmitt 109	36	(3)	Calais-Marck

Twin-engined Fighters

Destroyer Geschwader 26

Staff	Messerschmitt 110	2	(0)	Lille
I Gruppe	Messerschmitt 110	21	(10)	St Omer
II Gruppe	Messerschmitt 110	29	(7)	St Omer
III Gruppe	Messerschmitt 110	21	(12)	Arques

Destroyer Geschwader 76

Staff	Messerschmitt 110	2	(0)	Laval
II Gruppe	Messerschmitt 110	24	(6)	Abbeville
III Gruppe	Messerschmitt 110	12	(11)	Laval

Night Fighters

Night Fighter Geschwader 1

II Gruppe	Junkers 88 Dornier 17	14	(14)	Gilze Rijen

Coastal Aircraft

Coastal Flying Gruppe 106

	Junkers 88 Dornier 18 Heinkel 115	23	(7)	Borkum, airfields and seaplane bases in Brittany

Reconnaissance Aircraft

Long Range Reconnaissance Gruppe 122

3 Staffel	Junkers 88 Heinkel 111	11	(1)	Eindhoven
4 Staffel	Junkers 88 Heinkel 111	8	(2)	Brussels
5 Staffel	Junkers 88 Heinkel 111 Dornier 17	7	(2)	Haute-Fontaine

Tactical Development Geschwader 2

7 Staffel	Dornier 17 Messerschmitt 110	9	(3)	Grimbergen

Air-Sea Rescue Seaplanes

3 Air-Sea Rescue Staffel				
	Heinkel 59	5	(3)	Boulogne

AIR FLEET 3, HEADQUARTERS PARIS

Long Range Bombers

Tactical Development Geschwader 1

Staff	Junkers 88	2	(0)	Orléans/Bricy
I Gruppe	Junkers 88	19	(8)	Orléans/Bricy
II Gruppe	Junkers 88	16	(9)	Orléans/Bricy
III Gruppe	Junkers 88	18	(12)	Chateaudun

Bomber Geschwader 27

Staff	Heinkel 111	3	(2)	Tours
I Gruppe	Heinkel 111	12	(18)	Tours
II Gruppe	Heinkel 111	18	(16)	Dinard
III Gruppe	Heinkel 111	23	(2)	Rennes

Bomber Geschwader 51

Staff	Junkers 88	0	(0)	Orly
I Gruppe	Junkers 88	18	(7)	Melun
II Gruppe	Junkers 88	17	(13)	Orly
III Gruppe	Junkers 88	20	(7)	Etampes

Bomber Geschwader 54

Staff	Junkers 88	0	(0)	Evreux
I Gruppe	Junkers 88	20	(9)	Evreux
II Gruppe	Junkers 88	15	(9)	St Andre

Bomber Geschwader 55

Staff	Heinkel 111	3	(2)	Villacoublay
I Gruppe	Heinkel 111	27	(5)	Dreux
II Gruppe	Heinkel 111	26	(6)	Chartres
III Gruppe	Heinkel 111	23	(11)	Villacoublay

Bomber Gruppe 100

	Heinkel 111	19	(20)	Vannes

Bomber Gruppe 806

	Junkers 88	23	(9)	Nantes and Caen

Dive Bombers

Dive Bomber Geschwader 1

Staff	Junkers 87	3	(1)	Angers
	Dornier 17	3	(1)	Angers
I Gruppe	Junkers 87	28	(8)	Angers
III Gruppe	Junkers 87	28	(11)	Angers

Dive Bomber Geschwader 2

Staff	Junkers 87	3	(0)	St Malo
	Dornier 17	4	(1)	St Malo
I Gruppe	Junkers 87	24	(8)	St Malo
II Gruppe	Junkers 87	23	(7)	Lannion

Dive Bomber Geschwader 3

Staff	Junkers 87	5	(2)	Caen
	Dornier 17			
	Heinkel 111			
I Gruppe	Junkers 87	24	(14)	Caen

Dive Bomber Geschwader 77

Staff	Junkers 87	2	(2)	Caen
	Dornier 17	2	(4)	Caen
I Gruppe	Junkers 87	30	(9)	Caen
II Gruppe	Junkers 87	31	(8)	Caen
III Gruppe	Junkers 87	37	(1)	Caen

Single-engined Fighters

Fighter Geschwader 2

Staff	Messerschmitt 109	3	(1)	Evreux, Beaumont-le-Roger
I Gruppe	Messerschmitt 109	27	(5)	Beaumont-le-Roger
II Gruppe	Messerschmitt 109	24	(9)	Beaumont-le-Roger
III Gruppe	Messerschmitt 109	20	(9)	Le Havre

Fighter Geschwader 27

Staff	Messerschmitt 109	5	(0)	Cherbourg West
I Gruppe	Messerschmitt 109	39	(0)	Plumetot
II Gruppe	Messerschmitt 109	27	(12)	Crépon
III Gruppe	Messerschmitt 109	32	(7)	Carquebut

Fighter Geschwader 53

Staff	Messerschmitt 109	4	(0)	Cherbourg
I Gruppe	Messerschmitt 109	37	(2)	Rennes
II Gruppe	Messerschmitt 109	26	(4)	Dinan
III Gruppe	Messerschmitt 109	21	(18)	Sempy, Brest

Twin-engined Fighters

Destroyer Geschwader 2

Staff	Messerschmitt 110	2	(2)	Toussee-le-Noble
I Gruppe	Messerschmitt 110	19	(14)	Amiens
II Gruppe	Messerschmitt 110	23	(13)	Guyancourt

Tactical Development Geschwader 1

V Gruppe	Messerschmitt 110	24	(12)	Caen

Reconnaissance Aircraft

Long Range Reconnaissance Gruppe 11

2 Staffel	Messerschmitt 110	9	(2)	Le Bourget
	Dornier 17			

Long Range Reconnaissance Gruppe 123

2 Staffel	Dornier 17	8	(1)	

Long Range Armed-Reconnaissance

Bomber Geschwader 40

Staff	Junkers 88	1	(0)	Bordeaux
I Gruppe	Focke-Wulf 200	7	(2)	Bordeaux

Air-Sea Rescue Seaplanes

2 Air-Sea Rescue Staffel

	Heinkel 59	5	(4)	Cherbourg

AIR FLEET 5, HEADQUARTERS OSLO

Long Range Bombers

Bomber Geschwader 26

Staff	Heinkel 111	5	(0)	Stavanger
I Gruppe	Heinkel 111	28	(0)	Stavanger
III Gruppe	Heinkel 111	19	(1)	Stavanger

Bomber Geschwader 30

Staff	Junkers 88	1	(0)	Aalborg
I Gruppe	Junkers 88	26	(12)	Aalborg
III Gruppe	Junkers 88	21	(11)	Aalborg

Single-engined Fighters

Fighter Geschwader 77

II Gruppe	Messerschmitt 109	35	(4)	Stavanger

Twin-engined Fighters

Destroyer Geschwader 76

I Gruppe	Messerschmitt 110	20	(14)	Stavanger, Trondheim

Coastal Aircraft

Coastal Flying Gruppe 506

	Heinkel 115	22	(2)	Stavanger, Trondheim

Reconnaissance Aircraft

Long Range Reconnaissance Gruppe 22

2 Staffel	Dornier 17	2	(4)	Stavanger
3 Staffel	Dornier 17	4	(2)	Stavanger

Long Range Reconnaissance Gruppe 120

1 Staffel	Junkers 88	4	(0)	Stavanger
	Heinkel 111			

Long Range Reconnaissance Gruppe 121

1 Staffel	Junkers 88	5	(2)	Stavanger
	Heinkel 111			

LUFTWAFFE HIGH COMMAND RECONNAISSANCE GRUPPE

1 Staffel	Junkers 86P	17	(10)	Berlin Staaken
	Junkers 88			
	Heinkel 111			
	Heinkel 116			
	Messerschmitt 110			
	Blohm und Voss 142			
	Dornier 215			
	Dornier 217			
2 Staffel	Dornier 215	4	(5)	Berlin Staaken
	Heinkel 111			
3 Staffel	Heinkel 111	7	(4)	Berlin Jueterbog

NB High Command reconnaissance aircraft operated from bases in France, Belgium and Holland when flying sorties over England.

Aircraft Strengths and Locations of Units of Fighter Command 6 pm 17 August 1940

First figure, aircraft serviceable; in brackets, aircraft unserviceable

No 10 GROUP, HEADQUARTERS BOX

Middle Wallop Sector

234 Squadron Spitfires	9	(1)	Middle Wallop
609 Squadron Spitfires	13	(5)	Middle Wallop
604 Squadron Blenheims	9	(8)	Middle Wallop
152 Squadron Spitfires	13	(2)	Warmwell
249 Squadron Hurricanes	15	(5)	Boscombe Down

Filton Sector

92 Squadron Spitfires	16	(2)	Pembrey
87 Squadron Hurricanes	15	(4)	Exeter
213 Squadron Hurricanes	20	(4)	Exeter
238 Squadron Hurricanes	19	(3)	St Eval
247 Squadron Gladiators	5	(4)	Roborough

No 11 GROUP HEADQUARTERS UXBRIDGE

Kenley Sector

64 Squadron Spitfires	12	(5)	Kenley
615 Squadron Hurricanes	16	(6)	Kenley
111 Squadron Hurricanes	14	(7)	Croydon

Biggin Hill Sector

32 Squadron Hurricanes	13	(9)	Biggin Hill
610 Squadron Spitfires	19	(1)	Biggin Hill
501 Squadron Hurricanes	15	(7)	Gravesend

Northolt Sector

1 Squadron Hurricanes	16	(4)	Northolt	
1 RCAF Sqn. Hurricanes	22	(0)	Northolt	Became operational on 18 8 40
303 Squadron Hurricanes	15	(2)	Northolt	Polish. Not operational

Hornchurch Sector

54 Squadron Spitfires	12	(7)	Hornchurch	
266 Squadron Spitfires	7	(2)	Hornchurch	10 Spitfires delivered on evening 17 8 40
65 Squadron Spitfires	13	(7)	Rochford	
600 Squadron Blenheims	7	(5)	Manston	

North Weald Sector

| 56 Squadron | Hurricanes | 17 | (2) | North Weald |
| 151 Squadron | Hurricanes | 17 | (3) | North Weald |

Debden Sector

85 Squadron	Hurricanes	19	(3)	Debden
257 Squadron	Hurricanes	16	(6)	Debden
17 Squadron	Hurricanes	16	(5)	Martlesham Heath
25 Squadron	Blenheims	10	(7)	Martlesham Heath

Tangmere Sector

43 Squadron	Hurricanes	13	(1)	Tangmere
601 Squadron	Hurricanes	13	(3)	Tangmere
Fighter Interception Unit				
	Hurricanes	2	(0)	Tangmere
602 Squadron	Spitfires	18	(3)	Westhampnett

No 12 GROUP, HEADQUARTERS WATNALL

Coltishall Sector

| 66 Squadron | Spitfires | 15 | (3) | Coltishall | |
| 242 Squadron | Hurricanes | 21 | (1) | Coltishall | |

Duxford Sector

| 19 Squadron | Spitfires | 15 | (4) | Duxford | Cannon-armed |
| 310 Squadron | Hurricanes | 15 | (3) | Duxford | Czechoslovak |

Wittering Sector

23 Squadron	Blenheims	7	(7)	Wittering	
74 Squadron	Spitfires	17	(5)	Wittering	
229 Squadron	Hurricanes	18	(2)	Wittering	

Digby Sector

46 Squadron	Hurricanes	21	(1)	Digby	
611 Squadron	Spitfires	24	(3)	Digby	
29 Squadron	Blenheims	14	(5)	Digby	

Kirton-in-Lindsey Sector

141 Squadron	Defiants	14	(4)	Kirton-in-Lindsey	
222 Squadron	Spitfires	16	(3)	Kirton-in-Lindsey	
264 Squadron	Defiants	16	(5)	Kirton-in-Lindsey	

Church Fenton Sector

73 Squadron	Hurricanes	19	(3)	Church Fenton	
302 Squadron	Hurricanes	12	(5)	Leconfield	Polish. Not operational
616 Squadron	Spitfires	13	(4)	Leconfield	

No 13 GROUP, HEADQUARTERS NEWCASTLE

Catterick Sector

41 Squadron	Spitfires	16	(2)	Catterick
219 Squadron	Blenheims	11	(5)	Catterick
607 Squadron	Hurricanes	19	(5)	Usworth

Acklington Sector

| 72 Squadron | Spitfires | 14 | (4) | Acklington |
| 79 Squadron | Hurricanes | 18 | (4) | Acklington |

Turnhouse Sector

253 Squadron	Hurricanes	22	(2)	Turnhouse	
603 Squadron	Spitfires	14	(8)	Turnhouse	
145 Squadron	Hurricanes	8	(6)	Drem	
605 Squadron	Hurricanes	15	(5)	Drem	
263 Squadron	Hurricanes	8	(5)	Grangemouth	Not operational
	Whirlwinds	0	(5)		

Wick Sector

| 3 Squadron | Hurricanes | 18 | (3) | Wick |
| 504 Squadron | Hurricanes | 20 | (3) | Wick |

Sumburgh Sector

| 232 Squadron | Hurricanes | 8 | (0) | Sumburgh |

Aldergrove Sector

| 245 Squadron | Hurricanes | 14 | (8) | Aldergrove |

Fighter Types at Operational Training Units, 17 8 40

Spitfires	36	(19)
Hurricanes	49	(25)
Blenheims	15	(7)

Fighter Types Held at Maintenance Units, 17 8 40

	Ready for Immediate Issue	Ready in Four Days
Spitfires	118	34
Hurricanes	98	17
Defiants	73	1

Production of Fighters During Week Prior to 17 8 40

Spitfires	31
Hurricanes	43
Defiants	11
Whirlwinds	0
Beaufighters	5

Luftwaffe Intelligence Appreciation of Fighter Command, Issued on 17 August 1940

During the period from 1 July to 15 August 1940 the following enemy aircraft were confirmed destroyed by fighter action, flak and on the ground:

Spitfires	373
Hurricanes	180
Curtisses	9
Defiants	12
	574

To this figure of 574 enemy fighters destroyed must be added at least 196 due to machines involved in crash-landing, landings damaged beyond repair, accidents etc, giving a total loss of some 770 enemy fighters. During the same period some 270 to 300 new fighters were built, so the net reduction in enemy fighter strength is estimated at about 470. On 1 July the fighter units had 900 modern fighters so by [the morning of] 16 August there were 430 left; allowing 70 per cent serviceability, there are now 300 combat-ready fighters.

Unconfirmed but previously reliable reports distribute these combat-ready fighters at present as follows:

South and south-eastern England (south of the line The Wash – Bristol Channel)	200
The Midlands	70
Northern England and Scotland	30

The above figures relate to the German Intelligence picture for the beginning of 16 August, and from these must be subtracted the 92 British fighters claimed destroyed by the Luftwaffe on that day. The 'Curtisses' mentioned in the report were American-built Curtiss Hawk fighters, which had been used in large numbers by the French Air Force; the type was often mentioned in German combat reports during the Battle of Britain though, in fact, none was operational in the Royal Air Force.

Oberst 'Beppo' Schmid's 5th Directorate had calculated the strength of Fighter Command on the morning of 16 August by the simple expedient of subtracting the 770 aircraft thought put out of action, from the 900 thought to exist on 1 July added to the 300 new fighters believed delivered from the factories since then. It was a fundamentally unsound approach to the complex matter of Intelligence gathering and, as a result, the appreciation of Fighter Command's strength was wildly removed from the truth.

In fact, between 1 July and the evening of 15 August, wastage in Fighter Command had amounted to only 318 Spitfires, Hurricanes and Defiants, less than half the German estimate; and the factories had produced about 720 aircraft of these types, well over twice as many as Schmid's officers had calculated. Thus, instead of a net reduction over the period of 470 fighters, Fighter Command had ended it with over 400 more. On 1 July the Command had had 791 modern single-engined fighters on strength, 109 less than the German estimate. On 17 August, instead of being far weaker, Fighter Command was numerically greatly stronger than it had been on 1 July; it now had a total of 1,065 Spitfires, Hurricanes and Defiants on the strength of its squadrons of which 855 (80 per cent) were serviceable. A further 289 aircraft of these types were available at storage units ready for immediate issue. And 84 Spitfires and Hurricanes were held at Operational Training Units and could, at a pinch, be passed to the operational squadrons to make good losses. Thus, instead of the 430 Spitfires, Hurricanes and Defiants thought to be left on the 16th, dropping to 340 on the 17th, on the evening of the 17th Fighter Command could draw on 1,438 modern single-engined fighters – more than four times the number Schmid had estimated.

APPENDIX E

British Combat Losses, 18 August 1940

In this section a 'combat loss' is any aircraft destroyed or damaged while engaged in a combat sortie, whatever the cause, and those destroyed or damaged on the ground by enemy action

Unit	Type	Fate	Pilot	Remarks
1 1 Squadron	Hurricane	Damaged	Plt Off G. Goodman	Damaged in combat with a Messerschmitt 109, off Dover at about 1.50 pm
2 1 (RCAF) Sqn	Hurricane L1851	Damaged	Flt Lt V. Corbett	Ran into a refuelling vehicle at Hornchurch during scramble take-off at 2.40 pm
3 1(RCAF) Sqn	Hurricane P3757	Damaged	Fg Off H. Molson	Landing accident at Hornchurch, on return from operational mission
4 17 Squadron	Hurricane V7407	Damaged	Sdn Ldr C. Williams	Damaged in combat with Messerschmitt 109s, off Dover at about 1.50 pm
5 17 Squadron	Hurricane L1921	Destroyed	Plt Off N. Solomon *killed*	Missing after engagement with Messerschmitt 109s off Dover at about 1.50 pm
6 17 Squadron	Hurricane	Damaged	Sgt D. North-Bomford	Damaged in combat with Messerschmitt 109s, off Dover at about 1.50 pm
7 17 Squadron	Hurricane P3209	Destroyed		Destroyed on the ground at Manston, during strafing attack by Messerschmitt 109s of Fighter Geschwader 52 at about 2.10 pm
8 32 Squadron	Hurricane P 3147	Destroyed	Plt Off J. Pain *wounded*	Attacked and shot down by German fighter over Brenchley at about 1.45 pm. Pilot baled out

#	Squadron	Aircraft	Serial	Status	Pilot	Details
9	32 Squadron	Hurricane	V 7363	Destroyed	Flt Lt H. Russell *wounded*	Shot down by Messerschmitt 110 of Destroyer Geschwader 26 near Edenbridge at about 1.45 pm. Pilot baled out
10	32 Squadron	Hurricane	V 6536	Damaged	Sgt B. Henson *wounded*	Aircraft hit by return fire, while attacking a Dornier 17 of Bomber Geschwader 76 at about 1.45 pm. Forced-landed near Sevenoaks
11	32 Squadron	Hurricane	N 2461	Destroyed	Sdn Ldr M. Crossley	Shot down by Messerschmitt 109 of Fighter Geschwader 26 near Gillingham at about 5.40 pm. Pilot baled out
12	32 Squadron	Hurricane	V 6535	Destroyed	Plt Off R. De Grunne *wounded*	Shot down by Messerschmitt 109 of Fighter Geschwader 26 near Canterbury at about 5.40 pm. Pilot baled out
13	32 Squadron	Hurricane	R 4106	Destroyed	Sgt L. Pearce *wounded*	Shot down by Messerschmitt 109 of Fighter Geschwader 26 near Canterbury at about 5.40 pm. Pilot baled out
14	32 Squadron	Hurricane	R 4081	Damaged	Plt Off B. Wlasnowolski	Ran into a tree stump, landing back at Biggin Hill after combat sortie, at 7.30 pm
15	43 Squadron	Hurricane	R 4109	Damaged	Flt Lt F. Carey *wounded*	Pilot hit by stray bullet during mêlée over Thorney Island at about 2.30 pm. Forced-landed near Pulborough.
16	56 Squadron	Hurricane		Damaged	Fg Off I. Westmacott	Damaged in combat with Messerschmitt 110s of Destroyer Geschwader 26, off Clacton at about 5.30 pm
17	56 Squadron	Hurricane		Damaged	F.Sgt F. Higginson	Damaged during the mêlée off the Essex coast at about 5.30 pm
18	64 Squadron	Spitfire		Damaged		Damaged on the ground during the attack on Kenley by Bomber Geschwader 76 at 1.25 pm
19	65 Squadron	Spitfire	R 6713	Destroyed	Fg Off F. Gruszka *killed*	Missing from combat sortie around noon, aircraft crashed near Canterbury

#	Squadron	Aircraft	Status	Pilot	Details
20	85 Squadron	Hurricane P 3649	Damaged	Plt Off J. Marshall	Damaged in collision with Heinkel 111 of Bomber Geschwader 53, off Southend at about 6 pm. Landed at Debden minus starboard wing tip
21	85 Squadron	Hurricane V 7249	Destroyed	Plt Off J. Hemmingway	Shot down in mêlée off Southend at about 6 pm, probably by Messerschmitt 110 of Destroyer Geschwader 26. Pilot baled out into sea, picked up by boat from lightship
22	85 Squadron	Hurricane P 2923	Destroyed	Flt Lt R. Lee *killed*	Last seen at about 6 pm off Southend chasing Messerschmitt 109s out to sea
23	92 Squadron	Spitfire N 3040	Destroyed	Flt Lt R. Tuck *wounded*	Damaged in combat over Channel, pilot baled out near Tonbridge
24	111 Squadron	Hurricane R 4187	Destroyed	Flt Lt S. Connors *killed*	Shot down by return fire from Dornier 17s of 9th Staffel of Bomber Geschwader 76, or ground fire, south of Kenley at about 1.20 pm. Aircraft crashed near Wallington
25	111 Squadron	Hurricane P 3943	Destroyed	Sgt H. Newton *wounded*	Shot down by Uffz F. Bergmann, gunner on board Dornier 17 of 9th Staffel of Bomber Geschwader 76. Hurricane crashed at Tatsfield. Pilot baled out, 1.30 pm
26	111 Squadron	Hurricane N 2340	Destroyed	Sgt H. Deacon *wounded*	Shot down in error by ground gunners, crashed near Godstone. Pilot baled out, 1.50 pm
27	111 Squadron	Hurricane P 3399	Damaged	Plt Off P. Simpson	Damaged by return fire from Dornier 17 of 9th Staffel of Bomber Geschwader 76, forced-landed on Woodcote Park golf course near Epsom, about 1.40 pm
28	111 Squadron	Hurricane	Destroyed		Destroyed during attack on Croydon by Dornier 17s of Bomber Geschwader 76, 1.30 pm
29	111 Squadron	Hurricane	Damaged		Damaged during attack on Croydon by Dornier 17s of Bomber Geschwader 76, 1.30 pm

No.	Aircraft	Status	Pilot	Remarks
30	151 Squadron Hurricane R 4181	Destroyed	Plt Off J. Ramsay *killed*	Shot down in combat with German fighters at about 5.45 pm. Aircraft probably the one which crashed near Holliwell Point
31	151 Squadron Hurricane P 3940	Destroyed	Sdn Ldr J. Gordon *wounded*	Shot down in combat with Messerschmitt 110s of Destroyer Geschwader 26 near Rochford at about 5.45 pm. Pilot baled out. Aircraft crashed near Battlesbridge
32	151 Squadron Hurricane P 3871	Damaged	Wg Cdr F. Beamish	Damaged by return fire while attacking Heinkel 111s of Bomber Geschwader 53, near Chelmsford at about 5.45 pm. Aircraft forced-landed at Martlesham Heath
33	152 Squadron Spitfire	Damaged	Plt Off W. Beaumont	Damaged during the mêlée off the Isle of Wight at about 2.40 pm
34	152 Squadron Spitfire	Damaged		As above
35	234 Squadron Spitfire	Damaged		As above
36	257 Squadron Hurricane P 3708	Destroyed	Sgt A. Girdwood *died later of wounds*	Shot down over Foulness, probably by Messerschmitt 110 of Destroyer Geschwader 26. Pilot baled out, about 5.50 pm
37	257 Squadron Hurricane	Damaged	Flt Lt. H. Beresford	Damaged over Foulness, by Messerschmitt 110 of Destroyer Geschwader 26, about 5.50 pm
38	266 Squadron Spitfire X 4061	Destroyed		Hit during strafing attack on Manston by Messerschmitt 109s of Fighter Geschwader 52 at about 2.15 pm
39	266 Squadron Spitfire X 4066	Destroyed		As above
40	266 Squadron Spitfire X 4063	Damaged		As above

No.	Squadron / Aircraft	Status	Pilot	Remarks
41	266 Squadron Spitfire K 9850	Damaged		As above
42	266 Squadron Spitfire L 1088	Damaged		As above
43	266 Squadron Spitfire N 3127	Damaged		As above
44	266 Squadron Spitfire R 6762	Damaged		As above
45	266 Squadron Spitfire R 6920	Damaged		As above
46	501 Squadron Hurricane P 3208	Destroyed	Plt Off J. Bland *killed*	Shot down near Canterbury at about 1.05 pm by Oblt G. Shoepfel of Fighter Geschwader 26, in a Messerschmitt 109
47	501 Squadron Hurricane P 3059	Destroyed	Plt Off K. Lee *wounded*	As above, pilot baled out
48	501 Squadron Hurricane P 3815	Destroyed	Plt Off F. Kozlowski *wounded*	As above
49	501 Squadron Hurricane N 2617	Destroyed	Sgt D. McKay *wounded*	As above
50	501 Squadron Hurricane	Destroyed	Fg Off R. Dafforn	Shot down in combat with German fighters, near Sevenoaks, at about 1.30 pm. Pilot baled out
51	501 Squadron Hurricane R 4219	Destroyed	F.Sgt P. Morfill	As above
52	501 Squadron Hurricane P 2549	Destroyed	Flt Lt G. Stoney *killed*	Shot down near Chartham at about 5.40 pm by Hpt J. Foezoe of Fighter Geschwader 51, in a Messerschmitt 109
53	601 Squadron Hurricane V 7305	Damaged	F.Sgt A. Pond	Damaged by return fire while attacking a Junkers 87 of Dive Bomber Geschwader 77 over Thorney Island, at 2.30 pm. Aircraft further damaged during crash-landing at Tangmere

54	601 Squadron Hurricane	Destroyed	Sgt L. Guy *killed*	Shot down during the mêlée off Selsey Bill, about 2.40 pm
55	601 Squadron Hurricane L 1990	Destroyed	Sgt R. Hawkings *killed*	Shot down by Messerschmitt 109 of Fighter Geschwader 27, about 2.35 pm. Aircraft crashed near Pagham
56	602 Squadron Spitfire X 4110	Damaged *beyond repair*	Flt Lt J. Urie *wounded*	Severely damaged during attack by Messerschmitt 109 of Fighter Geschwader 27 near Bognor at 2.35 pm
57	602 Squadron Spitfire K 9969	Damaged	Fg Off P. Ferguson *wounded*	As above. Aircraft further damaged when it flew through high tension cables north of Littlehampton, and during the subsequent crash-landing
58	602 Squadron Spitfire X 4161	Damaged	Plt Off H. Moody	Damaged during attack by Messerschmitt 109 of Fighter Geschwader 27, near Bognor at 2.35 pm. Nosed-over after forced-landing at Ford
59	602 Squadron Spitfire L 1005	Damaged *beyond repair*	Fg Off C. Mount	Aircraft severely damaged during the mêlée near Ford at about 2.33 pm
60	602 Squadron Spitfire L 1019	Damaged *beyond repair*	Sgt B. Whall	Engine hit by return fire while attacking a Junkers 87 of Dive Bomber Geschwader 77 off Bognor at about 2.35 pm. Pilot ditched in shallow water off Middleton-on-Sea
61	610 Squadron Spitfire R 6694	Damaged	Plt Off C. Pegge	Damaged in combat with Messerschmitt 109. Further damaged when it ran into a bomb crater when landing at Biggin Hill at 1.50 pm
62	610 Squadron Spitfire R 6993	Damaged	Sdn Ldr J. Ellis	Damaged by return fire while attacking a Heinkel 111 of Bomber Geschwader 1, near Dungeness at about 1.45 pm

No.	Unit / Aircraft	Status	Pilot	Remarks
63	615 Squadron Hurricane P 2768	Destroyed	Sgt. P. Walley *killed*	Shot down by Messerschmitt 109 of Fighter Geschwader 3 near Kenley at about 1.23 pm. Aircraft crashed on Morden Park golf course
64	615 Squadron Hurricane L 1592	Damaged	Plt Off D. Looker *wounded*	Damaged by Messerschmitt 109 of Fighter Geschwader 3 near Kenley at about 1.23 pm. Further damaged by Croydon ground defences, while making a forced-landing
65	615 Squadron Hurricane R 4221	Damaged *beyond repair*	Plt Off P. Hugo *wounded*	Shot down by Messerschmitt 109 of Fighter Geschwader 3 near Kenley at about 1.23 pm. Crash-landed near Orpington
66	615 Squadron Hurricane P2969	Destroyed	Flt Lt L. Gaunce *wounded*	Shot down by Messerschmitt 109 of Fighter Geschwader 3 near Kenley at about 1.23 pm. Pilot baled out, aircraft crashed near Sevenoaks
67	615 Squadron Hurricane P 3158	Destroyed		Hit during attacks on Kenley by Dornier 17s of Bomber Geschwader 76, 1.23 to 1.25 pm
68	615 Squadron Hurricane P 3487	Destroyed		As above
69	615 Squadron Hurricane R 4186	Destroyed		As above
70	615 Squadron Hurricane	Destroyed		As above
71	615 Squadron Hurricane P 3161	Damaged		As above
72	615 Squadron Hurricane	Damaged		As above
73	615 Squadron Hurricane L 2075	Damaged	Plt Off S. Madle	Ran into a bomb crater landing after a combat sortie, at Kenley, about 4 pm
74	No 6 Flying Training School Anson	Destroyed	Sgt B. Hancock *killed*	Collided with, or rammed, Heinkel 111 of Bomber Geschwader 27 attacking the airfield at Windrush at about 11.50 pm. Both aircraft crashed at Northleach, Glos.

Other Aircraft Destroyed or Damaged, During Attacks on Airfields

Kenley: 1 Master, 1 Blenheim, 1 Proctor, 2 Magisters destroyed, 1 Magister damaged
West Malling: 3 Lysanders destroyed
Ford: 5 Sharks, 5 Swordfish, 2 Albacores, 1 Proctor destroyed, 16 Sharks, 1 Nimrod, 8 Walrus, 1 Roc damaged
Thorney Island: 1 Blenheim, 1 Anson, 1 Magister destroyed, 1 Wellington damaged
Gosport: 4 non-operational aircraft destroyed, 5 damaged

APPENDIX F

German Combat Losses, 18 August 1940

Unit	Type	Fate	Pilot	Remarks
Fighter Geschwader 2				
1 II Gruppe	Me 109	Destroyed	Oblt R. Moellerfriedrich *prisoner*	Shot down during action with British fighters near Portsmouth at 2.40 pm, crashed at Tapnall Farm near Freshwater. Pilot baled out and taken prisoner
2 II Gruppe	Me 109	Destroyed	*wounded*	Aircraft crashed into the sea at about 2.40 pm after combat with British fighters, wounded pilot picked up by the German rescue service
Fighter Geschwader 3				
3 I Gruppe	Me 109	Destroyed	Oblt H. Tiedmann *prisoner*	Aircraft forced-landed at Leeds near Maidstone, after suffering radiator damage during combat with British fighters at about 1.50 pm. Pilot left aircraft and was at liberty for about 12 hours before capture
4 II Gruppe	Me 109	Damaged *beyond repair*	Uffz F. Becker *died later of wounds*	Following combat with British fighters, this aircraft crash-landed near Calais with a gravely wounded pilot, who later died
5 II Gruppe	Me 109	Damaged *beyond repair*	Fw E. Dobrick *wounded*	Crash-landed near Boulogne, following combat with British fighters
6 II Gruppe	Me 109	Damaged	Fw Mueller	Crash-landed near Calais, following combat with British fighters
7 III Gruppe	Me 109	Destroyed	Ltn E. von Fondern *killed*	Shot down in action with British fighters over Kent, about 1.40 pm. Probably this aircraft crashed near Bredhurst
8 III Gruppe	Me 109	Destroyed	Obgef. W. Baesell *killed*	Shot down by Sdn Ldr D. Pemberton of No 1 Squadron after a long chase over Kent, at 6.15 pm. Aircraft crashed near Staplehurst
9 III Gruppe	Me 109	Destroyed	Uffz Keil	Ditched in the sea off Calais at about 2 pm, following combat with British fighters. Pilot picked up by German rescue service

Fighter Geschwader 26

10	III Gruppe	Me 109 Destroyed	Ltn W. Blume *wounded prisoner*	Shot down by Plt Off A. Eckford and Plt Off K. Pniak of No 32 Squadron at about 5.30 pm. Aircraft crashed at Kingston near Canterbury, pilot taken prisoner
11	III Gruppe	Me 109 Destroyed	Ltn G. Mueller-Duhe *killed*	Shot down by Flt Lt P. Brothers and Plt Off B. Wlasnowolski of No 32 Squadron at about 5.30 pm. Aircraft crashed at Chilham

Fighter Geschwader 27

12	I Gruppe	Me 109 Destroyed	Oblt M. Trumplemann *killed*	Shot down by British fighters, probably from No 234 Squadron, at about 2.30 pm off the Isle of Wight. Aircraft crashed into the sea
13	I Gruppe	Me 109 Destroyed	Ltn G. Mitsdoerffer *prisoner*	As above
14	I Gruppe	Me 109 Destroyed	Fw Sawallisch *killed*	As above
15	II Gruppe	Me 109 Destroyed	Oblt J. Neumann *prisoner*	Aircraft suffered radiator damage in combat with British fighters, forced-landed near Shanklindown, Isle of Wight, at about 2.35 pm
16	II Gruppe	Me 109 Destroyed	Uffz K. Nolte *killed*	Shot down in combat with British fighters near Selsey Bill at about 2.35 pm. Aircraft crashed into the sea
17	II Gruppe	Me 109 Destroyed		Shot down in combat with British fighters, off the Isle of Wight at about 2.35 pm. Aircraft crashed into the sea. Pilot picked up by German rescue service

Fighter Geschwader 51

18	I Gruppe	Me 109 Damaged	Oblt R. Leppla	Crash-landed at St Inglevert, aircraft damaged in collision during a combat mission

| 19 | II Gruppe | Me 109 | Destroyed | Hptm H. Tietzen *killed* | These two losses link with two claims by pilots of No 501 Squadron, Fg Off S. Witorzenc and Plt Off P. Zenker, of Me 109s destroyed near Whitstable at about 5.35 pm |
| 20 | II Gruppe | Me 109 | Destroyed | Ltn H. Lessing *killed* | |

Fighter Geschwader 54

21	II Gruppe	Me 109	Damaged		Damaged during attack on Flushing airfield by Blenheim of No 101 Squadron at about 10 pm
22	II Gruppe	Me 109	Damaged		As above
23	III Gruppe	Me 109	Damaged		Damaged in accident, during take-off for combat mission at Guines-West

Destroyer Geschwader 26

24	I Gruppe	Me 110	Destroyed	Oblt R. Proske *prisoner*	Shot down by Sdn Ldr A. MacDonell of No 64 Squadron. Crash-landed near Lydd at about 1.40 pm. Crewman wounded, taken prisoner
25	I Gruppe	Me 110	Destroyed	Uffz R. Mai *killed*	This aircraft and No 32 link with two Me 110s shot down over southern England at about 1.40 pm, one by Fg Off P. Weaver of No 56 Squadron which crashed at Bonnington, the other by Plt Off J. Flinders of No 32 Squadron and ground gunners, which crashed at Harbledown. There were no survivors in either case and the aircraft were completely wrecked
26	I Gruppe	Me 110	Damaged beyond repair		Damaged in action with British fighters, this aircraft crash-landed at Ypern
27	I Gruppe	Me 110	Damaged		Damaged in action with British fighters
28	I Gruppe	Me 110	Destroyed	Hptm H. Kaminski	Shot down into the sea off Clacton by British fighters, probably from No 54 or No 56 Squadron, at about 5.30 pm. Aircraft ditched. Pilot and radio operator rescued after four days in a dinghy

No	Gruppe	Type	Status	Crew	Remarks
29	I Gruppe	Me 110	Damaged	Ltn J. Koepsell	Damaged in combat with British fighter off the coast of Essex, possibly Sgt J. Ellis of No 85 Squadron, at about 6 pm
30	I Gruppe	Me 110	Destroyed		Damaged in combat with British fighters, crashed at Le Nieppe in France. No casualties
31	I Gruppe	Me 110	Destroyed	Oblt H. Kirchhoff killed	Aircraft crashed into the sea. May have been machine shot down by Flt Lt R. Tuck of No 92 Squadron off Beachy Head at about 1.40 pm. Both crewmen killed
32	I Gruppe	Me 110	Destroyed	Ofw W. Stange killed	See Remarks column for No 25
33	II Gruppe	Me 110	Destroyed	Hptm H. Luettke killed	Shot down by Plt Off C. Gray of No 54 Squadron and crashed at Smith's Sandpits, Clacton, at about 5.30 pm. Both crew killed
34	II Gruppe	Me 110	Destroyed	Fw F. Gierga prisoner	Shot down by British fighters off the Essex coast at about 5.55 pm, probably by Flt Lt H. Hamilton, Plt Off A. Lewis and Sgt F. Walter-Smith of No 85 Squadron. Aircraft ditched off North Foreland. Pilot rescued, radio operator killed
35	II Gruppe	Me 110	Destroyed	Uffz H. Jaeckel killed	Damaged in action with British fighters off Clacton, probably by Sdn Ldr G. Manton of No 56 Squadron at 5.30 pm. Finished off by ground fire, aircraft crashed at Eastchurch. Radio operator taken prisoner
36	II Gruppe	Me 110	Destroyed	Fw H. Stange prisoner	Probably damaged during attack by No 56 Squadron and finished off by Plt Off G. Goodman of No 1 Squadron at about 1.45 pm. Radio operator killed
37	II Gruppe	Me 110	Destroyed	Ofw A. Kiefel killed	Shot down by Sgt P. Robinson of No 56 Squadron at about 1.40 pm. Aircraft crashed at Pluckley. Both crew killed
38	II Gruppe	Me 110	Destroyed	Ltn H. Kaestner prisoner	Shot down at about 1.35 pm in combat with British fighters. Crash-landed near Newchurch, crew taken prisoner

39	II Gruppe	Me 110	Destroyed	Oblt H. Hellmuth *killed*	Engaged by Hurricanes of No 56 Squadron, finished off by Plt Off M. Mounsdon, at about 1.40 pm. Aircraft crashed at Lenham, both crew killed
40	II Gruppe	Me 110	Damaged		Damaged in action with British fighters at about 1.30 pm, this aircraft crash-landed at Wizernes in France. Radio-operator later died of wounds
41	III Gruppe	Me 110	Destroyed	Fw H. Klare *killed*	Probably shot down either by Plt Off J. Flinders of No 32 Squadron or Sgt H. Chandler of No 610 Squadron, this aircraft is believed to have crashed near Godstone
42	III Gruppe	Me 110	Damaged		Damaged in action with British fighters

Night Fighter Geschwader 1

| 43 | II Gruppe | Ju 88 | Destroyed | Ofw Zenkel *killed* | Shot down by Plt Off R. Rhodes and Sgt W. Gregory in a Blenheim night fighter of No 29 Squadron, off Spurn Head at about 3 am. Aircraft crashed into sea and all three on board killed |

Bomber Geschwader 1

| 44 | I Gruppe | He 111 | Destroyed | Ltn R. Ahrens *prisoner* | Shot down by Fg Off J. Quill, Plt Off E. Glaser, Sgt H. Orchard and Sgt M. Keymer of No 65 Squadron and Sdn Ldr M. Crossley of No 32 Squadron. Crash landed near Snargate at about 1.40 pm. One killed, rest taken prisoner |
| 45 | I Gruppe | He 111 | Damaged | | Damaged during fighter attack, near Biggin Hill at about 1.30 pm. One crewman killed, one wounded |

Bomber Geschwader 2

| 46 | II Gruppe | Do 17 | Damaged | | Damaged during fighter attack near Whitstable, at about 5.35 pm. One crew member wounded |

Bomber Geschwader 4

| 47 | II Gruppe | He 111 | Damaged | | Damaged in landing accident at Eindhoven following night combat mission |
| 48 | III Gruppe | Ju 88 | Damaged *beyond repair* | | Crash-landed at Vlaardingen after an engine failed during a night combat mission |

No	Gruppe	Type	Status	Crew	Notes
49	III Gruppe	Ju 88	Damaged		Crash-landed near Rotterdam, after running out of fuel during a night combat mission
Bomber Geschwader 27					
50	II Gruppe	He 111	Destroyed	Ofw A. Dreher *killed*	Collided with, or rammed by, Anson training aircraft while attacking the airfield at Windrush at about 11.50 pm. Both aircraft crashed at Northleach. All four on board killed
51	II Gruppe	He 111	Damaged *beyond repair*		Crash-landed at Laval, following a night combat mission. Three crewmen wounded
52	III Gruppe	He 111	Damaged		Landing accident at Rennes, when returning from a night combat mission. Ran into a Junkers 52, which was also damaged
Bomber Geschwader 53					
53	II Gruppe	He 111	Destroyed	Major R. Tamm *killed*	Shot down by Fg Off R. Milne of No 151 Squadron, over Essex at about 5.45 pm. Wreckage fell in the sea. All six men on board killed
54	II Gruppe	He 111	Damaged		Damaged in action, two crewmen wounded
55	III Gruppe	He 111	Destroyed	Uffz W. Grasser *prisoner*	Shot down off the Essex coast at about 5.50 pm, probably by Flt Lt L. H. Hamilton of No 85 Squadron. Aircraft ditched. Crew spent 26 hours in the water before rescue and capture
56	III Gruppe	He 111	Destroyed	Ltn W. Leber *prisoner*	Damaged during attack by Fg Off P. Weaver of No 56 Squadron, finished off by Plt Off W. Hopkins of No 54 Squadron at about 5.35 pm. Crash-landed at Smallgains on Foulness Island. One crewman killed, rest taken prisoner
57	III Gruppe	He 111	Destroyed	Uffz G. Gropp *killed*	Shot down off the Essex coast at about 5.55 pm. Probably aircraft attacked by Flt Lt H. Beresford and Sgt A. Girdwood of No 257 Squadron; or by Plt Off J. Marshall of No 85 Squadron. All five men on board killed

Bomber Geschwader 76

No	Unit	Aircraft	Status	Crew	Notes
58	I Gruppe	Do 17	Destroyed	Oblt W. Stoldt *killed*	Shot down by Plt Off A. Eckford of No 32 Squadron at about 1.20 pm. Aircraft crashed at Hurst Green near Oxted. Three dead, two crewmen taken prisoner
59	I Gruppe	Do 17	Damaged		Damaged in fighter attack, one crewman wounded
60	I Gruppe	Do 17	Damaged		Damaged in fighter attack, one crewman wounded
61	II Gruppe	Ju 88	Destroyed	Fw K. Geier *killed*	Shot down at about 1.30 pm by Flt Lt P. Brothers and Plt Off B. Wlasnowolski of No 32 Squadron, Fg Off J. O'Meara, F.Sgt E. Gilbert and Sgt A. Laws of No 64 Squadron and Flt Lt J. Sanders of No 615 Squadron. Aircraft crashed in woods near Ide Hill. All four crewmen killed
62	II Gruppe	Ju 88	Destroyed	Fw K. Krebs *killed*	Shot down by a fighter, possibly Sgt P. Farnes of No 501 Squadron, at about 1.35 pm. Aircraft crashed at Aylesford near West Malling. Pilot killed, other three crewmen taken prisoner
63	II Gruppe	Ju 88	Damaged		Damaged in action with British fighters at about 1.35 pm, made belly-landing at Creil in France
64	III Gruppe	Do 17	Destroyed	Ltn E. Leder *killed*	Possibly damaged over Kenley at about 1.25 pm by fighter of No 32 or No 64 Squadron. Finished off by Flt Lt H. Hillcoat, Plt Off C. Stavert and Plt Off G. Goodman of No 1 Squadron off Dungeness at about 1.40 pm. Aircraft crashed into the sea, all five crew killed
65	III Gruppe	Do 17	Damaged	Uffz Windschild	Attacked by Sqn Ldr C. Williams of No 17 Squadron at about 1.40 pm. Crash-landed near Calais
66	9th Staffel (III Gruppe)	Do 17	Destroyed	Fw J. Petersen *killed*	Shot down by ground fire at Kenley at 1.25 pm. Crashed just outside northern boundary of airfield, all five men on board killed

67	9th Staffel, (III Gruppe)	Do 17	Destroyed	Oblt R. Lamberty *wounded prisoner*	Set on fire by Kenley ground defences at 1.23 pm. Then attacked by Sgt W. Dymond and Sgt R. Brown of No 111 Squadron. Crashed at Leaves Green. All five on board taken prisoner, wounded
68	9th Staffel, (III Gruppe)	Do 17	Destroyed	Uffz G. Unger	One engine shot out by Kenley ground defences at 1.23 pm. Attacked and further damaged by Sergeant H. Newton of No 111 Squadron. Ditched in the Channel off Etampes, all crew rescued by the German Navy
69	9th Staffel, (III Gruppe)	Do 17	Destroyed	Uffz Schumacher	Damaged by ground defences, and exploding bombs, while attacking Kenley at 1.23 pm. Further damaged during attack by Hurricane of No 111 Squadron. Ditched in the Channel off Etampes. One crewman drowned, other three rescued by the German Navy.
70	9th Staffel, (III Gruppe)	Do 17	Damaged	Fw Stephani *wounded*	Damaged by Hurricane of No 111 Squadron near Kenley at about 1.25 pm. Crash-landed near Calais. Two crewmen killed, one wounded
71	9th Staffel, (III Gruppe)	Do 17	Damaged	Lt Magin *killed*	Damaged by ground fire while attacking Kenley at 1.23 pm, pilot mortally wounded. The navigator, Ofw W. Illg, took the controls and, after avoiding attacks by Hurricanes of No 111 Squadron, flew the aircraft back to France and landed it at St Omer
72	9th Staffel, (III Gruppe)	Do 17	Damaged	Fw Reichel	Damaged by Hurricane of No 111 Squadron near Kenley at about 1.25 pm. Crash-landed near Abbeville. One crew member wounded
73	9th Stafffel, (III Gruppe)	Do 17	Damaged	Uffz M. Maassen	Damaged by Hurricane of No 111 Squadron near Kenley at about 1.26 pm. Landed near Boulogne to initiate search for crew of No 69, later returned to base
74	9th Staffel, (III Gruppe)	Do 17	Damaged	Fw W. Raab	Damaged by ground fire over Kenley at 1.23, further damaged by ground fire during the return flight and navigator wounded. Landed at Amiens to off-load navigator, then returned to base

75	Bomber Gruppe 100	He 111	Destroyed		Crash-landed near Dinard during the early morning darkness, following mechanical failure after attack on Castle Bromwich

Dive Bomber Geschwader 77

76	I Gruppe	Ju 87	Destroyed	Hptm H. Meisel *killed*	Shot down by fighter at about 2.33 pm near Selsey Bill. Probably crashed in sea, both crew killed
77	I Gruppe	Ju 87	Destroyed	Uffz E. Weniger *killed*	As above
78	I Gruppe	Ju 87	Destroyed	Ofw W. Neumeier *killed*	As above
79	I Gruppe	Ju 87	Destroyed	Oblt H. Schaeffer *killed*	As above
80	I Gruppe	Ju 87	Destroyed	Oblt D. Lehmann *killed*	As above
81	I Gruppe	Ju 87	Destroyed	Lt H. Sinn *prisoner*	Shot down by Plt Off C. Gray of No 43 Squadron, aircraft crashed at West Ashling at about 2.30 pm. Pilot baled out, radio operator killed
82	I Gruppe	Ju 87	Destroyed	Oblt J. Wilhelm *prisoner*	Shot down at about 2.29 pm by Hurricane of No 43 or No 601 Squadron. Almost certainly this is the aircraft which crashed on mud flats at Fishbourne. Both crew taken prisoner, radio operator wounded
83	I Gruppe	Ju 87	Destroyed	Oblt F. Sayler *killed*	Shot down at about 2.29 pm by Hurricane of No 43 or No 601 Squadron. This is probably the aircraft that crashed near Chidham. Both crew killed
84	I Gruppe	Ju 87	Destroyed	Uffz A. Dann *killed*	Shot down at about 2.29 pm by Hurricane of No 43 or No 601 Squadron. Aircraft crashed at West Broyle, Chichester. Both crew killed
85	I Gruppe	Ju 87	Destroyed	Ofw G. Riegler *prisoner*	Shot down by a fighter at about 2.33 pm, this aircraft crashed into the sea about 5 miles south-west of Selsey Bill and the crew were rescued and taken prisoner
86	I Gruppe	Ju 87	Damaged *beyond repair*	Fw G. Meyer-Bothling *wounded*	Damaged in combat with British fighter, this aircraft crash-landed on the beach near Bayeux after returning to France. Radio operator killed

87	I Gruppe	Ju 87	Damaged	Oblt O. Schmidt *wounded*	Attacked by a fighter of No 43 or No 601 Squadron near Thorney Island at about 2.29 pm and suffered damage, radio operator mortally wounded
88	I Gruppe	Ju 87	Damaged	Lt K. Scheffel *wounded*	As above
89	I Gruppe	Ju 87	Damaged	Oblt K. Henze *wounded*	Attacked by fighter at about 2.32 pm off Thorney Island. Crash-landed in France
90	I Gruppe	Ju 87	Damaged	Fw Meier	Attacked by British fighter at about 2.32 pm; the radio operator Uffz K. Maier had *eight* machine gun bullets strike his body – and he survived
91	I Gruppe	Ju 87	Damaged	Oblt H. Bruck	Attacked by British fighter near Thorney Island at about 2.33 pm
92	II Gruppe	Ju 87	Destroyed	Oblt H. Sonntag *killed*	Shot down by fighter of No 602 Squadron near Bognor at about 2.32 pm. Both crew killed
93	II Gruppe	Ju 87	Destroyed	Oblt Merenski *killed*	As above
94	II Gruppe	Ju 87	Destroyed	Ofw K. Schweinhardt *prisoner*	Shot down by Sgt B. Whall of No 602 Squadron off Bognor at about 2.23 pm, this aircraft landed on Ham Manor Golf Course near Littlehampton. Radio operator died later
95	II Gruppe	Ju 87	Destroyed		Damaged by a British fighter near Bognor at about 2.32 pm, this aircraft crashed in France near Barfleur. Crew uninjured
96	III Gruppe	Ju 87	Destroyed	Uffz W. Moll *killed*	Shot down by Sgt B. Whall of No 602 Squadron off Bognor at about 2.25 pm. Both crew killed
97	III Gruppe	Ju 87	Destroyed	Fw H. Schulze *killed*	Damaged in action with British fighter after attacking Ford at 2.29 pm, crashed in France at Argentan, both crew killed
98	III Gruppe	Ju 87	Damaged		Damaged in action with British fighter after attacking Ford at 2.29 pm, landed with one crew member wounded
99	III Gruppe	Ju 87	Damaged		Damaged in action with British fighter after attacking Ford at 2.29 pm, landed near Caen.

Tactical Development Geschwader 2

| 100 | 7 (Recon-naissance) Staffel | Me 110 | Destroyed | Oblt A. Werdin | Intercepted and shot down over the Thames estuary at about 11.30 am by Flt Lt D. Gribble, Plt Off C. Gray, Plt Off W. Hopkins, F.Sgt P. Tew and Sgt J. Norwell of No 54 Squadron. Aircraft crashed into the sea off the French coast, both crew killed |

Note on Nos 76, 77, 78, 79, 80, 85, 86, 89, 90, 91, 95, 97, 98 and 99: because of the confused mêlée that took place over and off the south coast of England between 2.27 and 2.37 pm, it is not possible to link these Ju 87s with specific RAF pilots or squadrons. The following units claimed Ju 87s which cannot be accounted for:

No 43 Sqn: 8 destroyed, 1 probable
No 152 Sqn: 8 destroyed
No 235 Sqn (Coastal Command): 2 destroyed
No 601 Sqn: 6 destroyed
No 602 Sqn: 3 destroyed, 1 damaged

Several forward landing grounds

CHERBOURG

DINARD

RENNES

Fighter
Geschwad

Bomber
Geschwader 2

VANNES Bomber Gruppe 100

PAS DE
CALAIS

● BRUSSELS

LILLE ◉ Bomber Geschwader 53

ARRAS ◉   EPINOY
        ◉ Bomber Geschwader 2
CAMBRAI ◉

◉ ROSIERES-EN-SANTERRE
Bomber Geschwader 1
◉ MONTDIDIER

E HAVRE
◉ Fighter Geschwader 2

BEAUVAIS ◉   Bomber Geschwader 76
CREIL ◉
◉ CORMEILLES-EN-VEXIN

AIR FLEET 2

AEN
ve Bomber Geschwader 3, 77
hter Geschwader 27

AIR FLEET 3   ● PARIS

FIGHTER AIRFIELDS

PAS DE CALAIS AREA

DUNKIRK

CALAIS
• CALAIS–MARCK
• COQUELLES staff, I/FG52
• PEUPLINGUES II/FG 52
WISSANT • staff, I, II/FG 51
AUDEMBERT •   • GUINES I, III/FG 54
staff, I/FG 26   • CAFFIERS III/FG 26
MARQUISE II/FG 26   CAMPAGNE staff, /FG 54
                ST. OMER I, II/DG 26, III/FG 51
            HERMELINGHEN II/FG 54

BOULOGNE

DESVRES III/FG 3   ARQUES III/DG 26

SAMER staff, I, II/FG 3

Index